ALL GOOD THINGS MUST BEGIN

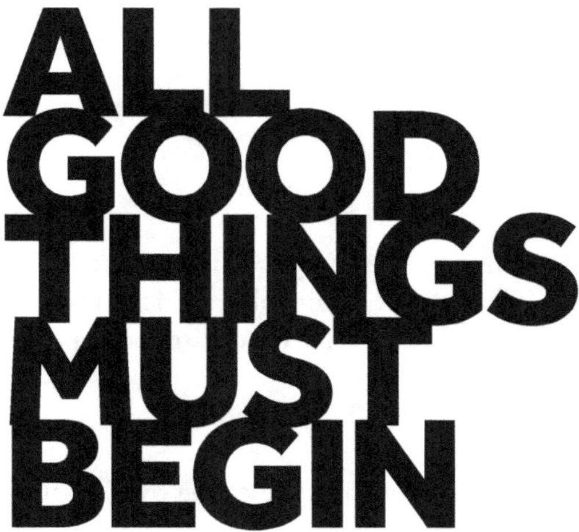

SHORT PLAYS IMAGINING THE FUTURE

EDITED BY
CHANTAL BILODEAU

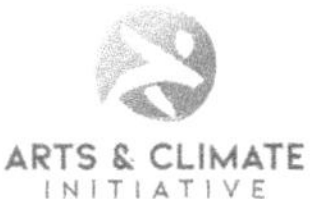

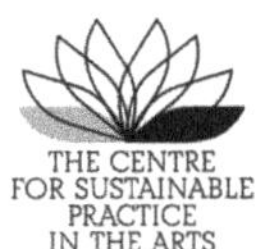

Published by the Arts & Climate Initiative and
the Centre for Sustainable Practice in the Arts
www.artsandclimate.org | www.sustainablepractice.org

First edition

Cover design and typesetting by Causality

Printed in the United States of America

ISBN 979-8-9905439-0-4
ISBN 979-8-9905439-1-1 (ebook)

I feel that the variety of plays performed took the audience on a real journey, one minute laughing and the next shocked or saddened. We got some amazing feedback and some people were quite emotional as they left the venue.

—Imogen Fraser, Lecturer
Suffolk New College, Ipswich, UK

I believe that the choice to collaborate with a community garden was an especially successful one for the nature of this performance, and that our combination of serious discussion with playfulness contributed greatly in reaching audiences of all ages and backgrounds.

—Sivan Raz, Founder & Artistic Director
Needs More Work Productions, New York, US

We had a thoughtful discussion with the audience after the event in which two themes emerged: the importance of the arts in getting people to change their thinking and behavior, and the need to continue sustained action rather than allowing our interest to wane.

—Curran Russell, Teacher, Theatre and Theory of Knowledge
UWC Mahindra College, Maharashtra, India

By selecting plays from a variety of genres, we were able to entertain, enlighten, and educate a student, faculty, and family audience about the importance of every single action we as humans make to effect change in any small or big way. This group of students expressed numerous times how this process will remain a highlight of their theatre training at York University.

—Jamie Robinson, Assistant Professor,
Department of Theatre, Dance & Performance,
School of the Arts, Media, Performance & Design,
York University, Toronto, Canada

CONTENTS

◊ ◊ ◊

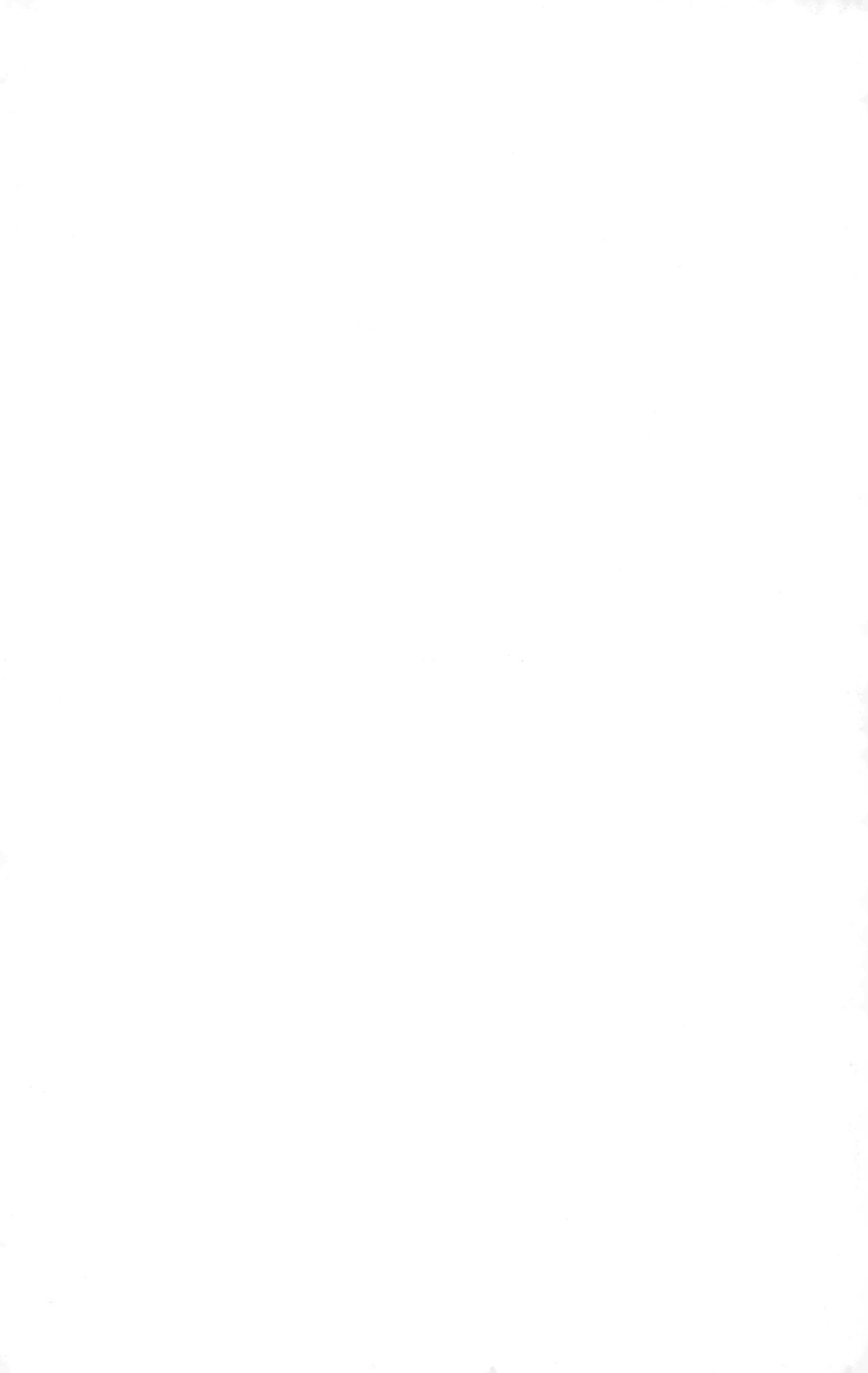

ACKNOWLEDGMENTS

When you hold this book in your hands, it might feel like a small object; after all, there isn't that much weight to it. But don't let this diminutive size fool you. It took nothing less than an entire community to put it together – dozens and dozens of people spread across five continents. So, I invite you to imagine how heavy this book would be if it were to truly represent the work and talents of everyone who contributed to it and join me in receiving its many offerings with gratitude.

I would like to first and foremost thank the fifty playwrights (forty-nine if I don't count myself) who wrote the plays included in these pages as a response to the prompt "All Good Things Must Begin." Without them, there would be no book to begin with. Originally commissioned for our Climate Change Theatre Action 2023 festival (CCTA), the plays offer visions of a complex, imperfect but also aspirational future, and, as such, provide thought-maps we can begin to follow to transition to a better world. I also am hugely grateful to the authors of the essays that comprise the first part of the book: Himali Kothari, Elspeth Tilley, Mark Wallace, Clare Preuss, Ian Garrett, and GiGi Buddie. Sharing their experience of interacting with these plays in different settings and countries provides unique perspectives on how theatre can address climate change issues, what personal and collective engagement might look like, and how playwrights' words impact audiences.

Because this book wouldn't exist without the CCTA festival happening in the first place, I owe huge thanks to the 2,500 artists and organizers who, in the fall of 2023, read and staged these plays all over the world, touching the hearts and minds of nearly 7,000 people, and embodying the very premise of CCTA 2023 – that positive change ("good things") must begin *somewhere*. One of the things that theatre does best is plant seeds of transformation. At a time when wide-scale transformation of our many systems is desperately needed, I take heart in the fact that so many seeds were planted.

I have no words to express my deep, deep gratitude for the work and support of my two extraordinary friends and colleagues, Julia Levine and GiGi Buddie, with whom I have been working for several years on bringing more climate stories into the world. They were key in the smooth running

of CCTA 2023 and in assembling this book, and they both bring passion and dedication to this herculean task. I am grateful for their presence, thoughtfulness, and for shining their bright light onto our world.
I am also indebted to my friend and colleague, Ian Garrett, from the Centre for Sustainable Practice in the Arts. A steady force and seemingly bottomless well of ideas and resources, he has been my CCTA partner since 2017, dreaming up collaborations, troubleshooting technological glitches, and constantly finding new ways for theatre to shape the climate conversation.

And last but not least, I offer my deepest thanks to Elizabeth Cameron, a friend from another life, whose editing and proofreading skills (and enthusiastic support) proved invaluable in bringing this book to life, and to Terri Gaines and Steve Gaines from Causality, whose design expertise turned a Word manuscript into a beautiful object.

INTRODUCTION

Chantal Bilodeau

As the fifth Climate Change Theatre Action festival (CCTA) – which commissioned the plays included in this book – was unfolding in the fall of 2023, the world broke an unfortunate series of records, with every month in that season becoming the warmest September, October, November, and December ever recorded. Furthermore, the year 2023 as a whole, marked the first time global average temperatures exceeded 1.5 degrees Celsius above pre-industrial levels for a twelve-month period.[1] If we needed a reminder of why we were doing what we were doing, it came loud and clear.

At the same time, in December 2023, at the UN Climate Conference in Dubai, thanks to a global Call to Action spearheaded by the Climate Heritage Network and signed by hundreds of arts and cultural organizations worldwide, the United Arab Emirates (hosts of COP28) and Brazil (future hosts of COP30 in 2025) announced the launch of the Group of Friends of Culture-Based Climate Action. An international coalition of UN Member States, the Group of Friends' stated goal is to build "political momentum for the recognition of culture as a uniquely powerful force in climate change policy."[2] It remains to be seen how much influence this group will have and how this influence will translate into meaningful policies, but, at the very least, it confirms what many artists and cultural workers have known for years: There can be no transition to a more just and regenerative world without culture as a key driver. As the Climate Heritage Network states on its website:

> Cultural heritage, including traditional knowledge, strengthens resilience, helps communities to adapt to climate impacts, protects places, and offers green, circular and regenerative solutions. The arts speak to hearts and minds, inspiring action and helping us to understand climate change through storytelling and shared experiences. The creative industries – design, music, fashion and film – shape our lifestyles, tastes and consumption patterns.[3]

[1] Dahl, Kristina. "First Year-Long Breach of 1.5 Degrees Celsius Could be More Enduring Without Accelerated Action by World Leaders." *Union of Concerned Scientists*, February 8, 2024. https://www.ucsusa.org/about/news/first-year-long-breach-15-degrees-celsius-could-be-more-enduring-without-accelerated

[2] "Call to Action." *Cultural Heritage Network*. https://www.climateheritage.org/jwd

[3] Ibid.

Arts and culture are so intrinsic to our lives that we sometimes barely notice them. They are just there, permeating our day-to-day experiences: the songs on the radio, the murals on the street, the languages we speak, what we eat for dinner. But take them away and it quickly becomes apparent that they are essential to our well-being, that they, in fact, create the meanings by which we live, organizing facts into personal and collective narratives, and connecting us to our physical environments. Now, as we struggle with a changed relationship to a changed world and are forced to rewrite the fundamental narratives that have buoyed humanity for the last few centuries, we would do well to harness the most important tools we have for that task.

In addition to giving meaning to our lives, arts and culture can help us envision and (re)create the future. While science and technology provide pathways for reducing global emissions of greenhouse gases, they don't, by themselves, dictate how these measures should be implemented, who should benefit from them, and how we need to adjust our identities and cultural practices to accommodate them. All of those decisions are mediated through culture:

> Cultural and creative processes make it possible for individuals and communities to explore their histories and sense of identity, imagine different futures, and promote a dialogue about needs, aspirations and rights. Active participation in cultural life provides the motivation and possibility of increased civic participation, lends cultural visibility to marginalised groups, and fosters mutual recognition and cooperation between different generations and cultures.[4]

There are countless arts and cultural organizations already working to address climate challenges with, and within their community, capitalizing on the strength of cultural networks, and the power of creativity and imagination. But we need more. As we know all too well, if we wait for change to come from the top, we will be waiting for a long time. The more we organize within our communities and work to dream up and implement the changes we want to see, the better prepared we will be to face the challenges ahead of us. In storytelling terms, this means we, artists, must be modern Jules Vernes[5] and imagine, not just the technology, but also the systems – economic, social, environmental, educational, moral, etc. – of

[4] Potts, Andrew. *The Role of Culture in Climate Resilient Development.* UCLG Committee on Culture Reports, n°10, and Climate Heritage Network (Working Group 5), 2021.

[5] In his book *Vingt Mille Lieues sous les mers* (Twenty Thousand Leagues Under the Seas), French author Jules Vernes (1828-1905) accurately described many features of today's modern submarines before they existed.

tomorrow, the systems that will support the lives of nine billion people on a finite Earth.

I am encouraged by the fact that the United Nations has taken the step to recognize the role of culture in climate change policy, and I will closely follow the activities of the Group of Friends at COP30 in Brazil and beyond. But, for now, I offer this book, and the stories it contains, as one more tool to engage in conversation around the climate crisis, to creatively explore who we are and who we want to be as a species, and to challenge ourselves to dream up and actualize what doesn't yet exist.

What Is Climate Change Theatre Action?

Inaugurated in 2015 and hosted biennially, CCTA is a worldwide festival of short plays about the climate crisis, presented to coincide with the United Nations Conferences of the Parties (COP meetings) – the annual meetings where world leaders gather to discuss strategies to reduce global greenhouse gas emissions. It is spearheaded by the Arts & Climate Initiative in partnership with the Centre for Sustainable Practice in the Arts, and aims to bring communities together and inspire them to take action on climate.[6]

Early in the year, we commission fifty playwrights, representing every inhabited continent, to write a five-minute play about an aspect of the climate crisis based on a prompt. We then make this collection of plays available to anyone interested in presenting an event in their community during a three-month window in the fall. Events can range from readings to fully produced performances, and from podcasts to film adaptations. Organizers are encouraged to design their event to reflect their own aesthetic and the needs of their community, and to include additional material by local artists.

To emphasize the "Action" part of Climate Change Theatre Action, we also invite organizers to think about an action – educational, social, or political – that can be incorporated into their event. These actions may involve collaborations with the scientific community or local environmental organizations, or they may take the form of donations or protests. In the past, organizers have pledged to reduce consumption and adopt plant-based diets, raised money for hurricane relief and tree-planting efforts, cleaned rivers, donated to food banks, and written letters to legislators to demand policy change.

[6] For more on the CCTA festival, visit www.climatechangetheatreaction.com

The five-minute format of the CCTA plays is not accidental. We want the plays to be as user-friendly as possible so they can be presented in different contexts, by people with varying levels of experience, and accommodate a wide range of budgets, including no budget at all. The plays can be performed individually as part of larger events – such as conferences and festivals – or grouped together in any number to create an evening of theatre.

All Good Things Must Begin

CCTA 2023 took place from September 17 to December 23, 2023. Once we had selected our fifty playwrights, we offered the following prompt:

> Our theme this year is inspired by the journal entry of American science fiction writer, Octavia Butler, "All Good Things Must Begin." Butler was determined to be a best-selling author. By setting intentions and visualizing this positive outcome, she defied the odds and became the author of many celebrated novels, winning each of science fiction's highest honors. She was also incredibly prescient, writing about extremism, racial justice, and climate change some thirty years ago. While the worlds of her novels depict the violent challenges of today's interlocking crises, her protagonists remain devoted to thriving, to achieving survival beyond the destructive and oppressive societies they come from.
>
> The climate crisis demands the same kind of imaginative leap: We will create a just and regenerative world only if we dare to imagine it first, and use that vision to guide us through the difficulties. We invite you to be solarpunks and envision radical pluralistic futures where nature and community thrive, and where we reject the apocalypse and embrace counterculture, post-capitalism, and decolonization. This doesn't necessarily translate into utopias, but into worlds where successes and failures exist side by side, and where hope, courage, and grief overlap.

While CCTA 2021 had a clear political overtone, with "Envisioning a Global Green New Deal" as our theme, in 2023 we chose a more poetic approach. We wanted to emphasize imagination and ways of being as opposed to political action. This, in no way, implies that action should be put on the backburner. Rather, we wanted to acknowledge an important aspect of the climate crisis that has long been overlooked but is essential to our ability to take any kind of action: emotional health.

Climate anxiety and climate distress are on the rise, especially among the younger generation.[7] While these feelings are healthy responses to the existential challenges we are facing, for any action to be possible, let alone sustainable, they must be addressed – and harnessed toward positive transformation. A way in which this can happen, we thought, is through keeping a sense of possibility alive. By reminding ourselves that "good things" don't appear fully formed but must begin somewhere, and what we aspire to can be put in motion anytime, we can hopefully keep despair at bay. After all, beginnings are always acts of faith. And there is no better antidote to feeling stuck than an unwavering faith in a different outcome.

Our prompt also invited playwrights to be solarpunks. A relatively recent sci-fi subgenre and aesthetic movement, solarpunk rejects dystopia and unapologetically embraces futures of hope. It seeks to answer and embody the question "What does a sustainable civilization look like, and how can we get there?" It is at once "a vision of the future, a thoughtful provocation, a way of living and a set of achievable proposals to get there."[8]

How to Use This Book

The goal of this anthology is to make the fifty plays of CCTA 2023 available to as many people as possible so they can continue to be studied, read, and performed. While the official festival season is over, there are no restrictions on using the plays in private or in classroom settings. We, of course, highly encourage you to perform them as well. However, if they are presented in a public space in front of an audience, we ask that permission from the playwrights be secured first. If you are charging admission, please consider paying royalties. Most playwrights are easily found online, but if you need help reaching anyone, email us at info@artsandclimate.org and we will assist you.

For ideas on how to use the plays and to see what organizers have done in the past, visit the Events page on the Climate Change Theatre Action website.[9] Throughout our five-season history, venues have ranged from city streets to national forests, from private backyards to farms, and from schools and universities to theatres, libraries, and churches. Some events are fully produced and presented on stages; others are intimate readings for family and friends. What they all have in common, however, is a desire to bring

[7] Moench, Mallory. "New Data Shows a Global Surge in Searches Related to 'Climate Anxiety'." *TIME.com*, November 22, 2023. https://time.com/6338759/climate-change-anxiety-google-search-trend

[8] Regenerative Design. "A Solarpunk Manifesto." *Res-des.org*, 2020. http://www.re-des.org/es/a-solarpunk-manifesto

[9] www.climatechangetheatreaction.com/events

people together around an important issue, and to facilitate inclusive and supportive conversations. Regardless of the size of your event, we encourage you to share it with us so we can add it to the CCTA website and publicize it on social media.

In addition to the plays, Part 1 of this book features six essays by members of the greater CCTA family, that provide insights on various aspects of the project. First, playwright Himali Kothari, who wrote plays for CCTA 2021 and CCTA 2023, and co-organized a CCTA event for Readings in the Shed in Mumbai in 2019, shares how getting involved with these initiatives made her more conscious of her role in protecting our planet. Second, Elspeth Tilley, a Professor of Creative Communication at Te Kunenga ki Pūrehuroa (Massey University), as well as a three-time CCTA playwright and five-time CCTA producer, describes how CCTA plays facilitated cross-cultural exchanges between New Zealand and Columbia, and between New Zealand and China, and surfaced unexpected connections. Next, Mark Wallace, Director of Beaford Arts, England's longest-established rural arts initiative, writes about working with teenagers from local schools and professional theatre makers to present CCTA performances that shook audiences and demonstrated how to take action collectively and make shared meanings across generations.

Fourth, Clare Preuss, Artistic Director of Downstage, a theatre company located in the heart of Canada's oil country, reflects on her experience presenting CCTA events in both 2021 and 2023, collaborating with the Immigrant Council for Arts Innovation to include newcomer artists, and supporting audiences who often have ties to the oil industry to participate in thoughtful conversation. Following Clare, Ian Garrett, researcher in the field of sustainability in arts and culture, as well as Associate Professor of Ecological Design for Performance at York University in Toronto and a co-organizer of CCTA, discusses three international design projects organized around CCTA plays in 2019, 2021, and 2023, and principles of ecoscenography and sustainable theatre practices. And last, interdisciplinary artist and climate activist, GiGi Buddie, who is my colleague and an Affiliate Artist with the Arts & Climate Initiative, tells us what we can learn about the impact of CCTA 2023 by crunching the numbers.

Going Forward

In 2023, Empatheatre, in collaboration with Shells & Spells animation studios and Triggerfish, premiered the short animated film *Indlela Yokuphila: The Soul's Journey*. The film is an exploration of South African spirituality that shows parallels between traditional beliefs and the scientific concept of the water lifecycle. It is without question a stunning work of art, but most astonishingly, the film

> was instrumental in three court proceedings in South Africa, brought successfully by Indigenous fisher leaders and ocean defenders against oil and gas giant Shell and the Department of Mineral Resources and Energy. These judicial decisions mark the first time that an animation has been used as evidence in a South African court, serving as a proxy for the intangible cultural heritage related to the ocean.[10]

This is a remarkable example of how arts and culture came together to protect an area of cultural and spiritual significance against a corporation bent on resource extraction. I find it is also a powerful antidote to despair and cynicism. It reminds us that there is good in the world (repeat: there is good in the world), that there is hope if we come together as communities and demand change, and that every time we use our creativity and imagination, we open up new possibilities. How we harness them is up to us.

[10] Empatheatre. *Indlela Yokuphila: The Soul's Journey*. YouTube, uploaded June 8, 2023. https://www.YouTube.com/watch?v=lNm-Yf8Dt10

PART 1

THOUGHTS ON CLIMATE CHANGE THEATRE ACTION

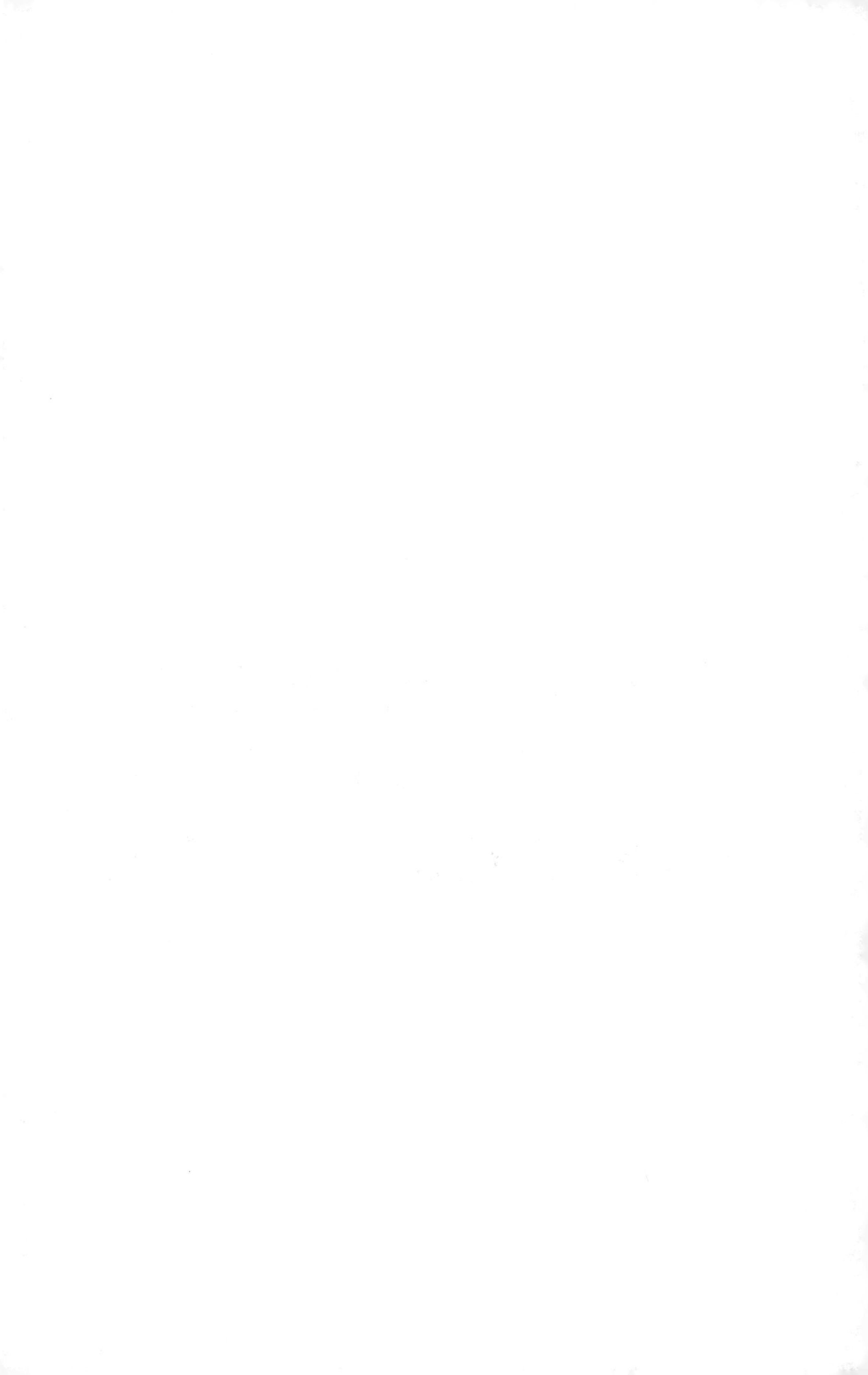

HOW CCTA MADE CLIMATE CHANGE PERSONAL

Himali Kothari

The alarm beeps from the beyond and jolts me awake. Its shrill notes persist until I locate the source and turn it off. It is 2:00 a.m., not my usual wake-up hour, and for a second, I consider crawling back under the sheets. *You just have to switch on the laptop. You don't even need to change out of your pajamas.* I coax myself out of bed and settle in front of the screen.

It was November 2021, and the world was emerging from the COVID-19 pandemic. During the twenty-odd months of intermittent lockdowns and travel bans across the globe, the world had shifted to online mode. Meetings, catching up with friends, birthdays, and even a wedding – I had done it all on Zoom. And, yes, I had whined, a lot. But, as the blue-and-white logo materialized on my screen, for once, I was thankful for this app. It was the reason I could catch the performance of my play by the students of the University of the Fraser Valley in Canada, thousands of kilometers from my home in Mumbai, India. The production was part of Climate Change Theatre Action 2021, and they had selected to perform ten plays from the collection of fifty. My play, *Friends For Life,* was one of them. This was my first time being commissioned to write a play for CCTA, and I was intrigued to see how my story would be interpreted and played out.

As the action unfolds on my fourteen-inch screen, sleep vanishes. The plays represent the voices of playwrights from multiple latitudes. A couple spotlight Indigenous issues, and others draw attention to global concerns. They are written in prose and verse. And they are all brought alive by the young students of the university. My play is seventh in the lineup, and, as the sixth play comes to an end, I feel the same flutter in my gut that I would feel if I were watching in person. The play is set in a small village in the arid heart of India, and the characters are based on the local women in that village. Their problem? Lack of rainfall, which means the lakes and rivers dry up. Every day, the women walk for hours to the nearest watering hole, and, as the drought continues, the walk to water becomes longer. These women cover their heads and part of their faces with a veil at all times. They have been raised in a patriarchal society where they must be submissive and keep their opinions to themselves. These are women from my country, but we are separated not simply by a few hundred kilometers; education, background, socio-economic class, opportunity, privilege … I have very little in common with them besides citizenship and skin color. And that had been the biggest struggle while writing the play, to convey their voice with clarity and honesty.

So, how were a group of Caucasians, who had even less in common with these women, and had likely not visited my part of the world, going to identify with their voice? How would students who had never walked more than a dozen steps to potable water identify with the desperation? My doubts were dispelled within seconds of the performance starting. The backdrop they had created was similar to the landscape of the region. Two girls appeared on the screen dressed in tan skirts and tops with long colorful scarves covering their heads. As I watched my words play out for the next ten minutes, I was overwhelmed by the spirit of the performers. It was evident that they had researched the play's setting and people, and had found resonance with their conflict. When the two young students twirled with joy at the end of the play, mimicking my stage directions closely, I clapped in my dark room lit only by the screen.

Six months later, in June 2022, I had the fortune to watch another version of my play at a playwright festival hosted by Schauspielhaus Graz in Austria. This time, too, it was part of an ensemble of CCTA plays. But unlike the previous year, as a guest playwright at the festival, I was present in person in the audience. The students of the University of Music and Performing Arts Graz were presenting the plays as staged readings. The stage featured an old refrigerator and some plants as props, and the actors positioned themselves at the perimeter of the stage. A few actors stepped in the center of the stage to narrate the stories in German while subtitles were displayed on a screen. Initially, my attention snapped back and forth between the subtitles and the stage, but after a while, I was swept up into the action on the stage. I don't understand German, but since I had read all the plays, I had context, and the emotions and body language of the actors filled in the blanks. There was a marked difference between the presentation in Graz and the one in the Fraser Valley. The students in Graz chose a narratorial approach instead of embodying characters. They infused movement that was generic rather than culture-specific. The story had details of a village in India, but their telling made it about the search for water at any time, on any place on Earth. They gave my very local narrative a very global resonance.

From reading groups to students to professional theatre artists, CCTA allows people from any corner of the world, irrespective of their theatrical experience and budget size, to access and perform these plays. As a playwright, one of the things I find most challenging to come to terms with is to let go of my story and detach myself from the form it will take based on the director's vision. While I cannot claim to have attained a Zen-like detachment, participating as a playwright in CCTA over two seasons taught me to ease off on the desire for control and submit to the process. After all, I had seen two very different performances of one play and had come away happily surprised. The variety of interpretations adds textures and layers to the original writing that can only augment its flavor profile. This becomes especially relevant because of the topic at hand. Climate change has global repercussions, and at the same time, it has specific local relevance based on physical, social, economic, and cultural contexts.

How It Started

I first learned of CCTA in November 2019. Writer-director Nikhil Katara and I were planning a staged reading for Readings in the Shed, a cultural initiative that Katara had launched in April 2018. Through the programs of Readings in the Shed, we had brought texts from different parts of the world to the Mumbai stage. There had been a myriad of written forms such as plays, essays, poems, short stories, letters, etc. Our hunt for "what next" on our program schedule led us to discover this festival called CCTA in North America.

I remember smiling when I first read the unabbreviated form of CCTA: Climate Change Theatre Action. Direct and no-nonsense, the festival's mission statement was in its name. We wrote to them with the concept for our performance and received an email with a link to the fifty plays of that season, and a load of encouragement. As I read the plays, images and voices from different parts of the world filled my head. Some were places I had seen, but not in that light. Others were places I had heard of but not seen. And some places I had not heard of at all. Some playwrights had recreated the stark reality. Some had twisted the real and presented it as a fable. Some had broken the fourth wall and involved the audience. From the fifty plays, we chose six that we felt would best connect with the Mumbai audience.

The email from CCTA indicated that alongside the performance, we must also include an activity that would mobilize the audience in some manner. For this purpose, we wrote to schools in the city with a question for the kids: What would you tell someone who says they do not believe in climate change? We invited the kids to send us a one hundred-word reply. The authors of the best twelve replies would be invited to the performance at the prestigious National Centre for Performing Arts (NCPA) and read their response to the audience. Over the next few weeks, we received scores of emails with replies ranging from educational to witty to passionate, and it was no mean feat to stick to our count of twelve best responses.

The plays were staged on a January evening in the *al fresco* garden setting of the NCPA, lit up by strings of fairy lights. An audience of about 120 Mumbaikars assembled to catch the performance of the CCTA plays interspersed by the responses of the selected twelve students. In a city not short on options on how to spend an evening, I was pleasantly surprised to see a sizable crowd for an event that would fall under activism theatre, for lack of better terminology. I positioned myself in the makeshift wings to watch the audience. Rapt, amused, thoughtful, dismayed ... multiple expressions played out on their faces during the seventy-five-minute performance. For the most part, the audience appeared engaged.

Would a talk on climate change have the same hold on an audience as these plays? Perhaps yes, for a climate activist already invested in the cause. However, the use of theatre attracted a different group of people who could potentially be affected by the issue highlighted on stage and become climate warriors. And the Earth needs as many climate warriors as it can get.

How Theatre Plays Its Role

Using theatre to draw attention to societal issues is not a new concept. It is as old as theatre itself. Theatre mirrors society and prods theatregoers to look closer at the goings-on. It stirs questions in their mind and conscience. Were they unaware or did they choose to not notice? And now, do they deny it? Accept it? Act on it? Theatre has the ability to move our collective conscience. The action may be difficult to measure but the impact is undeniable.

What makes CCTA's approach unique, however, is its global relevance. And it does so twice over: First, the commissioned playwrights come from countries across the six continents. This leads to building a collection that is rich in its range of themes, topics, and voices. Second, making the plays freely available allows these stories to scatter across the globe and germinate. Audiences leave a little more aware of and empathetic towards a corner of the world far, far away. And, considering the global relevance of both the cause and the fight, a unified mindset can only do good.

As I write this in April 2024, my social media feed is filled with apocalyptic images and videos of Dubai. According to the estimates of the World Meteorological Organization, the region saw more than two years of rain in one day.[1] In addition, the last few months have seen many worrying occurrences of extreme weather events, from flash floods to food shortages to extreme temperatures. And the cause of all of these can be traced to climate change. The World Economic Forum predicts extreme weather events will be the most severe global risks over the next ten years.[2] Climate change is a serious, if not the most severe, crisis that humanity needs to tackle. Shouldn't it be treated with more seriousness than by simply staging plays?

Naysayers will perhaps deny the impact of this exhaustive exercise that the festival carries out. Some will wave off theatre as entertainment and question its ability to take on an issue as serious as climate change. Is it not scientific reports and global policies that will be key in bringing about the desired changes? Is it not action that requires our attention and investment? Yes and Yes. Science and policies are crucial to safeguarding our planet, but do not by themselves cause a change in mindset; their effect is limited to the immediate point they address. Theatre, on the other hand, evokes rather than imposes. It invites theatregoers to listen and absorb. The messages that are conveyed through stories have the ability to bring about a change in how we perceive our world and our role in it. They have the potential to shake age-old practices and protocols. They do not tell us "Do this," "Don't do that." They prompt us to introspect on the "why" behind our actions. Thus, they create more profound and more lasting change. Therein lies the power of storytelling. And that is what CCTA has managed to harness.

As a writer and story-gobbler, mine may not be seen as the most unbiased view of the role of stories. But the realization of their potential power has crept in gradually. The stories I have read and seen over the years have shaped my perceptions and influenced how I interact with the world and its events. Every story, short or long, fiction or nonfiction, of my land or other lands, of the familiar or the alien, helps me better understand the world and myself. Each one alters my view of the world and impels me to introspect on how I interact with it. It was not that I was not aware of the impacts of climate change on our Earth. But, reading about it in headlines and news

[1] Deliso, Meredith; Peck, Daniel; Al-Tawy, Ayat; and Khan, Habibullah. "Dubai sees severe flooding after getting 2 years' worth of rain in 24 hours." *ABC News*, April 17, 2024. https://abcnews.go.com/International/dubai-flooding-heavy-rainfall/story?id=109321601
[2] Pandey, Kiran. "Extreme weather events most severe global risks over next 10 years: WEF." *Down to Earth*, January 11, 2024. https://www.downtoearth.org.in/news/climate-change/extreme-weather-events-most-severe-global-risks-over-next-10-years-wef-93824

broadcasts gave me a detached view of the situation. Being a part of CCTA for three seasons, on the other hand, as a presenter in 2019 and playwright in 2021 and 2023, provided access to 150 plays. These plays gave me a close-up view of climate change. They made me more conscious of my role in the life of our planet and helped me transition from the don't-do-harm approach to the do-protect approach.

As the Earth takes one more spin around the sun, CCTA approaches its sixth season. While the forecast for this third rock from the sun may appear gloomy, we could take heart in the fact that there is room to edit the existing narrative and script one headed for a happily-ever-after.

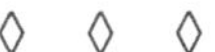

Himali Kothari lives in Mumbai, India. She compares her journey as an author to a trip down the rabbit hole, full of unexpected twists and turns. From writing website content to feature articles to short stories to plays, she is almost always inclined to say "Why Not?" when it involves wielding her pen (and keyboard) to do her bidding.

DRINKING IMAGINARY COSMOPOLITANS IN BEIJING: OR WHY KIWIS SOMETIMES FLY[1]

Elspeth Tilley

> I mua i muri (the past is in front of us, the future is behind).
> — Program Notes for the exhibition E Tu Ake: Māori Standing Strong[2]

> Listen is the key word here. We send time capsules through space and spend untold amounts of money looking for life on other planets, but we forget to stop and listen to what is around us.
> —Chantal Bilodeau[3]

When I was in my twenties, I thought "cosmopolitan" meant chic and flashy, like the magazine my older sisters read or the trendy cocktail they ordered at nightclubs. Later, I discovered it meant something quite different and more substantial: planetary solidarity or global citizenship. Even later, I grasped its fundamental necessity for responding to climate change. The philosopher, Fred Evans, writes that "Cosmopolitanism seeks a political ethics of world togetherness and a political aesthetics that can contribute to this task critically and imaginatively." Evans sees "the world as a 'cosmopolitan mind' composed of 'dialogic voices'" and he champions art's role in accessing, amplifying, and sharing human and more-than-human voices so that we can listen to each other as equal "citizens of the cosmos."[4] Some high-profile theatre directors have famously pledged never to fly again, and I admire and support that commitment, which has led to innovative international low-carbon digital theatre collaborations.[5] And,

---

[1] Although I call myself a "Kiwi" in this title, meaning New Zealander, I am a migrant to Aotearoa (New Zealand). Born in lutruwita (Tasmania), I now live and work on the homelands of Te Āti Awa, the *mana whenua* or Indigenous tribal authority for the region of Te Whanganui-a-Tara (Wellington). Te Āti Awa live in continuing relationship with their homelands and the ecologies within them, and my relationship to them and status as visitor to their lands are governed by Te Tiriti o Waitangi, the founding document of Aotearoa.

[2] Te Papa Tongarewa. Exhibition presented at Musée de la civilisation in Québec City from November 21, 2012 to September 8, 2013. https://www.mcq.org/en/mcq/expositions.php?idEx=w3594.

[3] "Decentering Humans: Writing Our Way out of the Apocalypse." *Decentered Playwriting: Alternative Techniques for the Stage*, edited by Dunn, C. M., Holmes, E. M., Hunter, L. Routledge, 2024.

[4] Evans, F. "Cosmopolitanism and the Creative Activism of Public Art." *The Journal of Aesthetics and Art Criticism 81*, 2023. https://academic.oup.com/jaac/article/81/2/213/7188942

[5] Cappelle, L. "This play is touring Europe: But no one's going anywhere." *The New York Times*, March 3, 2022. https://www.nytimes.com/2022/03/03/theater/a-play-for-the-living-in-a-time-of-extinction.html

of course, the Climate Change Theatre Action model in which plays, not productions, travel is ideal for creating low-carbon global dialogues. Since 2015, I have loved bringing CCTA voices and viewpoints from all corners of the planet to my classrooms, theatres, and the streets of my city every two years in ways that generate empathy across cultures. I have tried to also model climate action, including through a carbon neutral production in 2019. But, in 2023, I was able to be part of two cosmopolitan CCTA dialogues in ways that were even more profound, and these have led me to conclude that sometimes face-to-face listening brings something vital to the ability to ethically connect.

In April 2023, my colleague, Professor Leonel Alvarado, and I were awarded a New Zealand Prime Minister's Group Scholarship to take eight theatre students to Latin America to work with students and staff at the Universidad de Los Andes and a community-based creative group called "The Bronx." Our project centered on the ability of theatre to cross cultural and other boundaries and create mutual understanding around the shared issue of climate change.

My students prepared a CCTA play before leaving Aotearoa (New Zealand). They chose Katie Pearl's *The Earth's Blue Heart* because of its dual focus on the oceans that connect us all no matter where we are on the planet and on restoring Indigenous sustainability values to the forefront of climate conversations. There were several Māori students in our group, and they felt that the play connected with their own values from their Indigenous heritage as well as offering something universal that might resonate for Colombian audiences.

With Katie's permission, we showed *The Earth's Blue Heart* in Aotearoa as a pre-departure development performance then again on arrival as an icebreaker performance for our Colombian collaborators. The students were right: The performance sparked deep conversations and recognition of profound connections between Māori worldviews and Indigenous Colombian worldviews. Sparks of collaboration were lit and over the next four weeks, the two groups worked together to craft a multifaceted collaborative theatre piece of their own, exploring ideas of rivers, water, and sacred relationships to the Earth.

The devising culminated in a shared performance at Universidad de Los Andes in May 2023, called *What if the Rivers Could Speak?* Theatrically, we explored our two nations' histories of violence and dispossession from the viewpoint of water. We reimagined the Earth as a sacred space that nobody, whatever the challenges we face in any one group or nation, has the right to exploit. Together, we crafted a new set of dramatic stories that called for understanding climate change as a shared problem that affects all of humanity. It was a moving and life-changing experience and one which none of us, staff or students, will ever forget.

One of the epiphanies we had while working in Colombia was that while imagining the future is crucial to motivating change, the place we may need to look for the keys to that future is the past – or the ever-present. By exploring ecological values across cultures, we were reminded that for many Indigenous cultures worldwide, time is experienced not as linear but as concurrent or cyclical. In such temporalities, the consequences of our damaging actions are always with us, not something we can leave behind in the insidious "progress is inevitable and time heals" assumptions that fuel much non-Indigenous climate apathy. If our damage lives eternally alongside us, though, so do the solutions. Indigenous cultures hold answers, if we can find a way to hear them over the constant din of colonial thinking.

In her speech to the United Nations Paris Climate Conference in 2021 (COP26), Māori climate activist India Logan-Riley (Kahungunu, Rangitāne, Rongomaiwahine) noted that "Climate change is the final outcome of the colonial project and in our response, we must be decolonial, rooted in justice, and care for communities like mine who have borne the burden of the Global North greed for far too long."[6] Among the important pillars of decolonization is restoration: that is, "reinstating values and beliefs that existed before colonisation."[7] Of course, values and beliefs are only the start. As Logan-Riley added, "Land back. Oceans back. This is all part of following Indigenous leadership. This is what keeping warming below 1.5 degrees looks like. This is an invitation to you. This COP, learn our histories, listen to our stories, honor our knowledge, and get in line or get out of the way." As we worked together in Colombia, one of the questions we kept returning to was: How can we be better listeners to that which is much older and more enduring than the egocentric impositions of colonialism, patriarchy, and capitalism?

Increasingly, most non-Māori who work in sustainability roles in Aotearoa acknowledge that an understanding of Māori ecological values and

[6] Logan-Riley, I. "Indigenous activist India Logan-Riley's full speech at COP26." YouTube, uploaded by Doha Debates, 2021. https://www.youtube.com/watch?v=Qdxa1H4y-hw
[7] Tilley, E., Love, T. "The role of research in cross-cultural communication in Aotearoa/New Zealand." *Communication in the New Zealand Workplace: Theory and Practice,* edited by F. Sligo, R. Bathurst. Wellington, NZ: Software Technology New Zealand, 2005.

recognition of how fundamentally different they are from non-Indigenous ways of relating are central to achieving climate action. Advocating for a *tauiwi tautoko*[8] approach in which non-Māori study, support, and hold space for the importance of Māori values helps all of us improve our relationships with the environment. To quote from Logan-Riley's COP26 rallying call again, "In the impacts of climate change, our fates are intertwined."

So, when I received a second invitation to collaborate on climate theatre internationally in 2023, this time in Beijing as part of a research fellowship to Peking University, the play that I took with me on a USB stick behind the Great Fire Wall was (with her permission) by my Massey University colleague, Māori playwright Whiti Hereaka (Ngāti Tūwharetoa, Te Arawa, Tūhourangi, Ngāti Whakaue, Ngāti Tumatawera, Tainui, and Pākehā).

Whiti's play is called *Wayfinder*, and it is very much about that task of finding our way back or perhaps through to the values of those who cared for the land before us and continue to do so now, as well as figuring out how to hear the wisdom of the land itself. The play is also an acknowledgment that many Indigenous peoples are similarly finding their way on that journey, because of the violent disruption to intergenerational knowledge transfer wrought by colonization.

Wayfinder is an example of what Pasifika science fiction writer Dr. Gina Cole terms "Pasifikafuturism;" it imagines a science fiction future in which the science is Pacific traditional knowledge, showing "how it is possible to recover and affirm customary knowledge, impacted by the colonial project, as an evolving, living practice."[9] My Peking University host, Professor Zhao Baisheng, who has pioneered ecocriticism in China over the past three decades, had asked me to share with him and his students the writers who were leading the way in Aotearoa literature and theatre – who were at the cutting edge of bold literary innovation and new cultural developments. I shared Gina's Pasifikafuturism novel, *Na Viro*, with his students, and for our CCTA selection, I could not think of a better theatrical innovator to share than Whiti.

[8] In the Te Aka Māori Dictionary, *tauiwi* means alien, stranger, foreigner, or non-Māori and *tautoko* means to support, back, prop up, verify, or advocate. The concept came to prominence in Aotearoa through an important online anti-racism campaign, https://www.tauiwitautoko.com, encouraging non-Māori to speak up to address racism towards Māori, but is also now used in wider contexts to signal the importance of non-Māori learning how to be educated and respectful allies for Māori values.

[9] Cole, Gina. "'Pasifikafuturism:' The new genre of science fiction invented by author Gina Cole." *Stuff*, 2022. https://www.stuff.co.nz/life-style/130306614/pasifikafuturism-the-new-genre-of-science-fiction-invented-by-author-gina-cole

And so, in December 2023, in a spacious theatre in the School of Foreign Languages at Peking University as record snows fell outside, we presented a rehearsed reading, in English, and discussion, in both Mandarin and English, of *Wayfinder* by Whiti Hereaka under the banner of "CCTA Beijing 2023." The readers were my host Baisheng and Jiang Yuxin, a student from Duke University Shanghai with a passion for theatre.

In a practical sense, *Wayfinder* presented a challenge as a rehearsed reading because it has no dialogue. I split up and allocated the extensive stage directions that form the play in alternating blocks to Baisheng and Yuxin to read, as a kind of guided thought experiment for the audience. I encouraged audience members to close their eyes and build the visual world of the play in their minds as they listened.

Wayfinder is set in a perhaps dystopian, perhaps post-Apocalyptic future, but it is not bleak. Rather, it imagines a mechanism by which future inhabitants of the Earth can connect directly with the wisdom of the soil, the water, the birds, and the planet itself. It imagines listening. At its heart, *Wayfinder* is about Indigenous knowledge. It draws on Māori and Indigenous Pacific understandings of nature in which humans are inseparable from the ecologies that surround us, such that to poison a river is to poison the people. Or, as it is phrased more optimistically in a Māori *whakataukī* (proverb), "*Toitū te Marae a Tane, Toitū te Marae a Tangaroa, Toitū te iwi.* (If the land is well and the sea is well, the people will thrive.)"[10]

Of course, environmentalists have for decades understood that Indigenous knowledge has important climate solutions embedded in its ways of relating to the world, but that knowledge is difficult to communicate because it comes from a completely different conceptual basis to Darwinian forms of hierarchical classification and separation. Theatre, because it is also a different way of conceptualizing knowledge, an embodied, oral, aural, multimodal, and sometimes misty way rather than a linear, literate, well-lit way, offers a means to start to understand just how different Indigenous worldviews are.

In *Wayfinder*, Whiti uses that power of alterity – or if we were going to use Freud, we might call it the uncanny, something that is familiar and unfamiliar all at once – via the metaphor of a machine. She calls it "the instrument," and it provides a sort of bridge between a human and the inherent knowledge of stars and currents in the environment around them.

[10] Te Papa Atawhai / Department of Conservation. *Papatūānuku Thrives*, 2024. https://www.doc.govt.nz/about-us/our-role/our-purpose-and-outcomes

Whiti uses this metaphor of the instrument that connects humanity to nature's wisdom to help us imagine how we can merge our understanding with the environment around and within us, how we can better connect, as well as to point out that Indigenous knowledge of how to listen to the ecologies we are part of, is valid scientific knowledge.

In Whiti's own words, "Water and the ocean have always played an important role in the collective cultures of Te Moana Nui a Kiwa." (This refers to Oceania – the islands of the Pacific including Aotearoa.) "Rather than seeing the vast ocean that surrounds us as isolating, the ocean connects us." To me, her play embodied and brought to life in a powerful way the words of another eminent Māori author, Witi Ihimaera, who has written that:

> The sea … is not a resource for capitalism. There are human and non-human impacts, relationships between seen and unseen worlds that we are beginning to recognize. We must listen more closely to the Pacific narratives to ensure maintenance of the tapu, mana, noa, mauri, tika, pono and aroha of Te Moana Nui a Kiwa not only as a home but also as a food basket and water reservoir. We will survive. Then will come the next question: how will we thrive in the survive of the survival?[11]

In the introduction to her play, Whiti notes that, in a range of ways, Aotearoa "is currently trying to incorporate traditional ideas, or Mātauranga Māori, into our curriculum – as a complement, a mirror, a critique, and a lens to view 'Western' science." However, she notes that this "has been met by resistance – rooted in half-truths and frankly, racism. The opponents to this rail against traditional knowledge calling it 'myth' and 'fairy tale' while steadfastly clinging to their own myth and fairy tale of scientific objectivity." In *Wayfinder*, Whiti brings Western science and traditional knowledge together through the imaginary 'instrument' to show how we need to value all forms of knowledge. The instrument helps us envisage what is possible if we remove human greed and self-interest from the process of connecting across cultures and species and begin to work together for collective good. Whiti says, "It is a start, and I am hopeful that this is how we will find our way – as we always have done."

In Beijing, the discussion that followed Whiti's play was, once again, fascinating, and profoundly connective on many levels across cultural and linguistic differences. We discovered numerous values in common between

[11] Ihimaera, W. "Writing outward into the international world." *Journal of New Zealand & Pacific Studies 11*, 2024.

Chinese culture and Māori culture, such as respect for the wisdom of elders, a deep veneration for the land and, especially, an understanding of water as a transcendent resource that needs to be honored as so much more than a commodity to be exploited. My further reading about traditional Chinese environmental values since returning to Aotearoa has indicated that there is a strong affinity between long-established Chinese understandings of harmony and symbiosis between human and more-than-human worlds and Māori understandings of the interconnectedness of all things.

The audience at CCTA Beijing was, as it transpired, full of leading Chinese ecocriticism academics whom Baisheng had reached out to and invited. I discovered like-minded researchers who have been working intensively for years on the role that literature and theatre can play in promoting climate action. One, for example, teaches an environmental literature class and is editing an environmental literature reader to be published by the prestigious Tsinghua University Press next year. Another has been working to identify leading climate plays worldwide and obtain permissions to translate them into Mandarin for publication, with critical commentary, in top Chinese literary journals. It was thrilling to discover such an appetite for climate theatre, to learn just how much research is happening in China on ecocriticism, and to be able to build connections with people and ideas so directly relevant to what CCTA has been trying to do. We talked about the importance of cosmopolitanism; I joked about my sisters and their fancy cocktails, so we raised a hypothetical glass to toast our continued connection. The WeChat messages have been flowing ever since as I try with a range of Chinese academic colleagues to figure out how we can contribute to Fred Evans' goal of "a political ethics of world togetherness and a political aesthetics that can contribute to this task critically and imaginatively."

For both these trips, which have led to lifelong friendships and climate theatre collaborations that continue to unfold, I flew on airplanes. I did not pay to offset the flights, partly because that wasn't offered to me as an option through the particular booking mechanism I am required to use and partly because commercial carbon offsetting is controversial and may not be as effective as we hope. However, I did calculate my emissions and engage in my own form of carbon counterbalancing using a local tree-planting service. All my friends and family are accustomed now to having a tree planted for their birthday and other celebrations instead of directly receiving a gift. Many initiatives in Aotearoa plant trees (such as Trees That Count) or create carbon sinks (such as The Good Carbon Farm) and contribute to sustainability in ways that are more localized and accountable than international commercial carbon offsetting. Likely most regions of the world offer something similar in terms of regional tree-planting, carbon sink, or Indigenous-led waste reduction initiatives.

I still feel somewhat uncomfortable about the flying, but I think on these two occasions, it was worth it to take CCTA to new audiences and build such strong cosmopolitan bonds. For the young people who travelled to Colombia, Aotearoa is a long way from the rest of the world and they have limited opportunities to travel by any other means. It was important, especially after the isolation of the pandemic, for them to see themselves as global citizens and develop pan-Indigenous connections.

Working *kanohi ki te kanohi* (face to face) is recognized as an important aspect of building enduring relationships in the Māori world. It means "to see who or what is being communicated in the flesh using all the senses to hear, feel, smell, and taste the encounter through the sharing of the same air."[1] Likewise theatre, at its best, is about breathing the same air. As we struggle to understand how to act together as one worldwide community to combat the planetary issue of climate change, sometimes literally breathing the same air can help us figure out that we are in this together.

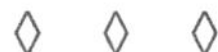

Dr. Elspeth Tilley, of Aotearoa-New Zealand, is a three-time CCTA playwright and five-time CCTA producer. She is Professor of Creative Communication at Te Kunenga ki Pūrehuroa (Massey University) where she teaches creative activism and writes political plays exploring issues ranging from climate change and homelessness to animal rights. Elspeth's plays have won awards worldwide, and she received the 2018 Playwrights' Association of New Zealand Outstanding Achievement Award. She is grateful for the support for her two 2023 CCTA international teaching and research collaborations from Education New Zealand and The New Zealand Centre at Peking University, respectively.

[1] Pātaka. Exhibition: Kanohi ki te kanohi, 2022. https://pataka.org.nz/whats/exhibitions/kanohi-ki-te-kanohi_faces-from-the-collections

SEVEN STARLINGS: OR HOW TO MAKE THEATRE MAKE CHANGE, PERHAPS

Mark Wallace

> Social capital – built on community connections, trust and norms – underpins the collective action needed to demand, enact and enforce environmental legislation.
>
> —Kate Raworth[2]

Getting teenagers out of bed on a school day isn't difficult in Croyde and Georgeham. When the early morning waves are strong, the five o'clock alarm is a fair price for a pre-school surf with the Croyde Bay dawn patrol.

Since 2022, this sheltered North Devon bay, along with thirty kilometers of English Atlantic coastline around it, has been designated a World Surfing Reserve, standing with just eleven other global exemplars. Putting your home village on a par with Malibu Beach and the Australian Gold Coast can do wonders for your sense of place.

"We were actually doing something about our environment rather than just talking about it," says Lexie, a fourteen-year-old student at nearby Braunton Academy.

Lexie chose *Clothes Minded*, written by American playwright, Klae Bainter, to be part of our Climate Change Theatre Action evening at her school in December 2023. A cast of fellow students and theatre professionals presented a total of twelve CCTA plays, along with opening and closing scenes devised by the students.

The next evening, we moved inland to Chulmleigh College, in the heart of rural North Devon, where the participating students chose to make their own work in response to the CCTA collection. Mentored by the cast, they performed their new pieces along with their selection of CCTA plays.

Their audience was not formed of the usual suspects. While there were a few eco-conscious theaterati, most were parents, friends, and neighbors from the

[2] *Doughnut Economics: Seven Ways to Think Like a 21st-Century Economist*, Chelsea Green Publishing, 2017.

village. After the final lines of the last piece, Chris Thorpe's *We Almost Died, Waiting*, they were silent. It was not the kind of knowing pause you'd expect from a specialist theatre crowd savoring a bittersweet closing scene. This was a little closer to shell shock.

The students had risen fully to the occasion. Our professionals had structured an evening that asked each member of the cast, regardless of age or training, to land their moment on stage. They had helped the students to shape their own pieces so that each burned with authentic hope, anger, and frustration. The audience had absorbed it all.

I stood up and thanked the cast, then explained to the parents and neighbors that evenings like this were taking place in many countries. CCTA plays were being performed in communities across the US, from California to Florida, across Europe, and from New Zealand to the Arctic Circle. "Thank you for helping North Devon to – quite literally – play its part on the world stage." It was a cheap line, but it landed.

> ... the increasing emphasis in social and political geography on rural, local communities as representing places of belonging and of shared knowledge which complicate and resist the apparent threat of globalization.
>
> —Jo Robinson[3]

In 2002, North Devon became the UK's first new-style UNESCO Biosphere Reserve. It's now one of 738 places on the planet asked to become a global center of sustainable development. UNESCO defines them as "sites for testing interdisciplinary approaches to understanding and managing interactions between social and ecological systems ... *They are places that provide local solutions to global challenges.*" (The emphasis is mine.)

Each Biosphere Reserve has a globally significant habitat at its core. For us, that's Braunton Burrows, a thirteen-square-kilometer dune system in the next bay along from Croyde. It's located at the estuary of two rivers, one of which, the Taw, runs just to the west of Chulmleigh, a long way upstream.

Can you guess which designation – World Surfing Reserve or UNESCO Biosphere Reserve – has more successfully captured the attention of the next generation?

[3] *Theatre and The Rural*, Springer, 2016.

To a large extent, it doesn't matter. Attention is no use if it's not converted into action. Organizations like Plastic Free North Devon straddle both, with regular beach cleans and a tourism support scheme to eradicate the piles of disposable bodyboards left on our beaches during the summer. The challenge, to which PFND has risen, is motivating enough people to come together and make a difference.

As the economist Kate Raworth notes, collective action is rarely spurred solely by personal gain. It's more often driven by shared social values: belonging, stewardship, and legacy. Writing in the journal *Ecological Economics* in 2015, Jasper Kenter defines these values as "the outcome of processes of effective social interaction, open dialogue and social learning … shared social values are closely allied to shared meanings."

At UNESCO's Dublin European Man and Biosphere conference in 2019, Estonia's Director of Biosphere Reserves led a session on the role of culture. He noted that science had tried to inspire these shared meanings for the past two decades with limited success. He suggested it was now time for culture to take the lead. Minds and hearts, respectively.

> … theatre-making implies a different division of labour to the previously established ones which feature clearly delineated playwrights, directors, designers, producers, and actors … Similarly, the work's relationship with the audience seems to be more important than any hierarchies between text and performance.
>
> —Duška Radosavljević[4]

"Our work with Beaford over the last six years has had a profound impact on our direction of travel," says Gill Nathanson, co-director of North Devon's multi story theatre company. The feeling is unquestionably mutual.

Multi story has been based in North Devon for over twenty years, surviving the slings and arrows of the touring scene with an unwavering commitment to independent small-scale theatre. "Our involvement with *Hefted*, a Beaford commission from playwright David Lane in 2018, meant confronting how our national and international touring pattern impacted on the environment," says Gill.

[4] *Theatre-Making: Interplay Between Text and Performance in the 21st Century*, Palgrave Macmillan, 2013.

"COVID meant that, for other reasons, we needed to embrace the local," she adds. "Early-career theatre makers were missing out on a lot of in-person theatre making. We worked to remedy that as best we could."

The pandemic had brought a number of recently trained professionals back home to North Devon to see out the lockdowns. Gill, and co-director Bill Buffery, established Theatre Workhouse in 2021 as a weekly session to keep professional skills in shape.

When COVID restrictions ended that summer, Theatre Workhouse was commissioned by Beaford to produce an evening for Climate Change Theatre Action 2021. They followed it with their own show, *Where To Begin,* in 2022, working with multi story and writer/director, Daniel Bye, to answer the tongue-in-cheek question, "What if the climate changed in North Devon?"

"The research and conversations around both CCTA 2021 and *Where To Begin* profoundly changed our lives. We can't unsee what we've seen and go back to our previous careless touring pattern, and we can't stop exploring how to draw back the veil – as happened to us," says Bill. "How to frame the arguments and engage in the conversations has become the topic that obsesses us." Multi story went on to make a beautiful new two-hander, *Last Dance Saloon*, a love story in which the protagonists' climate consciences, along with their passion for tango, shape the progress of a "September Song" affair.

CCTA 2021 had become a catalyst as well as a project. When CCTA 2023 came around, multi story and Beaford sought others with whom we could find common cause. We talked with our contacts in secondary schools.

"I want my students to know that theatre can tell their stories and needs their voices," says Sara Feasey, Head of Expressive Arts at Chulmleigh College, explaining her decision to take part. "I want them to believe that theatre can be a force for change and social justice – connecting us to others with shared purpose and meaning."

> But I didn't have to say anything. Because without any prompting, or any words from anyone ... every child in that classroom stood up, walked to the student, huddled around them, and hugged them. It was like the instinct to take care of each other was in them ... and they knew what had to be done.
>
> —Juan C. Sanchez[5]

[5] *Hurricane*, CCTA 2023.

In 2021, Arts Council England, our state-funded arts development agency, changed its approach.

"We launched our first Environmental Program in 2012 and embedded environmental reporting into our funding agreement," says Philip Butterworth, Arts Council England's Relationship Manager for North Devon. "By 2021, we strengthened this commitment with the launch of our ten-year strategy '*Let's Create,*'" he explains. "By asking partners to embed this thinking across their delivery, we increasingly see them take a leadership role on the subject in their area."

Arts Council England awarded a National Lottery Project Grant to multi story to deliver climate-focused workshops with teenage drama students from the two schools. The young people were alive to the issues raised by the CCTA 2023 plays, coming to the first session not only with a passion but with things they wanted to say.

"Theirs wasn't just an intellectual response – it was almost visceral," says Gill. Leadership, in this instance, meant holding a space for the next generation's voices. Gill and Bill shaped a process that kept ownership where it belonged. "It's that privilege of seeing young people express themselves full-bloodedly about the world," Bill says. "They wanted it to be an argument. They didn't want to pussyfoot around."

Over the course of several workshops, the students worked with the professional team to develop the pieces they had chosen or written. On the day itself, all that remained was to work through the ins and outs of each scene. By then, each cast's students and professionals knew each other well and could work fast and on their feet.

"The opportunity to work and perform alongside professional theatre makers, both seasoned and emerging, I knew would inspire my students," says Chulmleigh College's Sara Feasey. Braunton Academy's Head of Drama, Rob Carroll, concurs, adding, "CCTA was such an incredibly valuable experience for my students – and not just from the perspective of performing exciting new work on an issue that they care deeply about …"

> The world takes the shape we want it to take, but you want it to stay the same. Don't you see we can change it?
>
> —Nathan Joe[6]

[6] *Cassandra Drowning,* CCTA 2023.

CCTA's biennial invitation is collaborative from the outset. Its international writers combine to offer a global longlist of fifty short plays. Anyone anywhere can present a CCTA event "using at least one play from our collection," as long as they "include an action – educational, social, or civic – … to connect or galvanize people."

Our first performance, at Braunton Academy, was supported by volunteers from Plastic Free North Devon, who served refreshments and recruited audience members for the next beach clean. At Chulmleigh College, we distributed Biosphere Reserve information ahead of a three-year community climate action program starting in 2024.

Our third and final CCTA evening took place in Barnstaple, North Devon's regional center, a mile or two upstream from Braunton Burrows. It brought together our professionals, both student casts, and an audience including councilors, trustees, and regional stakeholders.

This was the first time the two schools had performed together. Braunton's Rob Carroll recalls "… my students' realization, through sharing their work with the community and seeing work from other schools, that there was a sense of common purpose, that they were all on the same page about what their contribution was, that they were a part of something bigger and that they were using theatre as their vehicle."

After the last line of *We Almost Died, Waiting*, four young women from Chulmleigh's cast stepped forward. Their self-penned coda was a call to action, uncompromising and rooted in the world their audience's generation had helped to shape. They ricocheted the lines between them until, as one, they set their gaze on the adults before them. "Stand with us," said one, in a tone combining invitation, instruction, and an underlying challenge to step outside and settle this right now. "Stand with us," they repeated together.

Blackout.

> The rapid, astonishing twists and turns of a murmuration are created by each starling just paying attention to its seven nearest fellow flyers … a similar kind of micro-attention in theatre, across all aspects of making work, can produce shifts in creative and social practice at a scale that collectively far outweighs any one of the actions.
>
> —Zoë Svendsen[7]

[7] "Climate Conversations: Making Theatre in the Context of Climate Crisis," Report commissioned by the Donmar Warehouse, 2023

Across three evenings in December 2023, three generations of North Devonians showed their audiences how it would be if we addressed our hopes and fears together.

Ours is a relatively small region, occupying just under 3,000 square kilometers of a corner of southwest England. Our rural villages contain farms that have been run by the same families for centuries, even as second-home buyers from elsewhere inflate property prices far beyond locally affordable levels.

We are at the same time insular and globally connected. It's a balance that tilts with each successive generation, from the retired smallholder who has never left the county to the teenage gamer talking to the world through his bedroom broadband.

A century ago, both would have found common cause in the land they worked together. The challenge for those of us managing our environmental assets today is to rebuild those shared social values. International designations give us validation, but without interpersonal connections they speak only to the mind and not the heart.

Climate Change Theatre Action enabled our cast to find these connections and raise their own voices in response. For three evenings, they showed their communities how to take action collectively – and in doing so, they made shared meanings across the generations and with others across the world. Hearts and minds, together.

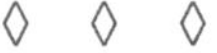

Mark Wallace has been the Director of Beaford Arts since 2007. He has served as chair of Theatre SW, representing South West England's theatre development agencies, and as chair of Audiences South West, the region's former audience development agency. He is a vice-chair of North Devon's UNESCO Biosphere Reserve Partnership, a member of Arts Council England's South West Area Council, and a Fellow of the Royal Society for Arts.

Beaford Arts, based in North Devon, is England's longest-established rural arts initiative, set up by the Dartington Hall Trust in 1966 and independent since the 1980s. Beaford's staff enable a network of volunteers in rural communities to bring professional arts performances, education, and exhibitions to North Devon's villages and towns. Beaford regularly supports and commissions new creative work at the intersection of arts, heritage, and environment. It is a member of Arts Council England's National Portfolio.

CREATIVE CLIMATE CONVERSATIONS IN THE HEART OF CANADA'S OIL COUNTRY

Clare Preuss

Climate change is a critical global issue. It's also an incredibly local issue for those of us who live and work in the province of Alberta, Canada. Alberta's oil sands have the fourth largest proven oil reserves in the world, after Venezuela, Saudi Arabia, and Iran. We are on the frontline of the climate conversation and it can be an emotional and taboo subject because so many people here rely on the oil and gas industry for their daily survival, or have loved ones who are embedded in the oil and gas economy.

Alberta is currently preparing for one of the driest summers on record. As of March 2024, there are fifty-one active water shortage advisories for Alberta according to our provincial government website.[1] In 2023, we had a record-breaking wildfire season across Canada. By September 5, 2023, more than 6,132 fires had burned 16.5 million hectares of land.[2] That is an area larger than Greece. Compounding these crises, it takes three barrels of fresh water to produce one barrel of oil from the Alberta oil sands.

I am the artistic director of Downstage, a professional theatre company based in Calgary. We create, produce, and present theatre that fosters conversations about important social issues and we are committed to addressing climate change in an artful, compassionate, and inclusive way. In 2019, Downstage honed-in on the need for artful conversation around the climate crisis and how it impacts us as a community. We wanted to host an event that allowed for various perspectives to be shared in a playful and future-focused way, while also acknowledging the complexities of the issue both locally and globally.

We began collaborating with Climate Change Theatre Action for our first series of staged readings entitled *Lighting the Way*. This one-night event sold out and we received excellent responses from our audience. Young audience members engaged passionately in the Long Table Discussion – a non-hierarchical invitation to partake in communal conversation. Conceived by

[1] https://www.alberta.ca/drought-current-conditions#jumplinks-0
[2] https://natural-resources.canada.ca/simply-science/canadas-record-breaking-wild-fires-2023-fiery-wake-call/25303#:~:text=Canada's%202023%20wildfire%20season%20is,than%20double%20the%201989%20record

performance artist and activist, Lois Weaver, it is inspired by the construct of a dinner party, with participants sitting around a table. Employees of The Pembina Institute, a think tank that advocates for strong and effective policies to support Canada's clean energy transition, remarked on the emotionally charged and insightful conversations after the show. It became clear to us that we had hit on something that served a vital need in our community.

We partnered with CCTA again for a two-day event in 2021 and invited new collaborators from the Immigrant Council for Arts Innovation. ICAI connects newcomer artists to the local arts community. It encourages diversity in expression and culture by creating a safe and welcoming environment where newcomer and immigrant artists feel confident to share their work. This was an incredibly nourishing experience. Because the CCTA plays are short and feature writers from around the world, it gave newcomer artists a chance to dive into a variety of theatrical storytelling styles in relationship to the topic of climate change. Also, because our CCTA events are formatted as staged readings, it was easier on actors who have learned English as an additional language. They didn't need to memorize their lines in order to be an effective part of the process. The conversations in rehearsals were rich with inquiry about the impact of climate change on ways of life around the world, and on human migration caused by drought, heat, and flooding, among other climate phenomena. After two successful events in 2019 and 2021, we realized that Calgary audiences were keen to participate in ongoing conversations about our lived reality within the context of climate change.

This past November, we embarked on our third CCTA project and once again partnered with ICAI for a series of staged readings followed by a Long Table Discussion. We entitled the series *All Good Things Must Begin* in keeping with CCTA's 2023 theme. Our collaboration with ICAI was an important one for this project. So many communities around the world are displaced because of climate change. This is a growing concern globally:

> Climate-driven movement of people is adding to a massive migration already under way to the world's cities. The number of migrants has doubled globally over the past decade, and the issue of what to do about rapidly increasing populations of displaced people will only become greater and more urgent.[3]

[3] Vince, Gaia. "The century of climate migration: why we need to plan for the great upheaval." *The Guardian*, August 18, 2022. https://www.theguardian.com/news/2022/aug/18/century-climate-crisis-migration-why-we-need-plan-great-upheaval#:~:text=Climate%2D-driven%20movement%20of%20people,become%20greater%20and%20more%20urgent

This quote, from a 2022 article in *The Guardian,* reflects thoughts that emerged during rehearsal. In working with ICAI and newcomer artists who have immigrated from the Global South to Canada, we discussed how climate change was one of many factors that caused migration. We have also hosted audience members who have seen massive shifts in climate in their countries of origin.

During the summer of 2023, our two lead curators, Ashley Bodiguel and Vicki Stroich, read all fifty plays commissioned by CCTA. Ashley works for the Pembina Institute. She received her BFA in theatre performance from Simon Fraser University and explores arts-based initiatives to prompt discussions about climate change and dispel taboos around the topic. Vicki is currently Artistic and Environmental Programs Manager at Caravan Farm Theatre. Prior to joining Caravan Farm Theatre, Vicki was based in Calgary and worked for four years as Engagement Director for Alberta Ecotrust Foundation, a long-standing and critical source of funding, training, and skill building for Alberta's environmental community. In recent years, Vicki had been exploring the intersection of the art and environmental sectors by participating in local and national programs and committees that bring the work of artists and environmental communities together. She has a BFA in Drama from the University of Calgary and an Extension Certificate in Social Innovation and Changemaking from Mount Royal University. Vicki was the initial instigator of the project back in 2019 when she met with me to discuss options for climate action through theatre. Both Vicki and Ashley have been with us since the beginning of our collaboration with CCTA and we are so thankful for their ongoing work on this vital project.

After Vicki and Ashley had read all of the plays, they shared a short list with the rest of our curation team. By early autumn 2023, the plays had been selected and our creative team was assembled. Five well-established local artists were be paired with five newly settled immigrant artists. This pairing allowed for organic conversations about climate to inform the work. The well-established local artists were quite familiar with the impact of the oil and gas industry on our region and how it informs political and economic decisions in terms of actions taken to mitigate climate change. Newcomer artists had lived experience of climate change in other parts of the world and knew how shifting weather patterns can affect economic and political choices. This knowledge sharing enriched the process. It also allowed artists with various creative traditions and practices to collaborate on plays that came from around the world. We collaborated with newcomer artists from Czech Republic, India, Iran, and Peru. Established local artists also had a multiplicity of lived experiences that included Indigenous, German, Irish, Nigerian, Somali, and Swiss roots. It was wonderful to hear the conversations that emerged from these collaborations, to see how each artist approached theatre making, and to learn what their perspective on climate change was.

For one week in November of 2023, we rehearsed eight plays in Motel Theatre, Arts Commons. Although actors kept their scripts in hand, all of the plays were fully staged. We included sound and lighting design as part of the experience. Downstage hosted three sold-out performances of *All Good Things Must Begin*, which featured *Actors Ready?* by Ethan King, *Wild Parsnips* by Tira Palmquist, *Duet* by Annie Furman, *A Little Green* by Charly Evon Simpson, *The Returning* by Emma Gibson, *50 Ways to End Mother Earth – In Under Five Minutes!* by Kirby Vicente, *You Are Not Alone* by Nicole Pschetz, and *A Hummingbird's Ululation* by Aleya Kassam.

It's always a fun challenge to find the most useful selection of plays for our CCTA events! There are so many great pieces to choose from. After a lot of deliberation, our team chose this mix of plays because they offered a variety of perspectives and they played with different styles of storytelling, providing a balance between poetry and humor. In addition, we wanted to incorporate a discussion into this theatre experience. We decided to have a two-act structure for the show: Act One included the performance of all eight plays; Act Two featured our version of a Long Table Discussion. At Downstage, we find that this format invites the public to engage in conversations with a sense of playful informality.

For our Long Table Discussion, there were twelve seats at the table. Audience members were invited to come to the table and take a seat any time they wished to engage in the ongoing conversation. They were also welcome to witness the conversation unfold from the comfort of their theatre seat. The fact that people could come and go from the table allowed for a multiplicity of voices and perspectives to be heard. Everyone was welcome to enjoy the free flow of ideas, the community gathering, and the sense of possibility that can come from this kind of collective energy.

We were lucky to have a group of climate-engaged professionals and activists join us for one or more of the Long Table Discussions. All seven guests offered valuable insights. I found that Jenin Ahmad's experience running the Climate Café – a forum for community members to get together to discuss the mental health impacts of climate change – at the University of Calgary was incredibly relatable for our younger audiences. Jenin was able to address the fear that many of us have in approaching the subject of climate change, and the many feelings that can arise including helplessness, anxiety, and despair. Jenin talked about ways to celebrate small victories along the way, even while being present with the bigger issues. Subashini Thangadurai has been working with us on CCTA projects since 2021. She is a seventeen-year-old climate advocate and centers her work with other teens on imagining creative solutions through societal innovation. Her approach is fresh and forward thinking. Subashini has a way of inspiring audiences of all ages with her impressive knowledge and genuine optimism. Hosting Jenin, Subashini, and other climate change specialists was a gentle yet profound way to inspire audience members to continue engaging with issues around climate change long after the event was over.

At every CCTA event, from 2019 to 2023, audiences acknowledged the need for this kind of work to happen here in Calgary. But because so many people have ties to the oil and gas industry, criticizing the work being done in the oil sands can bring up feelings of shame and guilt. Consequently, these climate conversations can be trepidatious, but they ultimately offer relief and even a renewed sense of optimism. The climate change conversation is inherently tied to capitalism. In one of the 2023 Long Table Discussions, there was a rich exchange around *rest* being a form of resistance. As we prioritize a slower and more thoughtful way of living, we can hone in on our sense of well-being and have the energy to do the important work of reshaping our relationship to the environment.

The amplified effects of climate change on our local environment have certainly shifted the discussion as well. The Downstage team has noticed the increasing need to address climate grief as part of our CCTA offerings. According to The Government of Canada's website, Canada experienced its warmest May to July period in over eighty years in 2023, breaking previous national temperature records for the three-month period by 0.8 degrees Celsius: "As wildfire risks will continue to intensify as the climate warms, Canada needs to reduce fossil fuel consumption and adapt fire management and mitigation strategies."[4] Alberta Economic Dashboard states that Alberta produced 18.2M cubic meters of oil in February 2024, which was 6.6 percent higher than in February 2023, when oil production was 17.1M cubic meters.[5] With Alberta's current drought, we are bracing for what

[4] https://natural-resources.canada.ca/simply-science/canadas-record-breaking-wildfires-2023-fiery-wake-call/25303
[5] https://economicdashboard.alberta.ca/dashboard/oil-production

could be the worst wildfire season on record while the oil and gas industry continues to function at top capacity. These truths can be overwhelming.

For every iteration of these CCTA events, we added additional performance dates – and every time the crowds came. Our 2019 and 2023 events were fully sold out and our 2021 event drew excellent crowds considering we were in the midst of COVID caution. For all three events, audiences were typically comprised of young people, climate activists, community leaders, and concerned citizens. The active participation of youth audience members in the Long Table Discussions in both 2019 and 2023 shows a true need for this kind of programming for young people. It is important to have these intergenerational, heartfelt conversations as we identify climate grief, address the current state of things, and stoke our imaginations so that we can create a future, which acknowledges the reality that *All Good Things Must Begin*.

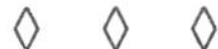

Clare Preuss is a multidisciplinary artist who has collaborated with creators across Canada as well as in Germany, Lebanon, Switzerland, Uganda, and the US. She is a director, actor, maker, and facilitator who works primarily with theatre, film, and live art. Clare played Mathlete Caroline Kraft in the cult classic, *Mean Girls,* among other film roles. She is a recipient of the Houselighters of the Citadel Theatre Award and has been nominated for various others. Clare is always keen to experiment with the intersections of art forms and is eternally curious. She is the Artistic Director at Downstage. www.downstage.ca

BEHIND THE SCENES OF CHANGE: THEATRE'S SUSTAINABLE PRODUCTION PRACTICES IN ACTION

Ian Garrett

"The world is on fire, and we're still fiddling while Rome burns." This poignant analogy may describe our collective inaction on climate change while there is an increase in the number of wildfires each year. It may ring truer each day as we witness the devastating consequences of our warming planet. However, to use another metaphor, theatre makers aren't waiting in the wings. From raging wildfires to unprecedented heat waves to devastating floods, the effects of climate change are no longer distant threats but stark realities causing regular cancellations of performances and arts events around the world, and many stage workers are taking action.

The Rising Curtain on Theatre's Vulnerabilities

The community of people working to design and build for theatrical productions in more sustainable and ecologically engaged ways has been increasing in recent years. But this hasn't mitigated the profound impact of climate change on the theatrical production industry and the future of entertainment. The performing arts, particularly theatre and live concerts, have historically thrived on the unpredictability of live performances. However, recent climatic events have introduced another unwelcome type of uncertainty.

In recent years, we've seen how natural disasters, exacerbated by climate change, have led to massive disruptions. Hurricane Harvey, which struck Houston, Texas, in 2017, inflicted damages upwards of $75 million on local theatres,[1] not to mention the loss of irreplaceable antique props, costumes, and custom wigs. More than the financial toll, the emotional and historical loss of such unique items underscores the irreparable damage inflicted by these climatic events.

[1] Kelley, Sonaiya. "Here's How Houston's Museums and Theatres Fared during Harvey." *Los Angeles Times*, September 6, 2017. https://www.latimes.com/entertainment/arts/la-et-cm-harvey-damage-on-houston-arts-institutions-20170906-htmlstory.html

At the Oregon Shakespeare Festival in Ashland, Oregon, nine performances were cancelled due to poor air quality from nearby forest fires in 2017. The situation worsened in 2018 with twenty-five cancelled performances. By 2019, all shows between July 30 and September 8 had to be relocated from an outdoor theatre with a capacity of 1,200 to a significantly smaller venue at Ashland High School, accommodating only 390 people.[2]

The changing summer weather patterns have further complicated the staging of outdoor performances. Shows have either been moved indoors or cancelled due to hailstorms, early fire seasons, intense heat, and smoke from distant wildfires. Such disruptions hint at a grim future where traditional outdoor theatre may become untenable.

The impact of climate change is not limited to theatre alone. It has also cast a shadow over the music industry, affecting concerts worldwide. In 2023 alone, high-profile events like Elton John's concert in Auckland, New Zealand, the shows in SXSW outdoor venues in Austin, Texas, and numerous festivals across the US and Europe were either cancelled or evacuated due to severe weather conditions, ranging from rain and flooding to extreme heat and poor air quality.[3] Each cancellation represents a missed opportunity for cultural exchange and community engagement.

In Jakarta, Indonesia, the implications of climate change are being felt, prompting drastic measures such as the decision to relocate the capital city.[4] What will happen to the newly established JIExpo Theatre, opened in 2020, when rising sea levels and more frequent flooding pose an ongoing threat to such infrastructural investments?

The narrative of climate change challenges us to confront the harsh realities of our changing environment and compels us to innovate in the face of adversity. For the theatre industry, this may mean embracing new technologies, redesigning traditional spaces, and advocating for stronger environmental policies, alongside the evolution of our personal approach to our work.

---

[2] Van Wing, Sage. "McKinney Fire Impacts Southern Oregon and Northern California." *Opb*, August 8, 2022. https://www.opb.org/article/2022/08/08/mckinney-fire-impacts-southern-oregon-and-northern-california

[3] Bain, Katie. "Here Are All The Concerts Affected By Climate Change In 2023." *Billboard*, October 20, 2023. https://www.billboard.com/lists/concerts-affected-climate-change-2023-full-list

[4] Beech, Hannah. "What's a President to Do When a Nation's Capital Is Sinking? Move It." *The New York Times*, May 16, 2023. https://www.nytimes.com/interactive/2023/05/16/headway/indonesia-nusantara-jakarta.html

While we adapt to these new realities, producing theatre is far from trivial. Sustainable theatre reshapes how communities perceive climate change by focusing on awareness, community engagement, and behavioral change.

Plays in the Climate Change Theatre Action (CCTA) collection highlight the urgency of climate action, presenting stories that make climate change tangible and immediate, thus elevating public consciousness. The plays often reflect local environmental issues, and their production worldwide fosters a sense of community and shared purpose through partnerships with local groups and the incorporation of regional concerns.

Ecoscenography and CCTA

Since 2015, CCTA has provided a platform for theatre makers to engage with sustainability through thematic scripts and projects that extend to design and production. CCTA not only raises awareness but also demonstrates practical applications of sustainable practices in the arts, with ecoscenography being a key component from the start.

Defined by Tanja Beer, the three Cs of ecoscenography – co-creation, celebration, and circulation – form a holistic framework for sustainable theatre production.[5] Co-creation emphasizes collaborative efforts among diverse human and non-human contributors. Celebration focuses on raising ecological awareness and appreciating collective efforts. Circulation promotes the sustainable use and reuse of materials and the ongoing relationships built during the process. Together, these principles ensure that theatre is both artistically enriching and environmentally responsible.

The CCTA design initiatives gained significant traction in 2019 when Triga Creative led the first CCTA EcoDesign Charrette. This collaborative workshop brought together artists, designers, and environmental experts to brainstorm and implement eco-friendly solutions in Triga's Toronto studio as well as online. It showcased how recycled and upcycled materials could be creatively used for sets and costumes, while exploring methods to minimize energy consumption and waste.[6]

---

[5] Beer, Tanja. *Ecoscenography: An Introduction to Ecological Design for Performance.* Palgrave Macmillan, 2022.

[6] "A Collective Exploration of Ecoscenography: Reflections on Triga Creative's CCTA Eco-Design Charrette" by Triga Creative in *Lighting the Way: An Anthology of Short Plays About the Climate Crisis*, Centre for Sustainable Practice in the Arts and The Arctic Cycle, 2020.

Furthering CCTA's commitment to sustainable design, the 2021 EcoDesign Charrette and Global Networked Learning course connected students and professionals worldwide from mid-October 2021 to mid-February 2022. Led by myself at York University in Toronto, Canada, Tanja Beer at Griffith University, and Tessa Rixon at Queensland University of Technology, both in Brisbane, Australia, participants learned to integrate sustainable design principles into their work using the three Cs of ecoscenography.[7] After months of collaborative workshops and studio work, an exhibition of these designs was showcased at cSpace King Edward in Calgary, Canada as part of World Stage Design 2022. The exhibition showed how powerful this work can be as an educational tool, often incorporating community workshops and discussions that highlighted the importance of sustainable practices.

For CCTA 2023, selected plays from this anthology were used in a results-driven workshop at the 2023 Prague Quadrennial of Performance Design and Space in the Czech Republic. Designers from around the world, and at various career stages, spent three days building full experiences of the plays. It continued to demonstrate the global reach of CCTA and has expanded awareness of the now 250 climate plays it has commissioned since 2015 that have affected all aspects of theatre making.

All Good Things Must Begin

A comprehensive view of all of the aspects of producing theatre is crucial to creating a more sustainable theatre. Using eco-friendly materials, repurposing sets, and incorporating energy-efficient technologies reduce productions' environmental footprints. But the concepts and thinking around how we perform in space can also push us to reimagine the way we interact with the world. This approach demonstrates how creativity coexists with ecological responsibility. Through the various ways that CCTA has sought to include design and production, we see how the plays inspire the realization of ecoscenographic priorities.

Eco-Efficiency

CCTA itself provides a new model for moving work around and "touring" through its distributed festival approach. We learned a great deal about how this can reduce environmental impacts during our partnership with Canada's National Arts Centre English Theatre on the second part of their

[7] "Global Network Learning EcoDesign Charrette" by Ian Garrett, Tanja Beer, and Tessa Rixon in *The Future Is Not Fixed: Short Plays Envisioning a Global Green New Deal*, Applause Theatre and Cinema Books, 2023.

two-year Climate Cycle in 2020. Originally intended as an in-person event, it was redesigned to take place across eight hubs to minimize long-distance travel, significantly reducing CO_2 emissions compared to traditional models. Due to the COVID-19 pandemic, the event moved online in June 2020, offering a third model for consideration. This final shift reduced emissions by over ninety-nine percent compared to traditional models.

Each iteration of that event was approached as a unique design challenge, adapting to the constraints and opportunities of the event's format while aiming to provide an impactful experience. Engaging with new technologies requires evaluating if they enhance our relationships in co-creation. We must consider if aspects of technology can expand how co-creators, including audience members, engage with the work to underscore our objectives. This prompts us to ask: What infrastructure do we need to support these relationships?

This thinking informed the global networking of the 2021 EcoDesign Charette, split between Canada and Australia, and spurred research into hybrid presentation models. The 2023 production of *Aionos* is a recent example. Conceived and produced by Toasterlab, and created by an ensemble of devisers led by Aisha Lesley Bentham, and consultation with Ari Tarr and Debbie Deer, it was performed in-person at ZOO venues in Edinburgh and online through the social VR platform Flipside, a Discord server, and conventional streaming. With cast and crew split between Edinburgh and Toronto, it leveraged online work developed during the pandemic to minimize the production's footprint and increase audience accessibility.

Advancements in technology hold significant promise for the future of sustainable theatre production. Innovations such as energy-efficient lighting systems can reduce energy consumption. The use of renewable energy sources can help power theatre operations. Innovative fabrication, used to create props and set pieces from biodegradable materials, can cut down on waste and the environmental impact of traditional manufacturing processes. Additionally, virtual and augmented reality technologies are emerging as transformative tools. These technologies can create immersive environments while reducing material use and waste.

Relationality

Working ecoscenographically emphasizes acknowledging Indigenous contexts and collaborating with communities. This approach involves deeply engaging with the locations where theatrical activities occur, understanding their historical and cultural significance, and respecting the Indigenous peoples who have historically stewarded the land. Consulting with Indigenous communities, incorporating their stories and knowledge, and ensuring their voices are represented in the production are essential steps.

Similar to CCTA's networking aspects, more projects now consider the broader context of their work. Each CCTA performance, even when based on the same selection of plays, prompts questions about the relationships and connections being established. We are encouraged to ask whose land we are on, acknowledging both historical stewardship and contemporary ownership. This reflection enhances the authenticity and relevance of the production. Establishing the right relationship with a site involves more than acknowledging its history; it means actively engaging with the community and environment. These practices ensure that the theatre's impact promotes a deeper connection between the performance and its environment.

The involvement of non-human characters in CCTA productions highlights the concept of non-human co-creators in ecoscenography. This perspective urges theatre practitioners to consider the array of non-human collaborators and acknowledge their significance within the creative process. Trees, mushrooms, and polar bears are not merely symbolic representations but active participants that bring their unique qualities and stories to the stage. By doing so, these characters challenge the anthropocentric view that often dominates theatre and encourage a more inclusive approach to storytelling.

Recognizing the agency of non-human characters is crucial. These entities exert influence within the narrative and have their own forms of presence and impact. For example, a tree in a production might symbolize growth, stability, or the consequences of deforestation. Mushrooms can represent the interconnectedness of life through their mycelial networks, while polar bears can symbolize the effects of climate change on Arctic habitats. By attributing agency to these characters, theatre acknowledges that non-human entities are integral to the world's ecological balance and have intrinsic value beyond their utility to humans.

Accessibility

Through these considerations, we observe a shared ethic of access across CCTA and ecoscenography. By making each collection of plays freely available during the festival season, and embracing an expanded view of co-creation, we are forced to critically evaluate how to include or exclude various groups. This involves considering how people can be brought to the place and how the place can be brought to the people, thereby emphasizing the importance of accessibility and inclusivity in sustainable theatre practices.

The affective qualities of theatre are most potent when they consider who has access to the celebration, how individuals arrive, and how they participate. It is essential to ask who is being included or excluded from the theatrical experience, and to explore innovative solutions to bridge these gaps. Are there ways to bring people to the performance venue that we haven't yet considered? For example, could we use community transportation services, offer sliding scale ticket pricing, or create partnerships with local organizations to facilitate attendance?

Equally important is how to bring the place to the people. This might involve creating mobile performances that travel to various communities, utilizing digital platforms to stream live shows, or incorporating virtual and augmented reality to offer immersive experiences for those who cannot physically attend. By exploring these avenues, we can expand the reach of theatre, making it more accessible to a diverse audience, and ensuring that the benefits of cultural engagement are widely distributed.

Fostering inclusivity means engaging with different community groups to understand their unique needs and preferences. This engagement can help tailor performances to be more relevant and resonant, thereby enhancing the overall impact of the theatre. It also involves creating spaces where diverse voices are heard and valued in the co-creation process, from the initial planning stages to the final production.

In practical terms, this approach to fostering inclusivity might look like collaborating with local cultural organizations, schools, and community centers to create satellite events or preview performances. It could also involve providing educational workshops and discussion panels that offer deeper insights into the themes of the plays, making the experience more enriching and engaging for all participants.

Conclusion

Sustainable theatre practices are critical to combating climate change. By integrating sustainability into their core practices, theatres can educate, inspire, and mobilize audiences toward environmental stewardship. These efforts show that artistic excellence and ecological responsibility are not mutually exclusive but can enhance each other. The theatre industry's adaptation to climate change can serve as a model for other sectors, showcasing the potential for creative solutions to global challenges. Though extreme weather and ash-filled air may force us to cancel performances, these adaptations are not trivial activities but crucial efforts in raising awareness and fostering community.

Beyond environmental benefits, sustainable theatre fosters a sense of community, inclusivity, and shared purpose. By addressing local environmental issues and incorporating diverse voices, an ecoscenographic approach strengthens community ties and resilience. It also highlights the importance of cultural engagement in addressing climate change, making the issue more tangible and immediate for audiences.

As we move forward, it is essential to continue supporting and expanding this work. This includes advocating for policies that promote environmental responsibility in the arts, funding research and development of eco-friendly technologies, and fostering collaborations among theatre professionals, environmental experts, and local communities.

You, dear reader, can contribute by attending sustainable theatre productions, participating in community workshops, and spreading awareness about the importance of sustainability in the arts. Theatre professionals can adopt the principles of ecoscenography, experiment with innovative design practices, and engage with local and Indigenous communities to create more inclusive and impactful productions.

Collaborating with CCTA is a great way to begin.

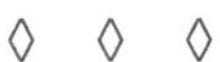

Ian Garrett is a designer, producer, educator, and researcher in the field of sustainability in arts and culture. He is producer for Toasterlab, a mixed reality performance collective, the director of the Centre for Sustainable

Practice in the Art, and an Associate Professor of Ecological Design for Performance at York University in Toronto.

CCTA 2023 BY THE NUMBERS: RETURNING TO THE STAGE

GiGi Buddie

In 2021, amidst the chaos of a global pandemic and a shifting theatrical landscape, Climate Change Theatre Action events across the globe pivoted to digital mediums. A faint blue light glowed in rooms as chat boxes filled with emoticon praise, and silent applause for the artists in their tiny Zoom screens. *Anyone* could tune in from *anywhere* – but this increased access to connection, which was bringing us closer together, was simultaneously pushing us further apart. I would click "leave meeting" and look up to find reality – quiet and detached from the show I had been watching mere seconds before. My yearning for a world reconnected by live performance grew and grew … and I knew I wasn't alone.

Fast forward to 2023 and the fifth iteration of CCTA, when I experienced firsthand the ubiquitous need for in-person theatrical connection. As part of my work with the Arts & Climate Initiative, I collected feedback from participating artists and organizers all over the world, and from mid-September 2023 to late February 2024, I received daily emails detailing the return of CCTA to the stage, whatever form a "stage" took for our different organizers. As in pre-pandemic years, performances were presented in theatres, universities, community gardens, libraries, coffee shops, churches, backyards, and even around a kitchen table. The plays were performed from Toronto to London to Auckland, and to new destinations like Baia Mare, Romania, and Tromsø, Norway. Audiences spanned over *four generations,* from ninety-year-old aunties to kindergarten-aged children, and presentations ranged in size from modest staged readings to productions featuring ensembles in full-on polar bear costumes. There were panels of scientists, talkbacks with local environmental nonprofits, and intentional climate rituals like the Climate Ribbon Project.[1] A complete archive of these performances is available on our website under the tab "Events."[2]

[1] www.theclimateribbon.org
[2] www.climatechangetheatreaction.com

The Numbers at a Glance

CCTA 2023 presented ninety-two events across twenty-three countries, with fifty-two of those events taking place in the US and reached roughly 10,000 people. Forty events took place at universities around the world, accounting for almost half of all events. Additionally, this year we saw a forty percent increase from our 2021 season in the number of events involving younger children in grade school, a number that may only continue to rise as this generation grows alongside our climate emergency. Overall, it's encouraging to see that the investment from educational institutions in climate education and creative action continues to increase. In fact, my own alma mater was my first introduction to CCTA back in 2018. It was through CCTA that I learned firsthand how powerful theatre can be in supporting social justice movements and environmental education, and I have since organized multiple events and performed in a few, as well. Being part of this movement opened my eyes to more creative and accessible ways to communicate data and intersectional information about the climate crisis, and to craft impactful narratives. It was because of my school's continued investment in creative climate education that I was empowered to get a minor in Environmental Analysis, write my undergraduate thesis on ecodrama and sustainable theatre, and why I wanted to stay connected with CCTA even after graduating. My story is but one example of the impact of this work on students and young scholars.

In total, the performances that made up CCTA 2023 were created by 2,500 students, educators, artists, organizers, and activists, and reached 7,000 audience members. On average, each event had an audience of fifty people. Altogether, the plays were presented 437 times across the ninety-two events. Each event presented roughly five of the fifty plays, and each play was presented an average of nine times globally.

Statistics by Location

Because most of the CCTA plays are written in English, performances have been heavily concentrated in English-speaking countries. As the initiative grows and we learn more with each iteration, we are working to secure translation resources that could expand the impact and accessibility of the plays. This year, to increase the overall accessibility of the initiative, our website involvement page was translated into Korean and Italian. Korea and Italy are two countries where we had close collaborators who could serve as a bridge between us and local non-English-speaking artists and organizers. However, performances were still heavily North American/Western

European-centric with around eighty percent of events occurring within three countries: the US (53), Canada (12), and the UK (9). Outside of these three countries, India and Norway held the largest number of events with three each. Additionally, only four of the ninety-two events were produced in countries from the Global South. To increase these numbers, we must strengthen our extensive CCTA network by selecting a more diverse range of playwrights and creating more relationships with Global South communities, artists, and educational institutions.

Within the US, Massachusetts and New York once again led the way with the most events at ten and eight, respectively. This was followed by Florida, Pennsylvania, and California, each at four. I find it interesting that these leading locations are remarkably similar to our pre-pandemic statistics. If we further analyze this consistent trend, it could provide insight into how we can leverage the tools we already know are succeeding to continue growing CCTA around the world. What is continuously working well in Massachusetts, New York, Florida, and California that can be replicated in countries within and beyond North America and Western Europe?

Beyond the Numbers

While these statistics paint an overall quantitative picture of CCTA 2023, we must journey beyond the numbers to fully understand the impact of CCTA in a post-pandemic world. The stories I received each day from the hardworking students, educators, artists, organizers, and activists creating events in their communities were ones filled with hope, excitement, and even the beginnings of plans for 2025. What the numbers cannot tell you is that the singular event held in China was a cross-collaboration between Peking University (Beijing) and Massey University (Aotearoa/New Zealand), where *Wayfinder* by Māori playwright, Whiti Hereaka, was translated into Mandarin by Professor and ecocriticism pioneer Zhao Baisheng. The scholars and students created a bridge across a myriad of barriers to explore a story of Indigenous knowledge. As event co-organizer and scholar, Elspeth Tilley, wrote in her essay, "Drinking Imaginary Cosmopolitans in Beijing: Or Why Kiwis Sometimes Fly," *Wayfinder* "draws on Māori and Indigenous Pacific understandings of nature in which humans are inseparable from the ecologies that surround us," and although it is "set in a perhaps dystopian, perhaps post-Apocalyptic future … it is not bleak. Rather, it imagines a mechanism by which future inhabitants of the Earth can connect directly with the wisdom of the soil, the water, the birds, and the planet itself." It was through this exploration in performance and dialogue, that these students and scholars uncovered many common values between Chinese and Māori cultures. In her correspondence with me, Tilley recounts that among their commonalities was their shared "respect for the wisdom of elders, a deep veneration for the land … [and] an understanding of water as a transcendent resource that needs to be honored as so much more than a commodity to be exploited." The numbers cannot tell you about this cross-cultural interrelation, which underscores connection and understanding – two components vital to climate activism. This story is but one from the many emails I received that detailed connection, collaboration, and excitement for discovery.

CCTA being live again was an accomplishment in and of itself, but further successes included sold-out evenings; over $1,000 being raised for the Neskantaga and Grassy Narrows First Nations in Toronto, Canada; the cleanup of a local river in Paud, India; and demands for yearly reprises. Other measurable successes I gathered from the feedback I received revolved around shared connection. Audiences created together, laughed together, shared knowledge and fears, were challenged, grew, and left feeling more connected, hopeful, and motivated to keep learning and taking action. And this time, when the performance ended, there was no silence from computer speakers or a lonely, faint blue light glowing in the darkness. Instead, there was laughter, applause, questions, palpable buzzing energy, and all the beauty that comes from human connection. The return to the stage was also a return to each other – and we were all welcomed with open arms.

However, returning to live productions after a multiyear global pandemic did not come without its setbacks, and so the emails sometimes told of disappointments: cancellations because of illness, or smaller audiences than expected. CCTA emerged from our Zoom theatre days with a comparable impression to the 2017 festival, and there was a slight decrease in participation from immediate pre-pandemic numbers. While CCTA has traditionally grown and expanded its reach throughout each iteration, 2023 did not align with this trend. However, amidst a shifting global and theatrical landscape, this deviation from the norm does not mean that progress was evaded altogether. I believe 2023 saw a different type of growth – one that celebrated the significance of *returning*.

A Shifting Landscape

Through my journey across the ninety-two global events, I found that traditional theatrical spaces were seemingly utilized less, and budget restraints led to more intimate events – like eight friends around a kitchen table in

Seoul, or a climate open mic in the Napa County Library. The creativity around performance spaces was remarkable. Perhaps it stemmed from the desire to create more accessible and more intimate art within smaller communities. Perhaps it was aided by the innovativeness of the Zoom theatre days where being forced to think outside of theatrical boxes was the norm.

A commonality of many of the events this year was a celebration of the *process* of returning to each other and to artistic activism. During their CCTA event, Professor Alyssa Schmidt and her community at the Boston Conservatory at Berklee talked openly about eco-anxiety and what it feels like to be living on Earth at this exact moment in time. They shared stories about places they felt connected to and sat with each other in their hope, grief, and wants. Schmidt wrote, "We also simply reveled in the rarity that it is to slow down and storytell together, especially when process – rather than product – is centered and celebrated." This approach to creating and sharing art sets us up to be more empathetic, compassionate, and courageous artists and activists because the focus is on learning while working in community. And just a few states over at Lansing Community College in Michigan, Melissa Kaplan poignantly drove this point home in her correspondence with me, writing "strangers when the night begins but not when it ends."

CCTA is about sharing, learning, and growing as humans, artists, activists, caretakers, scholars, friends, and even as strangers. The 2023 season brought many of us back to the theatre, and co-founder, Chantal Bilodeau, says it best as she reflects on our achievements: "Collectively, we created a movement." And it is one to be proud of.

Final Thoughts

Four friends are standing in front of the Herald Corp building in Seoul, South Korea, the site of the world's third Climate Clock.[3] The clock reads "5 years, 228 days, 15 hours, 1 minute, and 4 seconds" – the time we have left until our global average temperature is predicted to rise 1.5 degrees Celsius above pre-industrial levels, taking us past Earth's "safe" warming point. As time continues to flow around them, Juntae Choi and their friends gather around a kitchen table and ask: "What will we do in this flowing time?" And as simple and delicate as this may seem, they decide to talk about their

[3]The Climate Clock is an art and technology project that counts down the critical time window to reach zero emissions, while tracking our progress on key solution pathways. https://climateclock.world

friendship and love for the Earth. Somewhere in the distance, the clock is counting down, and they begin.

Climate Change Theatre Action will always be more than a collection of statistics and numbers. It is a chance to return to each other, to return to our love for the Earth, to return and return and return. We are the engineers planning for a future together on this beautiful planet. We keep showing up, we unite, joining together at kitchen tables, in backyards, on amphitheater stages, and we share hopes, dreams, grief, and joy as we work to inspire action. The clock is still counting down. And so now I ask: what will *you* do in this flowing time?

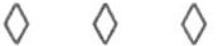

GiGi Buddie is an interdisciplinary artist and climate activist currently based in the Bay Area on the traditional homelands of the Coast Miwok People. She is a graduate of Pomona College with a degree in theatre performance and environmental analysis. As an American Indian of Tongva and Mescalero descent, GiGi creates and contributes to art that uplifts marginalized voices, and shares stories of creation, resilience, and beauty from frontline communities. GiGi currently works as a writer and an affiliate artist for the Arts & Climate Initiative, as well as an organizer for Climate Change Theatre Action.

PART 2

THE PLAYS

PHOTOGRAPHIC REALISM

Javaad Alipoor

This is a short play about the Women, Life, Freedom movement in Iran. It's written to be performed by one voice, although this voice can be divided up between as many performers as your production wants to use. The text is broken up to describe the way it could be delivered by a chorus. The imagery could be explored through projection, movement, or just through the text.

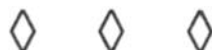

This is a short play about the Women, Life, Freedom movement in Iran. It's about how we think of that movement. It's about how the people in that movement think of themselves. It's about how we imagine doing something that has never been done before.

Consider one image. A thin baton. Designed to cut and make bleed as much as smash. Paused. A millimeter from a human head. Tip already grazing hair.

There is also another image. The precise one created in your head; the layers of televisual cliché, let's say. Or that particular memory. Your particular mind flicking when you hear those particular words.

A scar on a human face. A corner of a scar just peeking beneath dark hair. Dark hair falling across a woman's face. On a woman's face. A woman in a town called Saqqez in Kurdistan, Iran.

Think scar, think hair. Think woman. Woman's face. Saqqez, Kurdistan, Iran.

Think, is this right? Think, is this what I am supposed to be thinking? Think, is this me just like, I don't know, putting things on people I haven't met?

Think, is that how you pronounce "Saqqez"?

Imagine this woman walking through town for the first time without wearing a headscarf. There is an image of, probably, a bazaar. There is perhaps a sound. There is potentially the audio-drone that follows any scene-setting shot in a TV show set in the Middle East. Half call to prayer, half traditional lute or reed flute.

The bazaar is busy. The woman's head is full of her own images. Her own picture meanings and contexts.

She is twenty-four.

There are twenty-four years of memory in her head.

There are twenty-four years of memory in her muscles, so when she passes an older man or woman who she thinks is looking at her judgmentally, her forearm twitches in instinct.

An instinct to grasp at where her headscarf used to be, an instinct to readjust the way it sits. An instinct to redraw the battle line, sometimes a point to her, sometimes one for the police.

The battle line that separates private freedom from public obedience. The battle line across every woman's forehead and hairline.

Imagine when she comes across other women who have also thrown the headscarf away. See a moment of shared conspiracy among young women. Or see an older woman. Pride and encouragement.

Imagine our young woman. Kurdistan. Iran. No hijab. Meets young women. Meeting old women.

Also, the triggered images. Is there a woman from an American TV show? Is there the memory of a Muslim woman? There might be some half-recollected discussion of the politics of hijab?

In her head, there might be pride. There might be an image of a previous moment of shame when she didn't do this. An image that makes her think her life has been wasted up to this point.

There might be two images sitting together. There might be the memory of a beach holiday, far from the eyes of the militia where she could sunbathe how she wanted, sitting weirdly with the suffocating feeling of town. The town might not be suffocating. All these images sit together. Pasts and what could or should have been.

In the same way.

When I tell you about the murder of Gila Mahsa Aminio at the hands of the Iranian police, when I say that it inspired large sections of Iranian women to decide to stop wearing the mandatory head coverings enforced by the Islamic Republic of Iran, that it became one part of a general rising against dictatorship, the same thing happens.

Those particular images immediately fire up related ones in your mind. Enforced mandatory hijab. An image. A whole series. Feminism. Islamophobia. A third-generation Algerian in a Parisian banlieue. A racist politician in Holland or England.

Insofar as we can try and imagine something really new, we put down the images that we have collected before. When we try and let go of the pictures we rely on to reinterpret, we go through the same mental process that allows people to do something new for the first time. We break rules that seem unbreakable.

Whether we want to really understand what is going through the mind of a woman in another corner of the world, or we want to step outside and feel the wind through our hair in the open.

Picture a woman being beaten with a thin baton, designed to cut as much as to smash. Picture healing. Picture an old woman's finger many years later, running over a scar.

Picture nothing more than a young woman slipping very briefly and catching herself. Picture a tiny cut, and one or two drops of blood, but enough to leave a little mark.

It's only in the space between the things we can already imagine that there lies the possibility to act.

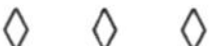

Javaad Alipoor is an award-winning playwright, director, filmmaker and performer based in the UK. *The Believers Are But Brothers* (2017) opened in Edinburgh where it won a Fringe First Award, before transferring to London's Bush Theatre, and on to an international tour. The sequel, *Rich Kids: A History of Shopping Malls in Tehran* (2019), premiered at the Traverse Theatre. His latest play, *Things Hidden Since the Foundation of the World*, the last part in the trilogy that began with *Believers*, opened at HOME Manchester and Battersea Arts Centre, London in 2022 and toured internationally in 2023.
www.javaadalipoor.co.uk

CLOTHES MINDED

Klae Bainter

I created this piece as a satirical response to feeling overwhelmed. Recently, I learned about the dumping of fast fashion in the Atacama Desert and was inspired to explore the idea of a corporate fashion house unintentionally promoting the right thing.

◊ ◊ ◊

An advertisement.
Lights up.

TWO FASHION ICONS …

Any race, any gender. Maybe they're in all black … maybe they're in something dingy, maybe something chic. Whatever it may be, it's fashionable.

MALIBU: Fashion *is* a language.

LEAF: Fashion *is* a language.

MALIBU: Chic. Punk. Retro.

LEAF: Athletic. Minimalist. Preppy.

MALIBU: Casual. Hip Hop. Goth.

LEAF: Just a series of words until you …

MALIBU & LEAF: *Add-A-Comma.*

LEAF: Introducing the hottest new voice in fashion: *THE Add-A-Comma Collection.*

MALIBU: "In these clothes. With this voice. I am me. And you are you."

LEAF: Lonely independent clauses until you … *Add-A-Comma.*

MALIBU: When you want your clothes to give an introduction. YES, *Add-A-Comma.*

LEAF: Do you want to set off an expression that interrupts the flow? It is, *after all*, your style.

MALIBU: *Add-A-Comma*.

LEAF: If you can *fill out a dress*, you can *direct address. Add-A-Comma*, kings & queens.

MALIBU: Rebrand, *comma.*

LEAF: Relearn, *comma.*

MALIBU: Reuse, *comma.*

MALIBU: We are innovators, always looking ahead to the linear future of fashion. That's why for years we've been aging our clothes in gargantuan piles in the Chilean Desert, patiently waiting for them to mature into a language designed for a generation like yours.

LEAF: You may ask: Is this the same Chilean Desert where, for years now, the fashion industry has been dumping its quick & cheap trends?

MALIBU: The same Chilean Desert that has sixty thousand tons of fashion waste from companies like H&M, Nike, & Old Navy?

LEAF: You won't find any of our waste in the Atacama Desert …

MALIBU: *Add-A-Comma* to your life.

LEAF: Because we're putting the *collect*, in *Spring Collection.* Taking out as much as we can from the sun-soaked sands of Chile to …

MALIBU: Reimagine, *comma.*

LEAF: Remove, *comma.*

MALIBU: Reboot, *comma.*

LEAF: Resell, *comma.*

MALIBU: We're bringing the heat home from the desert this summer.

LEAF: Atacama Desert.

MALIBU: *Add-A-Comma* to your life.

LEAF: Is this the same Chilean Desert full of synthetic fabrics that can take hundreds of years to decompose?

MALIBU: Atacama Desert.

LEAF: *Add-A-Comma* to your personal brand.

MALIBU: We can't concern ourselves with toxic textile drip …

LEAF: We're too busy concerning ourselves with *your* drip …

MALIBU: *Add-A-Comma …*

LEAF: … from head to toe.

MALIBU: We like to think of it as a gestation period for new trends.

LEAF: One person's discarded waste …

MALIBU … is another person's fall collection.

LEAF: A rebirth.

MALIBU: A new beginning.

LEAF: Atacama Desert.

MALIBU: *Add-A-Comma* to your wardrobe.

LEAF: But these clothes are messed up. They're dingy. Burned. Soiled. Bleached from the sun. Odorous. Bug infested. Home to all kinds of critters. They're torn & tattered. Ripped & ragged. Missing buttons. Zippers with broken teeth.

MALIBU: Pockets full of stones. Sheared sleeves. Smudged collars. Lost draw strings. Rusty rivets. They let the rain in, & they let the heat out. They're stained. Shabby. Down to the heel. Cracked soles. Tarnished leather. Knotted laces.

LEAF: Shredded & slovenly. Worn down & windblown.

MALIBU: That's what they said about grunge too & look how that turned out. We say *Add-A-Comma …*

LEAF: … & extend the life of discarded fashion.

MALIBU: Fashion is a language.

LEAF: Don't let your sentence end …

MALIBU & LEAF: *Add-A-Comma.*

Lights fade.

Klae Bainter (he/him) is a playwright currently based in Cleveland, Ohio, US. His plays use poetic language to examine the grotesque nature of people, their values, and the spaces they hold sacred. His work has been produced in Cleveland, Spokane, Seattle, and Houston. Klae received his MFA in Playwriting from Ohio University, and his BA in English Literature & Creative Writing from the University of Washington. He lives with an obnoxious orange cat named Cormac.
https://newplayexchange.org/users/38310/klae-bainter

UNDERTOW

Keith Barker

Undertow emerged from numerous discussions with people across diverse political perspectives, reflecting my concern about the prevailing lack of empathy or understanding for differing viewpoints. In a political world determined to polarize us, I attempted to write something that is closer to a real conversation, emphasizing not the dichotomy of right versus wrong, but rather the hopeful idea of right versus right, and the art of finding a middle ground.

Notes

The play is meant for any gender, any age, any nationality. Please change the pronouns to fit the preference of the artists reading the play. If words like "dude" or "bud" feel gendered, feel free to change them to fit the player. It is important to note these two people, regardless of their opposing political views, love each other. Everything should be said with that in mind. The closeness of the siblings should make the quips quick and sparring.

GREY is outside on the balcony. It is fall. There is a nip of cold in the air. EMBER enters.

GREY: Mom sent you out to apologize?

EMBER: No.

GREY: It's ok if she did.

EMBER: Not everything is about you, bud. I came out to get some fresh air.

GREY: Uh-huh.

EMBER: Dude, your house is way too small to be hosting this many people.

GREY: You say that every year.

EMBER: And yet here we are.

GREY: You're just bitter you had to spend two hundred bucks on gas to get here.

EMBER: Why do you gotta be like that?

GREY: Hey, I wasn't the one yelling at the dinner table.

EMBER: You started it.

GREY: Then don't ask me what I think about your truck.

EMBER: I was talking about the color, not your opinion on tailpipe emissions.

GREY: How many trees do you think you'll have to plant to offset the CO_2?

EMBER: Do you ask that question to all your lawyer buddies who drive SUVs to work?

GREY: I try to lead by example. I ride my bike.

EMBER: So, you don't.

GREY: I say to them what I say to you: Little changes go a long way.

EMBER: Well, here's a little change I'd like to see: Stop telling everyone you're a vegan. Every second word out of your mouth is vegan this, or vegan that. Yes, we know, because you never shut up about it. It's embarrassing.

GREY: Auntie Bev asked me what being a vegan means and Razi wanted to know if I still eat cheese, so I had to explain it to them, AGAIN.

EMBER: You don't eat cheese?

GREY: Dude. How many times –

EMBER: I don't keep track of what you eat.

GREY: Actually, I found a really nice, fermented cashew cheese you need to try.

EMBER: Stop. Those words don't make any sense to me.

GREY: Plant-based alternatives are the way of the future.

EMBER: Yeah, a sad future.

GREY: Hey, I love a good cheese, but I hate factory farming and the impacts it has on the environment, so I gave it up.

EMBER: You fly for work. Isn't that bad for the planet?

GREY: I choose my airlines carefully, and I fly far less than I ever did.

EMBER: Wow, you have an answer for everything.

GREY: Dude, I think about these things all the time. There's not a day goes by –

EMBER: Stop it, stop talking, please. I came out here to get away from people.

Beat.

GREY: I'm just going to say one more thing, and then I'll drop it. There are seven billion people on this planet, and if everyone looked at their choices, considered their footprint, and understood that small actions make a difference –

EMBER: Why can't you just be normal.

GREY: How is talking about the environment not normal?

EMBER: I have neither the time nor the crayons to explain it to you.

GREY: You have a one-year-old, and another baby on the way.

EMBER: So?

GREY: You know what? Forget it.

EMBER: No. I'd like you to finish.

GREY: You're getting mad.

EMBER: It's too late for that. Spit it out.

Beat.

GREY: Here's what I don't understand: Even if you don't believe in climate change, or you think it's a hoax, why not do the little things scientists are asking us to do, in case you're wrong?

EMBER: What if they're wrong?

GREY: Not the point. Small actions will make the world a better place regardless. Don't you want to make better choices for your kids?

EMBER: You don't know the first thing about my choices.

GREY: You refuse to own a recycling bin.

EMBER: Not true.

GREY: You don't have one in your house.

EMBER: It's more complicated than that.

GREY: And what about the composter I bought you a year ago? It's still sitting in your garage.

EMBER: Well, yeah, but –

GREY: You roll your eyes at the mention of renewable energy.

EMBER: Cause it pisses me off.

GREY: And you talk about being a meat eater like it's a badge of honor, with your guns and your hunting rights.

EMBER: No no no –

GREY: And when the world is shifting to electric vehicles, you go out and buy the biggest truck you can find.

EMBER: Cause I need it. The only reason you ride your bike to the office is cause it's twenty minutes from your condo. I need my truck on job sites because I keep all my tools in it. I may not be perfect, but at least I don't go around lecturing people about things I don't understand.

GREY: No, you just scream terrible things at them at the dinner table in front of their family.

Beat.

EMBER: You're right. I shouldn't have yelled at you like that.

Beat.

GREY: And I shouldn't have made fun of your truck. I like the gray. It's a good choice.

EMBER: Thanks … It's electric.

GREY: What? Why didn't you –

EMBER: Cause I'm exhausted. The baby's not sleeping, so we're not sleeping. I was excited to show it to you, but then you started lecturing me, and it pissed me off.

GREY: You're so stubborn –

EMBER: Ok there, judgy pants.

GREY: I wasn't judging you.

EMBER: And just so you know, I'm proud to be a hunter because I like to know where my meat comes from. I don't want to buy something on white Styrofoam, full of hormones, that's been fed GMO corn its whole life.

GREY: What about tofu?

EMBER: Hey, if it was in a forest and I could shoot it, then sure. But again, you're buying something factory farmed, made with potential GMO soy, and who knows what else.

GREY: Fair.

EMBER: And the reason I don't own a recycling bin is because the town won't extend curbside pickup outside city limits, and the only recycling depot is over forty-five minutes away.

GREY: Maybe I can help?

EMBER: What, on your bike?

GREY: Whoa –

EMBER: And yes, it's true I haven't set up the composter yet, but that's because when the baby arrived our lives descended into chaos.

GREY: Right.

EMBER: And the only reason I roll my eyes at renewable energy is because it's way too expensive. I wanted to get solar panels for the shop, but I can't afford it.

GREY: I'm sorry. I was judging you on things I didn't know about.

EMBER: You were. But I was too.

GREY: I'm the worst.

EMBER: Listen. I'm only going to say this once. You repeat this, and I will murder you in your sleep. I read the articles you send, I look at the websites you tell me to look at, I even listened to that podcast you sent me. That stuff can be annoying, like really annoying … but I kinda like it too.

GREY: You do?

EMBER: I just wish you'd acknowledge these things are more complicated than black and white sometimes.

GREY: I know, I will. I promise.

EMBER: K.

GREY: You're really going to like that cashew cheese.

EMBER: Red Tupperware?

GREY: You tried it?

EMBER: Damn, it *is* good.

GREY: Told ya.

EMBER: Yeah yeah, of course you did. Let's get back in there. I gotta tell mom I fixed this.

GREY: I knew she sent you out here.

They exit together.

◊ ◊ ◊

Keith Barker is a citizen of the Métis Nation of Ontario, Canada. He's a playwright, actor, and director from Northwestern Ontario. Formally the Artistic Director at Native Earth Performing Arts, currently the Director of the Foerster Bernstein New Play Development Program at the Stratford Festival. Awards include a Dora Mavor Moore Award, The Carol Bolt Award, a SAT Award, and a Yukon Arts Award. Keith was a finalist for the Governor General's Award in 2018. His plays are published through Playwrights Canada Press.

THE POLAR BEARS

Nicolas Billon

As the conversation around climate change mitigation continues to grow over the next few years, I worry that too much faith will be put in "market-based solutions." My hope is that more emphasis is placed on political action and policy changes. This wish was the seed for *The Polar Bears.*

◊ ◊ ◊

Two performers, dressed as polar bears, address the audience.

POLAR BEAR 1: So, the problem –

POLAR BEAR 2: Is really simple.

POLAR BEAR 1: Straightforward.

POLAR BEAR 2: We're hungry.

POLAR BEAR 1: Very.

POLAR BEAR 2: And there aren't enough seals.

POLAR BEAR 1: No, no –

POLAR BEAR 2: Sorry, no, that's not exactly it. There's not enough *sea ice* for us to hunt seals.

POLAR BEAR 1 nods.

POLAR BEAR 2: Because of climate –

POLAR BEAR 1: Yes, yes, yes. They *know.* We know, we all *know.* No one needs to hear another rant about climate change.

POLAR BEAR 2: Yeah. Who wants that?

POLAR BEAR 1: No one.

POLAR BEAR 2: Exactly.

POLAR BEAR 1: But the fact remains: We're two hungry polar bears.

POLAR BEAR 2: Very.

POLAR BEAR 1: So, let's solve our problem. Let's talk *solutions.*

POLAR BEAR 2: Ok!

POLAR BEAR 1: I've been educating myself about this. Like, a lot.

POLAR BEAR 2: Oh yeah?

POLAR BEAR 1: YouTube has tons of great videos about this. And it's pretty clear that what we need, what will *actually* work, is a market-based solution.

POLAR BEAR 2: Sounds great.

POLAR BEAR 1: It's not like our diet is complicated.

POLAR BEAR 2: Seal. Seal. More seal. And the occasional glaciologist.

POLAR BEAR 1: That was only the once.

POLAR BEAR 2 nods, sighs: That was a good day.

POLAR BEAR 1 rustles through their back pockets (yes, this polar bear has back pockets) and pulls out a cigarette pack. They flip it open, pull out a lighter from the pack, and put a cigarette in their mouth.

POLAR BEAR 2 watches, half horrified and half hoping they'll be offered one.

POLAR BEAR 2: You smoke?

POLAR BEAR 1, *shrugs*: Helps me think …

POLAR BEAR 1 flicks the lighter, but it doesn't work. They try again. Nope.

POLAR BEAR 2: That's the universe telling you smoking is bad for you.

Annoyed, POLAR BEAR 1 glances at POLAR BEAR 2, then throws the cigarette away.

POLAR BEAR 1: The universe's a jerk.

POLAR BEAR 2: Yeah?

POLAR BEAR 1 nods.

POLAR BEAR 2: I guess that's why we're hungry.

POLAR BEAR 1: No, that's the sea ice … *(grasps at an idea)* What if we diversified our diet? That would help, wouldn't it?

POLAR BEAR 2: I love it! More glaciologists, fewer seals.

POLAR BEAR 1: I was thinking more like cheaper sources of calories.

POLAR BEAR 2, *disappointed*: Oh. Ok. Like what?

POLAR BEAR 1: Like … pizza.

POLAR BEAR 2: Oh, yeah! That's good. We could get it delivered.

POLAR BEAR 1: Now you're thinking. See? Market-based solution. Boom!

POLAR BEAR 1 pulls out a smartphone from another pocket.

POLAR BEAR 2: You have reception out here!?

POLAR BEAR 1: It's spotty, but … *(taps on the phone)* What do you want on your pizza?

POLAR BEAR 2: Seal?

POLAR BEAR 1 shakes their head.

POLAR BEAR 2: Glaci –

POLAR BEAR 1: How about pepperoni?

POLAR BEAR 2: Sure.

POLAR BEAR 1: Great.

POLAR BEAR 1's claws click-click-click as they place the order.

POLAR BEAR 2: This is great. And for dessert, we'll eat the delivery person.

POLAR BEAR 1: Well, no. We'll want them to deliver again, right?

POLAR BEAR 2, *disappointed*: I guess.

POLAR BEAR 1: Ugh.

POLAR BEAR 2: What?

POLAR BEAR 1: "We're sorry, you are outside of our delivery zone."

POLAR BEAR 2: Jerks.

POLAR BEAR 1: What's the point of providing exact GPS coordinates …? *(shrugs, frustrated)* Fine. Pizza's out. What else can we get delivered?

POLAR BEAR 2: We are pretty far from, you know, anything …

POLAR BEAR 1: I know, but surely someone's figured out how to monetize their snowmobile. Or use a drone or something?

POLAR BEAR 2: Weather's a bit rough for drones …

POLAR BEAR 1: Of course, yeah, just … Ok, maybe diversifying our diet isn't the solution. Maybe we need a better way to hunt seals.

POLAR BEAR 2: Or get more of them at once.

POLAR BEAR 1, *lightbulbs*: Of course. We should get seals in bulk!

POLAR BEAR 2: Yeah!

POLAR BEAR 1: What we need is a Costco.

POLAR BEAR 2: Genius.

POLAR BEAR 1: Imagine? Twelve-packs of seal. We just load up our carts and feast in the parking lot.

POLAR BEAR 2: And eat the employees for dessert!

POLAR BEAR 1: No.

POLAR BEAR 2: Why not?

POLAR BEAR 1: Because then you'll have a labor shortage, which'll push prices up, and we won't be able to afford the seals.

POLAR BEAR 2: So? *Then* we can eat the employees!

POLAR BEAR 1: If we can't afford the seals, the Costco will close and we'll be back to square one.

POLAR BEAR 2: Right. Hungry.

POLAR BEAR 1: Yeah.

POLAR BEAR 1 takes out a clear water bottle (think Nalgene) and takes a swig.

POLAR BEAR 2: Vodka? Are you serious …?

POLAR BEAR 1: It's *water*.

POLAR BEAR 2: Of course it is.

POLAR BEAR 1: It's water.

POLAR BEAR 2: Did YouTube tell you it helps with thinking?

POLAR BEAR 1: I don't hear you putting forward any ideas.

POLAR BEAR 2: Actually, why don't we begin by –

POLAR BEAR 1: Ugh! Not this again … *(mimics a whiny Polar Bear 2)* "Let's write to our representative! Let's make our politicians accountable! Blah-blah-blah …"

POLAR BEAR 2: It's something.

POLAR BEAR 1 rolls their eyes, and takes another swig from their water bottle.

POLAR BEAR 2 scoffs.

POLAR BEAR 1 glares at POLAR BEAR 2, then offers them the bottle. Dares them to take it.

POLAR BEAR 2 takes the bottle. Sniffs the content, frowns. Takes a sip.

POLAR BEAR 2: It's … water.

POLAR BEAR 2 returns the bottle to POLAR BEAR 1.

POLAR BEAR 1: I told you. Why did you think it was vodka?

POLAR BEAR 2: We're in the *Arctic.*

POLAR BEAR 1 shrugs: So?

POLAR BEAR 2: Alcohol won't freeze in the cold. But water *should*, shouldn't it?

POLAR BEAR 1 looks at the bottle, swirls the water around.

POLAR BEAR 1: Yeah … It should. *(realizing what this means)* It used to.

POLAR BEAR 1 and POLAR BEAR 2 share a look.

POLAR BEAR 1: Maybe we can also, you know, write a letter. I mean, in addition to finding market-based solutions.

POLAR BEAR 2: Sure.

POLAR BEAR 2 looks out at the audience and nudges POLAR BEAR 1.

POLAR BEAR 2, *whispers*: We could always eat the audience.

POLAR BEAR 1: Now look –

POLAR BEAR 2: There'll be another audience after this one. They're a renewable resource!

POLAR BEAR 1: That's not –

POLAR BEAR 2: And it would reduce carbon emissions. One of them probably drives a gas-guzzler!

POLAR BEAR 1, *firm*: They're our guests. Where are your manners?

POLAR BEAR 2, *disappointed*: That's true.

POLAR BEAR 1: Plus, it's illegal to feed performing polar bears.

POLAR BEAR 2: What if someone volunteers?

POLAR BEAR 1, *puts a paw around Polar Bear 2's shoulder*: Let's go write some letters.

POLAR BEAR 2: But … I'm hungry.

POLAR BEAR 1: I know. Me too.

POLAR BEAR 1 heads off. POLAR BEAR 2 stares at the audience, licking their lips, in the vain hope someone might volunteer.

POLAR BEAR 2, *whispers*: Anyone …?

POLAR BEAR 1 stops and turns back.

POLAR BEAR 1: Come on. We gotta start somewhere.

POLAR BEAR 2 slumps their shoulders and heads off with POLAR BEAR 1.

Lights fade –

BLACKOUT.

◊ ◊ ◊

Nicolas Billon is based in Canada and writes for theatre, television, and film. His work has been produced around the world and garnered many awards, including a Governor General's Award for Drama, a Canadian Screen Award, and a Writers Guild of Canada Screenwriting Award. www.nicolasbillon.com

MAGICAL FUNGI IN TIMES SQUARE

Chantal Bilodeau

When writing this play, I was searching for a BIG IDEA. But nothing I came across was quite doing it. Then, it occurred to me to look for something smaller, something in my own backyard so to speak, and to imagine how this little piece of the world could change for the better. The following two articles also provided interesting material to build on: "Rising Groundwater Threatens New York City – Researchers to Study How Much"[1] and "Do You Dare Enter a Fairy Ring? The Mythical Mushroom Portals of the Supernatural."[2]

Notes

A, B, and C can be any gender and ethnicity.
This should be played over the top. Keep the pace, milk the humor.
Feel free to clean up the language if swear words are not appropriate for your setting.

◊ ◊ ◊

New York City's Times Square, sometime in the near future. A enters with B and C in tow and gestures to the ground. Given how the three are dressed, it's clear that they are performers. One of them might be in drag.

A: Here! See?

B: Oh – my God.

A: Right?

C: What?

B: That's a – shit – that's what it is, isn't it?

---

[1] Maldonado, Samantha. "Rising Groundwater Threatens New York City – Researchers to Study How Much." *The City*, January 18, 2023. https://www.thecity.nyc/2023/01/18/rising-groundwater-threatens-new-york-city

[2] Leafloor, Liz. "Do you dare enter a fairy ring? The mythical mushroom portals of the supernatural," *Origins*, August 28, 2018. https://www.ancient-origins.net/human-origins-folklore/do-you-dare-enter-fairy-ring-mythical-mushroom-portals-supernatural-003677

A: Looks like it.

C: What??

With a huff, A gestures in an exaggerated way.

A: Can't you see?

C: The mushrooms?

A & B, *gasp, offended*: IT'S A FAIRY RING!

C: It's a bunch of mushrooms growing in a circle.

A: In the middle of Times Square?

C: Uh, ye-ah. The water table under the city is rising.

A: So?

C: So, mushrooms love moisture. It's the perfect environment for them.

A: Ok, first of all, don't call them mushrooms –

A & B: THEY'RE FUNGI!

A: And second, isn't it amazing how quickly nature rebounds once you remove the pavement? I mean, Broadway should have been turned into a pedestrian street a long time ago.

B: This is a sign.

A: You think?

B: Yes. I hear it. Loud and clear.

C: Yeah, it's a sign that the city needs to do something before the problem gets worse. I don't wanna wade through a foot of water and ruin a perfectly good pair of shoes every time it rains.

C moves as if to kick the mushrooms. A & B hold them back.

A & B: DON'T!

A: What are you doing?

B: Are you out of your mind?

A: Stop it!

A & B: DO NOT TOUCH THE FAIRY RING!

C: Jeez. Chill. What do you think is gonna happen? I'm gonna get cursed?

B: You don't wanna chance it, trust me. Because even if this is just a circle of –

A & B: FUNGI –

B: – these fungi are connected by mycelium. And that mycelium is like a giant underground internet. See the trees over there? They're probably googling us and the mycelium is telling them what we're talking about.

C: All the more reason to squash them.

B: All the more reason to respect this highly sophisticated nonhuman communication system which, by the way, is the only thing that's free and working properly in this city.

A: Should I step in?

A moves as if to step into the ring.

B: Wait! *(to C)* Give me your hat.

B doesn't wait, grabs the hat from C's head, and gives it to A.

C: What the fuck?

A puts the hat on.

B: Backwards. You have to put the hat on backwards.

A: Ok.

A turns the hat around.

C: So, I can't touch the – the – *(gestures)* but this clown here is gonna –

A & B: SHUT UP!

A: I'm stepping in.

A dramatically steps into the ring. They wait for something to happen.

B: You feel anything?

A: No.

C: This is ridiculous. Give me my hat back.

B: See anything?

A: Uh, no, not really. Should I run around the ring or –

B takes out their phone and googles.

C: How about you kiss every mushroom while standing on one foot and screaming "I love me some filthy fairy fungi!"

B, *finding the answer*: Nine times. Not more, not less. Run around the ring exactly nine times.

A: Ok.

A starts running and counts silently.

C, *to B*: Why are we doing this? We need to get back to rehearsal.

B: It's good luck.

C rolls their eyes.

B: Don't roll your eyes at me. There's enough shit going on in the world, a little good luck is not gonna hurt. It might even help.

A: Nine!

B: Now step out. Quick!

A steps out of the ring. As soon as they're out, something happens. All three feel it.

A & B & C: Whoa.

They look around.

A & B & C: Whoa.

C: What's going on?

B: I feel so weird.

All three look around, amazed.

C: Well, slap my ass and call me Sally. Are you seeing what I'm seeing?

A, *pointing*: That's a – that's a food stand … selling – selling oysters. From the harbor.

B, *pointing*: The building over there … its entire wall is covered in plants.

A, *pointing*: That one too.

C: There are no cars … Oh, yes, there are a few.

B: But there are no cars parked on the street.

C: Right.

A: It smells better than usual, doesn't it?

B: You mean, there isn't a cloud of weed smoke floating over the entire city?

A: That. And garbage.

C, *pointing*: Look! That's kale growing on the corner!

A & B & C: Aaaaawww …

A: I see some buildings have solar windows.

B: People seem happy. Or happier.

A: It's beautiful.

B: Yes.

A & B & C: SO, SO BEAUTIFUL …

Suddenly, poof! It's all gone.

A: Wait. What? No!

C: Fuuuuuck …

B: Where did it go?

A: Come back!

C: That was crazy!

A: I'm stepping back in.

B & C: NO!

A: Why? If we can just –

C: This is as much magic as I can handle in one day.

B: And the second time might not be so lucky.

A: But it was so nice.

B: I know.

C: It was wonderful.

Beat.

A: Do you think we might – like – I mean I know it takes time but –

B: You mean whether it's possible to uh – to –

C: Good question. I guess – I don't know but –

A: Maybe?

B: Well, we saw it.

C: We did. And, you know, now I'll never be able to look at a circle of mush –

A & B: FUNGI –

C: – fungi – a circle of fungi – in the same way ever again. I mean … that's a step forward, isn't it?

A puts the hat back on C's head.

A: That's the kind of magic we need.

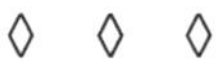

Chantal Bilodeau is a Montreal-born, New York-based playwright whose work focuses on the intersection of storytelling and the climate crisis, and the founding artistic director of the Arts & Climate Initiative. She is writing a series of eight plays that look at the social and environmental changes taking place in the eight Arctic states. In 2019, she was named one of "8 Trailblazers Who Are Changing the Climate Conversation" by Audubon Magazine.
www.cbilodeau.com

NOW

Wren Brian

I'm not a particularly optimistic person. I try to be a realist, but more often than not dip into pessimism (and sometimes even have a good long swim in it). The truth is it takes more energy, imagination, and strength to imagine better, but we need to. As hard as it is, we need to dare to dream.

Note

Every effort should be made for the play to be cast primarily, if not entirely, with actors who identify as disabled, female, BIPOC, and/or LGBTQIA2S+.

◊ ◊ ◊

One or more voices. Staging is completely up to the artists. May say lines together or apart.

Take a deep breath
In and out
That's it
Two more, just like that
In and out
In and out
We need something from you
It's not much
And it's everything
It's not hard
It is
It shouldn't be
Focus
Now …
Dream

Dream?

Dream
Dream of the future

What future

Focus
Now …
Dream in spectacular color
Grand scale
What might be
What could be
What would be ideal
What would save us

What is this about dreams
What dreams may come type-of-dreams?

No
Dream of life
Humanity's future
Not its past
What is the magnificent future?

It doesn't exist
Destruction
Death
Decay
That is the future

Take a deep breath

Why dream of a future I will not see?
Look around
We aren't getting a future
There is no point

Yes there is
If enough dare to dream it

They'll never see it

And?

There is no point in dreaming of a future I will not see

Take that "I" out of it

There is no future for us

Think bigger
Generations
Centuries
If enough of our ancestors thought of our future
If only
We wouldn't be here
Now
Dream ahead
Two
Five
Seven
Generations
Centuries
Dreaming isn't for now
It's not for us
It's not for "I"
This type of dreaming
This type of dreaming we need
Our future blood needs
Now
Is big
Is beyond
Is bold

I want your hope

Try

But I know too much

Take a deep breath
In and out
Try now
Breathe
Can you do that?

I'll try

Breathe deep
In and out
In and out
Feel the earth underneath
Billions of years old
In and out
The water in the veins
Carried down through generations
In and out
Air flowing through centuries
Sustaining everything
Connect
Connect to everything
It is wonderful
It is horrifying
It is everything
Connect
Do you feel it?

Maybe

Maybe is enough
Be in this moment
In this time
In this now
This brief life
Feel all that came before
Pushing
Moving
Out of this moment
Listen

I'm listening

Be bold
Go beyond
Grow big
Dare to dream
Dream with us
Then
Then

Then

When enough of us are dreaming
We can dare to begin
...
...
...
...
...
Now
Now
What is your dream?

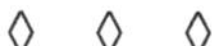

Wren Brian is a playwright born and raised in Whitehorse, Yukon, Canada (territory of the Kwanlin Dün and Ta'an Kwäch'än) and is of mostly settler ancestry (seven great-grandparents were white settlers, one was Métis). After twelve years living in Manitoba (Treaty 1), she is now living in Scotland. Wren is dedicated to creating characters that can be played by actors of any gender, ancestry, ability, and/or age while exploring complicated themes relevant to our times.
www.wrenbrian.com

BONBIBI AND DAKSHIN RAY MEET THE BUREAUCRACY

Manjima Chatterjee

The Sundarbans is a critical ecosystem on the India-Bangladesh deltaic coastline. A mangrove forest, it is home to a vast variety of creatures, most important of which is the Royal Bengal Tiger. The Sundarbans is peppered with large and small islands, which have for years hosted nomadic boat people and land-based communities who practice agriculture, as well as hunting and gathering. Intricately syncretic in its culture, this fiercely inhospitable land is governed by a confederation of gods.

Up until now, Sundarbans has defeated sea level rise by way of its protective system of mangroves, and kept a large tract of the Indian subcontinent from sinking altogether. However, in recent years, the politics of the land have led to communal and industrial conflicts. I felt that it was time the omnipresent gods came down to speak to our governments and helped them set their priorities straight!

Much gratitude is due to Choiti Ghosh and Tram Arts Trust, from whose research-led object theatre project this play branched out, and to the people of Sundarbans, particularly Annpur, who took time out to explain the issues at hand and allowed us to participate in their daily lives and rituals.

Characters

BONBIBI: A goddess of the forest. Born of Muslim parents, she and her brother, Shah Jangali, were asked to travel to the Sundarbans, the Land of 18 Tides, to take care of the people there and broker peace between the people and tigers, led by Dakshin Ray. She is usually represented as a young woman dressed in bright clothing, mounted on a tiger or a rooster.

DAKSHIN RAY: A lord of the forest. The treasures of the forest – its wood, honey, and animals – belong to him, and people must ask his permission if they want to take anything. As per the lore, he initially refused to share these treasures with humans, attacking them at will, until Bonbibi intervened and brokered a deal, keeping people safe from tiger attacks if they obey the rules and chant her name. He is usually represented as a middle-aged man bearing a stick or a gun, and sometimes as a tiger.

MRS. MOYNA CHAKROBORTY: A government official in her late thirties.

ASSISTANT: A young man, mild mannered and generally a little terrified.

Time

Now.

◊ ◊ ◊

A government office with harsh neon lighting. BONBIBI sits on a bench, wearing a simple saree with a Muslim head scarf. DAKSHIN RAY stands at a window, his back to the audience, wearing a mishmash *– a tightly bound up* dhoti *with a* gamchha *towel and a sacred thread, and a two-faced mask with a tiger on one side and human on the other, which he mostly wears like headgear. A formal coat, which looks incongruous, completes his getup. DAKSHIN RAY suddenly growls, but it doesn't come out right. He turns to BONBIBI.*

DAKSHIN RAY: Maybe I should bite her.

BONBIBI continues to sit there, smiling placidly at all she sees.

DAKSHIN RAY: What do you think? Just a bite? Or go in for the kill?

BONBIBI: You will stay down, Dakshin *bhai*. You promised.

DAKSHIN RAY: Not even one bite?

She gives him a look. He shakes his head and walks off to one side.

DAKSHIN RAY, *singing in Bangla*: *Shundi'r debo pindi chotke!*

BONBIBI: So very bloodthirsty all the time!

DAKSHIN RAY: At least I am true to my nature! How am I wrong? You told me to stay away from them as long as they played by the rules. But look at what they've done! Salt in the water, smoke in the air. See how ragged you look! You're supposed to be the Lady of the Forest! Everyone runs to you, all the time, saying "Bonbibi, save me!"

BONBIBI: You're a fine one to talk! Didn't you scale up your attacks? We had a deal, Dakshin Ray!

DAKSHIN RAY mutters under his breath.

BONBIBI: Speak up if you have something to say!

He struts up to her, then slams down on his haunches and whispers confidentially.

DAKSHIN RAY: They're not listening to me anymore.

BONBIBI, *attentive*: They? Your tigers?

DAKSHIN RAY: It's the salt in the water. It's too much. It's making them weak. Lethargic. They don't want to hunt prey that runs faster than them.

BONBIBI: And so, the humans?

DAKSHIN RAY: Exactly. Pathetic creatures. *(darts a look at her)* My tigers, I mean, of course!

BONBIBI: I'll handle this conversation. Don't lose your calm, ok?

DAKSHIN RAY: Me? I'm struggling to even summon a proper growl … *(demonstrates softly)*

The ASSISTANT appears as a buzzer rings. DAKSHIN RAY growls again and the ASSISTANT jumps in fear. BONBIBI stands up, smartly, a bright smile pinned to her face. They are escorted into an office by the ASSISTANT, where they are greeted by MRS. MOYNA CHAKROBORTY, the Block Development Officer (BDO).

MRS. MOYNA CHAKROBORTY: Complaint?

BONBIBI: We're here to meet the Block Development Officer.

MRS. MOYNA CHAKROBORTY: Yes. So. Complaint?

BONBIBI: We would like to make some recommendations, please.

MRS. MOYNA CHAKROBORTY: No recommendations, only complaints. This is a government office. Do you have an appointment?

DAKSHIN RAY, *softly growls*: Do you know who this is?

BONBIBI: Dakshin *bhai*! *(to officer, pleasantly)* Madam, I am Bonbibi, from the Sundarbans. You can listen to me now, or I can haunt your dreams …

MRS. MOYNA CHAKROBORTY, *astounded*: Bonbibi! The Lady of the Forest! *(scoffs)* And then this, I suppose, is Dakshin Ray, Lord of the Tigers!

DAKSHIN RAY: Lord of the entire Land of 18 Tides, actually.

BONBIBI: Listen to me. It's urgent. There's a disaster brewing. We're here to warn you about it.

MRS. MOYNA CHAKROBORTY: Right. Thank you. Next!

BONBIBI: What do you mean, next? Didn't you hear us? We're the gods of the forest and we need to talk to you …

MRS. MOYNA CHAKROBORTY dismissively begins to ring a bell, muttering "Of all the crazies," etc. under her breath. DAKSHIN RAY emits an enormous growl. Everybody freezes. The light changes and becomes dappled. A soft drum beat plays in the background, and we hear the swishing of leaves, grass, and the creatures in the forest. It is as though the forest itself has arrived in the office. DAKSHIN RAY's mask is on his face, tiger face front, as he advances on her, menacingly.

DAKSHIN RAY, *soft, menacing, like a great cat about to pounce*: Listen to me, Mrs. Moyna Chakroborty. Everyone here is in grave danger. You understand, don't you? Now, do you know us?

MRS. MOYNA CHAKROBORTY: Y-you are Dakshin Ray, Lord of the Sundarbans Forest, and she is Bonbibi, Lady of the Forest, protector of human beings and holder of the contract of peace between humans and tigers.

BONBIBI: Between humans and the forest, in fact. It's a bit unusual, our being here. We're here to say something.

BONBIBI and DAKSHIN RAY circumambulate MRS. MOYNA CHAKROBORTY as they speak.

Normally, our people would know the rules of the forest and protect it –

DAKSHIN RAY: But you allow anybody in, and you don't ask the people.

BONBIBI: We've tried to reach out to you through your dreams –

DAKSHIN RAY: But your dreams are TV storylines, and you thought we were characters in a soap! *(mild, disgusted growl)*

MRS. MOYNA CHAKROBORTY: R-right!

BONBIBI: My creatures are letting you know of their distress –

DAKSHIN RAY: But you don't know how to read them anymore, either. What's with you, humans? You don't know how to read animal behavior, or the weather, or even each other! Which planet do you think you live on, anyway?

MRS. MOYNA CHAKROBORTY: I-I- … w-what do you want?

BONBIBI: What do I want?

Signals DAKSHIN RAY, who takes out a long list from his jacket and starts reading out.

DAKSHIN RAY, *staccato*: Stop your policies of dividing people. We don't care who worships which god and how. We need people to work together and pay attention to the forest. If humans have uncontrolled access to the forest at any given time of the year, taking honey and precious wood whenever they want, using up all the fresh water in the rivers, picking up the baby fish before they are even old enough to reproduce, fishing licenses going off the charts, then …

MRS. MOYNA CHAKROBORTY: Those licenses are useless anyway …

BONBIBI: Yes, they are. You know why? Because you aren't paying attention to the land. Can people exist when the land does not?

DAKSHIN RAY, *quoting*: "The trees, the animals, the rivers, and the sea, they are all a part of this land, let's protect them with all our might." "If we destroy the land, we destroy ourselves, for we are all connected in this web of life."

MRS. MOYNA CHAKROBORTY: This is … this is … from her book of worship!

DAKSHIN RAY: Bonbibir Johuranama, yes.

MRS. MOYNA CHAKROBORTY: What do you – what do you want from me?

BONBIBI dips into the folds of her saree and brings out a small rootlike object. She gives it to MRS. MOYNA CHAKROBORTY.

BONBIBI: It's the sucker shoot of a Sundari mangrove. Did you know they're almost gone, my beautiful Sundari trees? There's just too much salt in the soil and the rivers! And you can't stop cutting them down because their wood is so beautiful and sturdy? *(shakes her head in distress)*

MRS. MOYNA CHAKROBORTY: Human needs …

BONBIBI: No, you will stop. You will, because you have to. Plant this. Plant this, and water it. No, it will water itself. Find fresh water for it. Send the water back to the rivers. Bring the communities together to plant these and find solutions to the problem of fresh water. They are my people! Stop trying to make them fight among themselves and find ways to make them work together!

DAKSHIN RAY: That's your job.

MRS. MOYNA CHAKROBORTY: You see, the politicians …

BONBIBI: They're human, too, aren't they? If the planet dies, where do they go? Now get to work. Together! By the way, if you don't do something about the salinity soon, the tigers will attack more and more people …

MRS. MOYNA CHAKROBORTY: We're working on that, making the fences stronger and increasing their coverage …

DAKSHIN RAY: Fences! *(growls)* You fools! If the tigers die out, do you think you will survive?

He moves as if to attack MRS. MOYNA CHAKROBORTY, who runs to BONBIBI for her protection.

MRS. MOYNA CHAKROBORTY: Bonbibi! Save me!

BONBIBI, *sighs*: Dakshin *bhai! (to Mrs. Moyna Chakroborty)* I'm bound by my vow to protect both of you, but sometimes I really wonder ... Listen to me and listen well. The waters are rising. The ocean is coming to claim us all. Protect the land, and it will protect you. This is your time, BDO. Use it well. Build bridges between people, between species, the planet! Bridges, not fences. Beginning now.

BONBIBI and DAKSHIN RAY walk out. The light slowly changes back to the harsh neon lighting from the beginning of the play. MRS. MOYNA CHAKROBORTY sits on her seat with shaky legs and rings the bell. The ASSISTANT comes running.

ASSISTANT: Yes, ma'am?

MRS. MOYNA CHAKROBORTY: Come, Ramesh, we have work to do. Building bridges, not fences!

ASSISTANT: Bridges, ma'am?

MRS. MOYNA CHAKROBORTY: Bridges, yes.

She laughs nervously. They get together and start making plans.

◊ ◊ ◊

Manjima Chatterjee is an Indian drama explorer, school administrator, and writer. She won The Hindu Metro Plus Playwright Award in 2013 for her play *The Mountain of Bones*, which has since been published by Dhauli Books. Her dramatic and academic writing has been published and presented in India and abroad, and she has been a part of podcasts, web shows, and other public conversations. She lives in Noida, India, with her husband and two children.

DIRT!

Karen Elias

In creating the character of the God of Wisdom, I was inspired by Enki from Sumerian mythology, who does indeed have red-painted fingernails and is generous to a fault. The character I have created is not tied to Sumerian culture, however; I imagine my God of Wisdom being played by a white male since they represent here a kind of generic paternalism. The character of Riya came from reading about the wonderful work being done by Barefoot College International to empower impoverished grandmothers with limited education to become Solar Mamas, giving them the technical know-how to electrify their local communities – and light up the world.[1] Since Barefoot College draws participants from ninety-three different countries, I imagine Riya being played by a woman of color who hails from an impoverished area in one of these regions.

Characters

GOD OF WISDOM: Nonbinary man no longer young, well-meaning but impulsive, capable of learning from their mistakes. They are seated on a garden bench, knitting something colorful with oversized yarn and needles. They are wearing heavy garden boots and have red-painted fingernails. Piled around them are garden implements and bins labeled "Recyclables," "Compost," "Greens," "Browns," "Mulch," "Healthy Spores," etc.

RIYA: Woman of color, no longer young. She has recently completed Barefoot College's six-month training program to become a Solar Mama. She is confident, a bit sassy, and very much alive, possibly dressed in a mix of Eastern and Western clothes.

Setting

A room in the pantheon, a bit messy but with touches of green plant life.

Time

Arc that moves from past to present to future.

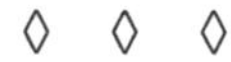

[1] www.barefootcollege.org

GOD OF WISDOM: Every pantheon should have one. A God of Wisdom, that is. Let me tell you, though, the job isn't all peaches and roses.

I'll tell you a story. Back when I was young and gorgeous, they paid me a visit, the humans. I laid out the best silver. We feasted at the Table of Heaven. We drank beer together. We drank more beer together. We drank more and more beer together. In short, we got sloshed.

We played a toasting game.
"To Free Will," they said.

"To you," I said, "the grand experiment!"

My heart was open. "What's mine is yours," I said. "Let me give you a gift." And they lit up. The robe? The crown? "We'll take them!" they said. And they did. Carried them back to their boat, unloaded them at their docks. My powers, given away in a moment of high hilarity. Everything. The high priesthood, the noble enduring crown, the holy measuring rod. Addition. Subtraction. Multiplication … and division.

Well, you can imagine.

When the beer had gone out from the one who had drunk beer, as they say, I was confused. I asked around. Everyone said the same thing: I had given my powers away, and there was no getting them back. The people were already dancing in the streets. The priests were already giving thanks at their holy shrines. I realized what was done was done.

Beat.

Anyway, it was a relief, really. Getting out from under. As you can imagine. But it made me think. What kind of god was I anyway? A god with no powers is like a bird with no song. I looked around. I thought: Where is there an empty space that I, the God of Wisdom, can fill? And it came to me. Dirt! I did research. I asked the sages, the scholars. They were in agreement. Dirt was beneath them. As it were, ha ha. So, I thought: Perfect! This is the spot for me.

Very slowly, over many days, I fashioned my new powers. The broadfork. The fungi. The compost and the cover crop. The art of no-till and planned grazing. The rejoicing of the holy, regenerated earth!

So, there I was with a pocketful of newly minted powers. Plus, a whole waiting-list of architects and artists and engineers, with the seeds of my new ideas germinating in their brains … And nothing happened.

How long was it? I can't be sure. One day, out of the blue, the God of Justice sent an SOS. Humans were running amok.

"Is it bad?" I asked.

"It's bad," she said. "A great chasm looms between the present and the future we've dreamed of for so long. They might lose the planet."

She said it was about time we put our heads together. We went three days and three nights without sleep. And then we declared a climate emergency! The planetary fires must be put out, and those responsible tried in the Grand Chamber of the Court of Unassailable Rights. All those with their hand on the spigot of deadly gases – and there were many, as you can imagine – would be rendered powerless, and their plans made harmless, in perpetuity.

We watched as the measure of noxious gases slowly began its long-awaited descent. And then, something completely unexpected: The women of the world joined hands across the planet. The Solar Sisters, the scientists, the spies, the students, and the storytellers! It was like a knock upon the door.

RIYA knocks. She is holding a solar lantern aloft and carrying a bundle.

It began slowly, the headwaters gathering silently. Not one of us was looking in that direction as women became green entrepreneurs.

GOD OF WISDOM mimes welcoming RIYA, bowing to her and inviting her to sit on the bench.

Then, the waters became rivers, and all at once the world was giddy with new beginnings.

RIYA bows, sets her lantern down, and sits.

(knitting as they talk to RIYA) Now, Riya, you have come knocking at my door. I wasn't expecting visitors. My place is a bit messy. I apologize.

RIYA looks around, likes what she sees.

RIYA: No problems. I am now a woman of the world! At first, I was feeling nervous to come here. But, after six months at the place called Barefoot College, I am now the Solar Mama who knows how to turn light from the sun into study lamps for my children. All this is giving me the bravery to come knocking at your door.

GOD OF WISDOM: Welcome, Riya. You're a sight for my sore heart …

RIYA opens her bundle to reveal another solar lantern.

RIYA: And I am bringing you a gift.

GOD OF WISDOM takes the lantern.

GOD OF WISDOM, *moved*: Thank you, thank you. I –

RIYA, *rushing, speaking over him*: And I have this to say: I am very proud to be a strong woman. It's always being said that we are the lower sex. Good for almost nothing.

GOD OF WISDOM: Yes, all the old prejudices! It's time we let them go.

RIYA: So. We will start with you! You, who have been keeping your eyes closed for too long. I am a messenger – how do you say, envoy? – from the places on the planet that have been prisoned in the dark. What are you for, the immortal one who is seeing the big entire picture, if you do not even know that I exist!

GOD OF WISDOM: You make a good point …

RIYA: Perhaps we are not considered capable because they are not giving us the opportunity, or the tools. If they do, then we can move the mountains!

GOD OF WISDOM: I agree it's way past time for us to hear your story.

RIYA: Good. Then I will be telling it. The world must open up a new and wider circumference if it wishes to contain me!

GOD OF WISDOM: Barefoot women begin knocking on my door. They tell me their stories. Some so sad the telling would melt the very stones.

(holds up knitting) I've been knitting these stories into our tapestry library. Lest we forget. *(pauses, knits)*

RIYA's action and the following from the GOD OF WISDOM happen simultaneously. She picks up her lantern and switches on the light, holds it high and begins slowly walking across the stage. The lights dim on GOD OF WISDOM as they continue talking. A path of light appears at RIYA's feet as she walks. Halfway across, RIYA stops. After a beat, a path of light moves from the opposite side to meet her halfway. She holds her lantern high and walks across the bridge of light to the other side. Smaller lights blink around her like fireflies.

So … the great chasm that opened between the present and what seemed an impossible future now appears capable of being crossed. One by one, the women set out, each holding their lantern against the dark. We hold our breath. Halfway across they stop. Some say the women are doomed to failure, that they are doing nothing more than walking the plank of despair. But their light is unwavering! They've become a force to be trusted. Slowly, slowly, the future extends a hand from the other side and meets them halfway.

RIYA exits. Stage lights come back up.

So here we are. All my tools suddenly in great demand. Mosaics of new green appearing everywhere, even in the dark places and in the deserts and along the abandoned coalfields.

They switch on their lantern, hold it aloft, step forward. Sound of light rain, to end of play.

Tonight, I listen as the falling rain seeps slowly into the welcoming Earth. The human and natural worlds replenishing each other. The population learning to flourish within the planet's limitations. It takes a village – and then another. And another. *(beat)* Yes, as every one of us is able to imagine …

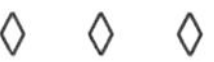

Karen Elias fell in love with theatre as a child. Now living in Pennsylvania, US, she is assuaging her need to speak from the frontlines of the climate crisis by writing plays of her own. Those who are passionate about combating the crisis know we need to have conversations with others. A play, happening in a room where living, breathing people are sitting and listening, is one way to advance those conversations.

NACHTFLUG

Nathan Ellis

Things are getting very bad, aren't they? And as we wake up and realize things are already much worse than we imagined, we have to remember to take care of ourselves, that life is not all about the endings. This is a text for performance by one voice, many voices, or no voices. It can be performed by anyone of any gender, age, and from anywhere. Play with it, cut it up and put it back together; make it yours: It's not finished until you perform it.

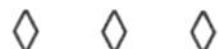

I was flying over the Indian Ocean, thirty-five thousand feet up in the air, and I was sleeping. I always sleep well on flights, I find the sound of the plane, the sound of the engines, very calming, very soothing. It's not just the sound, though, it's also the idea of flying, the sense of disconnection. The idea of being somewhere up above the Earth, no contact, just us, on our own. It's a space where you can disconnect yourself, feel completely separated from the world, from humanity. You might think that sounds strange, but I like that feeling. It helps me sleep. Anyway, it was several hours into the flight, when I woke and I'm not sure how, but I sensed something was very, very wrong, something dreadful was happening. As I say, I'm not sure how I knew, or even what it was. I couldn't tell if it was in the plane or down on the ground, but I had this sudden overwhelming sense that something terrible was happening. You know sometimes you feel that way, a sense of impending doom, they call it, in medical-speak, a sense of impending disaster. So, I woke up, feeling completely rotten, as I say, and the person next to me was awake, the rest of the cabin was dim, everyone else on the plane seemed to be sleeping, but the person next to me was awake, they were watching something on a screen, something romantic, it had that sheen of romance behind it: pretty, American actors with nice teeth smiling at each other. The person took out their little earbuds and they said, "Are you alright?" and I said, "Yes, I'm fine." though I felt very far from fine, in fact I felt almost nauseous with worry. I asked, "What time is it?" to have something to ask, and they said, "Hard to know, we're somewhere over the Indian Ocean, but it's hard to know, isn't it." and I said, "Yes." "You woke with a real start, were you having a bad dream?" I didn't quite know how to answer that question, so I just shrugged and said, "No, it's all ok. I'm fine."

And they smiled and they put back in their earbuds and pressed play and the film went on. That was almost an hour ago now. The film is still playing. It seems like the two pretty people might live happily together after all. I've seen several flight attendants rushing back and forth, one of them was crying, I am certain of it, but all the other passengers are still sleeping, and it seems cruel to wake them. At some point in the next few hours, as the sun rises in the windows and the passengers awake, I imagine the captain will speak through the intercom: "This is your captain speaking. I'm sorry to say, something terrible has happened, something truly awful." And I will turn to the person next to me, the droning sound of the engines will be so calming, and I will hold their hand, like we are in a movie, and say, as the credits roll, and the tears on their cheeks glisten in the flashing lights of the cabin, "It's fine. It's alright. Go back to sleep. Wherever we are now, it's not time to wake up yet."

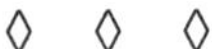

Nathan Ellis is a writer-director originally from the UK, currently based in Berlin. He was a member of the Royal Court Invitation Writers' Supergroup 2018-19 led by Alice Birch and Ali Mcdowall. He is a current member of the Channel 4 4Screenwriting group and was a member of BBC Writers Room Drama Room 2021-22. His plays include *Super High Resolution* (Soho Theatre, London; Staatstheater Kassel, Germany), *work.txt* (a play without actors) (Summerhall, Edinburgh, International Tour), and *No One Is Coming to Save You* (Bunker Theatre, London). His work has been performed on six continents.

THIS PLAY

Kendra Fanconi

This little play is a love story; all about the love, power, and possibility of theatre. When I was writing this, I was thinking about these questions:

- What is the theatre's role in this climate moment?
- How does actor = citizen, a play = society, and the theatre = the world?
- How do we create change within small places, like the stage, as a way to practice societal change?
- How does transformation happen and are we ready to transform to the post-fossil world?

◊ ◊ ◊

Lights up on ACTOR ONE. The lighting cue is beautiful. We are in the theatre.

ACTOR ONE has script in hand, which they occasionally refer to. They are looking downstage in the near distance into an immense and affecting storefront window display, and there is a beat of their looking, which is nuanced and compelling. We, the audience, see what they see.

ACTOR ONE: It's a Marvel. Not a Marvel Movie Franchise, which is also completely wonderful and later tonight you should line up for it, but a capital-M-Marvel you can almost touch.

ACTOR ONE touches the storefront window. Their mime is excellent.

Behold. The New Fall Line. *(sighs with desire)* If I wore *(points and we get a sense of how they might carry themselves differently)*. If I had *(ditto, an accessory, that might make them speak differently)*. If I lived *(ditto, and we have a sense of how it might make them feel differently)*. If I only could be *(and we get a sense of the transformation they desire)*. I hanker. I crave. I FAMINE.

Licks the window, and, hungrily, might try to gnaw through the glass, but cannot get the things on the other side of the glass. ACTOR ONE suffers defeat.

But I don't have enough to … I don't make enough for … I am a failure at … but I will I must I can't I won't I want I can't I need I suck I will I won't I must I wa-ha-ha-ha.

ACTOR ONE sobs convincingly from the searing pain of incomplete consumption.

Beat. ACTOR ONE sighs. Speaks to the audience.

This play hates itself.

I know, right? You think you are the one who gets to love a play or hate a play, but this play beat you to it.

Hey, this is not my fault, I didn't ask to be *(repeats moments from the gesture score from the last paragraph)*. I'm just an actor, I didn't even get a full week on this thing. If you want to lay blame, blame the play –

Mid-word, ACTOR ONE slumps forward, an empty vessel with the play pulled out of them. Beat. Resurrection.

This play is powerful.

Play tries to shut ACTOR ONE down, they shake it off.

Yeah, it can get a little carried away.

Play tries to distract ACTOR ONE.

It has a seductive design aesthetic orbiting around a spiritually devoid center.

ACTOR ONE wrests themselves away.

This play will leave you with longing.

Play tries to push them off the stage.

You know This Play, it raises the stakes, and hastens the time signature. That hockey stick curve, who do you think invented it? That's right! This Play! It loves crisis. This Play is emitting carbon at 250 times the 1990 baseline. It has gone too far, said too much. You forget, I'm a super-feeler, I can sense what you are trying to do to me!

(aside, to audience) I know I am in this thing, and as such am a presumed ally, but I hate this world, do you hear me? It has a weak ending. *(hissing)* Thissssss Play falls apart in the second act! I beat out six others, three of whom were taller than me, and three of whom were skinnier than me to get this role, but I know what all seven of us actors know, and that is that there is something bigger than the play, that's right, that I may be stuck in this world, but I am also in the theatre.

(taunting the play) C'mon, what do you have to say about that?

Play responds on the page and the actor sees.

This Play just released a flash flood of fear.

A chair slides on stage from stage left. ACTOR ONE stands on chair, watching the fear level rise, looking all the way to the distant horizon, with rising terror but then –

(checking the script) Suddenly, a stage direction reads: "Actor One stands on chair, watching the fear level rise with rising terror, looking, eventually, all the way to the distant horizon."

(struggling) Well … as a citizen of the theatre, as the one who acts, I invoke the ancient device of Breaking the Fourth Wall.

Jumps off the chair and crosses downstage right.

I'm (actor's name). I had (____) for breakfast and I have a huge crush on (name of company member) and at the very beginning of this play, I farted completely silently because I have control of my instrument!

The Play takes away ACTOR ONE's voice. They speak but no sound comes out. But because ACTOR ONE is a remarkable actor, they turn their own volume up, during this next paragraph, from one to ten.

I cannot be silenced, I have a BFA. I have done seven years of Fitzmaurice voicework, I am highly trained in the art of speaking up. I am an actor, I act!

Perhaps the audience claps a little, or whoops, which pleases ACTOR ONE.

And, to be completely transparent, I am an actor who benefits from a little encouragement. The theatre only exists if one is not alone. I'm up here, you sit across from me there, and we *see each other*. I mean, not when I gaze at the far-off edge of the horizon but even when I gaze at the far-off edge of the horizon …

ACTOR ONE stares at the far-off edge of the horizon.

… I can still feel that you are with me. I look for you. You see through me. Together, we experience the awesome yawn of the horizon. I see for you, plus, I am one hundred percent biodegradable, folks! Believe it! I don't work for This Play, I work for The Theatre and don't forget that, right here, in my back pocket, all the time, I have Deus Ex Machina!

DEUS EX MACHINA enters.

(recognizing Deus Ex Machina) Hmm, we might want a fly cue for you, there.

They both look up, to see if the fly system might work for an aerial entrance.

DEUS EX MACHINA: There is time to work that out.

ACTOR ONE: We are still rehearsing?

DEUS EX MACHINA: Yes, the future. That is what the theatre is for. Could you look to the far-off edge of the horizon?

ACTOR ONE does so, beautifully.

DEUS EX MACHINA: This is our rehearsal for our post-fossil future, small ways of being and extraordinary acts of bravery, new ways of connecting with strangers and community and family, and dealing with gestures to the storefront window, all of this …

Their focus changes to short-distance storefront window.

ACTOR ONE: Stuff.

DEUS EX MACHINA, *narrating their personal stage direction*: "Deux Ex Machina takes enormous mime hammer and strikes the marvelous storefront window. Sound cue of enormous destruction of consumer culture."

ACTOR ONE: Oh, shame, because I did like that *(mimes the accessory).*

DEUS EX MACHINA: You did. You wanted it. So, now we must hold rehearsal on the small stage of your hand not grabbing at what you do not have but –

ACTOR ONE: But rather, a hand that swings the Sword of Truth through the guts of post-consumer society because we have Level 4 certification in Stage Combat! Oh my god, I've been training my whole life for this!

DEUS EX MACHINA: Here *(holding out their hand),* on this new, this empty stage, we are acting.

ACTOR ONE: We are? Is this the future?

DEUS EX MACHINA, *taking ACTOR ONE'S hand*: It depends, *(calls ACTOR ONE by name)*. Did something change?

ACTOR ONE: Yes, *(calls DEUS EX MACHINA by name, it happens to be that person in the company who they admitted they had a huge crush on).*

Hand, hand, they hold hands. Something definitely changes. Light out.

Wait, is this the end?

Not the end

◊ ◊ ◊

Kendra Fanconi co-founded, and for eighteen years, acted as artistic director of The Only Animal, a company that was uniquely dedicated to theatre that springs from a deep engagement with place. She created more than forty original pieces with the company, conceptualizing, directing, writing and sometimes designing work that was often site-specific, immersive, interactive, installation-based, and cast landscape as the lead character. The outcomes of her work have been focused on solutionary impacts on the climate crisis with her current freelance artistic pursuits featuring eco-restoration. Kendra now works from her land in Sunshine, Colorado, where she lives with her philosopher husband and two kids, who are real characters.

INFERNO

Angie Farrow

So many people have lost their homes either through flooding or fires. The play *Inferno* asks: How do we recover when we lose everything we own and, despite loss, can we stay strong enough to address the larger issues of climate change?

◊ ◊ ◊

The stage is full of orange light and the sound of fire raging. LOLA, a woman in her middle years, speaks to the audience.

There is no warning.
One minute you're lying on the couch,
Tucking into a bag of Turkish delights;
The next minute, you're hurtling out of the house,
Screaming blue murder.

"Fire! Fire!
Charlie! Charlie! Get out! Get out!"
But Charlie is already in the garden trying to get the hose started.
"That won't do it, you pratt!
You'll be dead before the water starts!"

The hose has been leaking for weeks.
(to Charlie) "How many times have I told you?
It's what happens when you buy cheap from Bunnings!"

And I don't remember much after that,
Just the heat of the inferno.
The flames nearly licking our faces,
And me and Charlie running for our lives.

LOLA runs for her life. Then the orange light dims and the sounds of the flames and the cracking disappear. LOLA surveys the damage.

And here we are the next morning,
Looking at what used to be our house:
Nothing but charred wood and smoke.
Everything burnt as far as the skyline.
No kidding, it's like the surface of the moon.
Charlie says: "I guess nature is just doing its thing."
And I don't know how we have the energy for another row,
After all we've been through,
But we do.

We've always been good at bickering.
My sister says we've made it an artform.

(to Charlie) "Nature?
Maybe you have to wait for your house to burn down
Before you see reason?" I say:
"Forty odd degrees every day
Swimming in sweat,
No rain for months,
And you still say it's just nature doing its thing.
What planet are you on, Charlie?"

And I know that Charlie is about to tell me
That climate scientists are in it for the money,
Because we've been here before.
But then he does something really weird.
Seriously weird:
He walks away.
Fifteen years of marriage,
And I don't know this then, but I know it now:
I never see him again.

LOLA watches Charlie walk away.

You see when you lose your stuff,
You lose who you are.
It's the truth.
You lose your memories, photos, passport,
The fluffy bunny mum bought me that time I was crook.
I called him Ernie.

And even when you remember what you've lost,
You forget what you remembered.

I have to keep touching my skin to know I'm here.

They fix me up with a counselor
And she tells me to meditate.
But when I close my eyes, all I can see
Are the flames eating everything alive.

My sister Sue tries to sort me out;
"You've got to stop thinking about the apocalypse, Lola.
Just because you lost your house.
Doesn't mean the world's going to end."

I know she's making sense,
But I can't shake myself out of things.

(as sister Sue) "It was a shit house anyway.
Always smelled of dry rot and Charlie's armpits."

Oh, she tries everything.
Even tries fixing me up with a man.
"Not all men are like Charlie," she says.
"Some of them can string a decent sentence together."
But after one date,
They always know there's nothing to me.
I'm like an old toy without the stuffing.

She puts on a backpack.

Then one day, I can't explain this,
I hand in my notice at the brewery,
And I kit myself out with some hiking gear.
My sister Sue thinks it's funny.
"You? Hiking?
You need a lie down just walking to the dairy."
And without even a plan or a proper goodbye,
I start walking.

LOLA starts walking.

I know it seems crazy,
But what else can you do when you've lost yourself,
Except go looking?

I guess months go by with me in this nothing space.
But I don't really feel the time.
I see a lot of the country.
Wear out plenty of shoe leather,
But I start to realize: You can't walk yourself alive,
No matter how far you go.

What happens next?

Look, none of this makes sense.
But one day I'm in a town north of the country,
It's a mid-summer scorcher,
And I stop in the library to cool down.

I mean, libraries have never been my thing, ok?
At home we used all our books to shore up
The broken coffee table.
But I notice a small crowd gathered,
And there's this woman on a podium,
Flashing images onto a screen.
Oh, you can tell a mile off,
She's one of these smart-arse academics –
All brains and no sense of humor.

LOLA sits to watch more carefully.

At first, not much of what she's saying makes sense,
Because she's using these fancy words.
Something about solar power:
People building commercial power stations in orbit.
A lot of science that does my head in.

I'm looking around at these posh people,
With their nice frocks and expensive skin
And I feel like I always do:
Like I don't belong.

And this woman is banging on about
These huge satellites.
She reckons they can convert the sun's rays into power.
It's all pretty science fiction.
And, I dunno …
I start paying attention.
You see, they beam these rays down to Earth.
It's a whole new project on a massive scale.

Look, there's no point in going into it all:
You can find out for yourselves.
But these giant things that float in space …
Maybe they can reduce carbon emissions enough to, you know …
Make a big difference.
Turn things around.

I guess it means there's hope.

And this academic woman says it could change everything.

Everyone has left and I'm the only one seated.
And I realize I can feel myself breathing.
Nothing dramatic, but enough to let some light in.

LOLA gets up and walks outside and looks up at the sky.

And then I walk out into the heat.
It's dark now and I see the sky is full of stars.
And I wonder why I never looked before.

Lights fade to blackout.

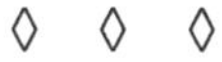

Angie Farrow is a Professor Emerita at Massey University, New Zealand. She has been writing plays for radio and theatre for most of her adult life. She has published five volumes of theatre plays, and her work continues to be performed in festivals overseas. She has won numerous national and international awards for her plays which, in recent years, have focused largely on issues around climate change.

DUET

Annie Furman

This piece comes from a network of inspirations: Dr. Jennifer Atkinson's writings on eco-grief and eco-anxiety and how these feelings can immobilize youth on issues of climate crisis; discussions with fellow artists about how climate anxieties have changed how we create; the visitors who came up to me when I was working as an environmental educator on ancestral and unceded Haudenosaunee land, colonially known as Upstate New York, and asked me countless variations of the question, "But where do I start?" I'm still asking myself that question, and I'm still learning how to answer it. This is one version.

Notes

The only stage direction is that there intentionally are no stage directions here. This piece can be performed by any number of performers, and lines may be attributed as the group imagines they ought to be. Where do you need to hear/have this conversation right now, in this moment? In your head, across the internet, at midnight on a logged hillside? Who do you need to have it with? Yourself? Another generation? Your favorite childhood tree?

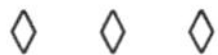

Is it lonely there
In the dark
And the cold
All alone
alone
Am I alone?
I have you for company
so far
so very far
Through all the nothing
In between
Through space and time
And the shattered song of starlight
Chiming clear on all the notes of nothing

What do you fill the
s p a c e s
In-between with?
With wind
        And light
                And memory
Do you ever feel small?
Surrounded by all that

emptiness

echoing

        echoing

                echoing

No.

No?

Am I alone?
I hold multitudes within me
I am microcosm and cosmos
I am made of a myriad of songs
And I will sing

Sing?

sing
Of falling snow and falling stars
Of sap and dreams that flow
Of voices strong in chorus
Of futures that could grow
Filling all the nothing
The apathy in-between
Filling it with harmonies
Of worlds both bright and green

For if I am alone
Then so, I think, are you

And if we are both alone
Well then
I do not think we are

What are we then?

Hm?

At our core
In our heart
Wood
If we knew what we were
Could we break the rules
That hold us in orbit?
Could we change?

We do change
Season to season
Month to month
We are made
Of change

But could we grow beyond the law of gravity?
Could we imagine
A world untethered?

Re-tethered
Hm
What would we do
In your world?

Tell stories
Sing songs
Weather time
Grow

Then do it

What?

Change it
Throw out all of yesterday's rules
Set them down with the sun

But I can't
Gravity is
Sap and
Seasons and
Starlight
Law of land
And light-years

Humor me

Ok …

Close your eyes
Turn it off

What?
Gravity?

Or whatever else it is
That holds you
Frozen
In the moment before reaching
Too scared to touch
To try
Turn it off

And what?

If you could reach
Without fear of falling
What would you touch?

The stars
Undimmed by smog
A sunrise
Over clean water
Soil

Nourishing and nourished
. . .
You

Well then
That is not
Such a bad place
To start

◊ ◊ ◊

Annie Furman (she/her) is a theatre maker and environmental educator from Upstate New York, whose most frequent co-workers/performance partners are horses and pigeons. She is currently pursuing her MFA in Interdisciplinary Studies with a focus on performing arts and sustainability at the University of British Columbia Okanagan on the unceded and ancestral territory of the syilx people. She has recently been a contributor to *(Be)longing: Tiny Stories for Radical Futures.*

GIVING DAY

Justine Garrett

What if we gave ourselves collective permission to reimagine what it means to celebrate a holiday? As the rhythm of the seasons change around us, we might take the opportunity to align how we celebrate with the values we actually hold, rather than engage with holidays that ask us to enact rituals that feel inauthentic.

Characters

WELCOMER: Any gender, any ethnicity. A hopeful parent.
NEWCOMER: Any gender, any ethnicity. Older. Has lived and traveled alone for a long time.

Setting

Any part of an urban home – could be backyard, porch, kitchen, or living room – decorated modestly for a celebration.

Note

/ indicates an overlap

◊ ◊ ◊

WELCOMER adjusts several baskets of food and fabric or clothing on a table. They hum or sing to themselves. There are a few chairs around the table. The table doesn't appear to be set for anything in particular, but WELCOMER is satisfied with the arrangement.

NEWCOMER enters and lingers out of the sight of WELCOMER, seemingly waiting for the right moment to say hello. NEWCOMER wears a bag – it could be handmade – and a large scarf wrapped around them in a creative way.

NEWCOMER: Boo!

WELCOMER: Oh!

NEWCOMER: I'm so sorry.

WELCOMER: Sorry? Oh, goodness, no.

NEWCOMER: I didn't do it right, did I?

WELCOMER: You did! No, I get so distracted. I'd make effortless prey, if it came to that.

NEWCOMER: Joy does that anyway, makes us all easy marks.

WELCOMER: I should be welcoming you. So let me be the first to welcome you to Giving Day. Welcome.

NEWCOMER pulls several small handmade dolls out of their bag.

NEWCOMER: I brought a few things, for the kids. I made them.

WELCOMER: Oh, they're beautiful. My daughter will turn pebbles into dolls, anything. The tiniest dramas. So, these will be something special. They even smell good. Lavender?

WELCOMER takes the dolls from NEWCOMER and adds them to the table.

NEWCOMER: Just a few grains in their bellies. Reminds me of the island.

NEWCOMER sits.

NEWCOMER: I feel tired every time I try to do something new. Except for the dolls. Those don't tire me out. Is she here?

WELCOMER: No, she's out with other children. They still hunt around for candy for a bit before we eat. Take a look and see if there's anything you need.

NEWCOMER adds a few things from the table to their bag. WELCOMER watches them in silence for a beat.

WELCOMER: Am I right to say that I like your costume?

NEWCOMER: Thanks, yes, I tried something. I don't think I look like myself at least.

WELCOMER: Then you got it right. Sharing whatever you have, taking what you need. Costumes optional but encouraged.

NEWCOMER: My kids would have liked it.

WELCOMER: You must miss them. *(pause)* Are they /

NEWCOMER: / I wasn't planning on staying.

WELCOMER: / coming soon to see you?

NEWCOMER: / I'm making you go out of your way.

WELCOMER: / No. You're not. Really. This is why I'm here.

NEWCOMER: I'm out of rhythm. I think my last costume was something like a cat, but when was that? I haven't celebrated anything for so long.

WELCOMER: I couldn't do everything the same way again, and instead of waiting for kids to come knock on my door, I put everything I had in my pantry on my porch – the old clothes we didn't need, cans of whatever, all of it – and I sat there waiting for anyone to come by and take anything. Just to see. At first, the kids came around because they were curious. And the next morning, another neighbor put out a table, and, you know the guy at the end of the block? You've met him? He started cooking on a camp stove, right there in the middle of the street.

NEWCOMER: I smelled something good as I was walking over.

WELCOMER: We'll head down there in a minute for dinner. Some of the neighbors really hated me for changing everything at first. But, eventually, loneliness or need wore them out. That's a terrible way of putting it. You've come so far alone.

NEWCOMER: It's ok. I am alone. When I was living out on the island, I thought I liked being alone, you know? That was it, I was going to hunker down and live with the seagulls. But here I am.

WELCOMER: I could squawk, if you want.

NEWCOMER: Let's hear it.

WELCOMER squawks like a seagull. NEWCOMER is pleased.

NEWCOMER: Needs a bit more desperation.

WELCOMER: I guess I'm all out.

◊ ◊ ◊

Justine Garrett is a writer and filmmaker from Los Angeles, living in Toronto. With the arts collective Toasterlab, she creates place-based immersive experiences, including *Transmission* (Future of Storytelling Festival and Edinburgh Fringe) and *Virtual Parkway Forest Park* (Arts in the Parks). She wrote and produced *Groundworks*, a documentary about California Native artists that aired on PBS, and she directed and produced the *Captain Me* musical kids' series. She teaches in the Scriptwriting & Story Design program at Toronto Metropolitan University.
www.justinegarrett.com

THE RETURNING

Emma Gibson

My inspiration for this play came from reading about pearl divers. From the Ama (the female Japanese pearl divers) to certain pearl diving companies and their dedication to sustainability and the environment, I learned that with every dive, these pearl farmers adopt the same underwater rhythms as the tide, so their dive has no impact on the delicate marine life they must maintain to ensure their pearls are perfect.

In this play, I wanted to explore the lives of three generations of women and imagine a world which we are hopefully returning to – a world in which we are deeply connected to the rhythms and cycles of the planet, allowing us all to flourish and live with joy.

Characters

ANNA (past): A pearl diver. Any ethnicity.
ANNE (present): A survivor. Any ethnicity.
ANI (future): A bride. Any ethnicity.

Setting

An ocean
A city
A beach

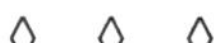

ANNA, ANNE, and ANI are in different worlds. Perhaps separate pools of light.

A soft chime

ANNA: First, I must pray

ANI: I must get dressed

ANNE: I must eat

ANNA: The shrine is on the top of a small hill, overlooking the sea

ANI: I open the wardrobe

ANNE: I look in the fridge

ANNE crouches down

ANNA: Inside the temple it is cool, quiet

ANNA kneels down

I kneel on a small, silk pillow

ANI: The dress is hanging there, full of expectation

ANNE: There is half a rind of cheese and a bulb of garlic

ANNA: I pray to the resident deity for a safe passage through life and at sea

ANNE: Unfortunately, the air pollution is high today, and the nearest store is seventeen minutes away

ANI: This dress has been in my family for years

ANNA: Then I pray to the resident deity for those who will come after me

ANNE: But I need to eat

ANNE stands. ANI turns slightly towards her

ANI: I think of my mother in this dress

ANNA: Then I rise

ANNA stands. ANI turns slightly towards her

ANI: And my grandmother

A soft chime

ANNA: The changing hut is a short walk from the temple. There

ANNA/ANI/ANNE: I put on my

ANI: White silk dress

ANNA: My white cotton tunic

ANNE: My white paper mask

ANI: Here is my veil

ANNA: My headscarf

ANNE: I pull up my hood

ANNA: My headscarf has a five-pointed star embroidered on it

ANI: The lace on the veil matches the detailing on the dress

ANNE: I put on my gloves

ANNA: I wipe the inside of my mask with mugwort

ANI: I apply my makeup

They all look in imaginary mirrors in front of them

ANNE: I am safe

ANNA: I am protected

ANI: I am beautiful

A soft chime

ANNA: I pick up my chisel that is engraved with a lattice pattern that keeps danger away

ANNE: I pick up my inhaler

ANI: My flowers

ANNA: One final prayer

ANNE: Slowly open the door

ANI: Here I come

ANNA: I flood my lungs with oxygen and take

ANNE/ANI/ANNA: One final breath

ANNE: Step outside

ANI: Step into the sunshine

ANNA: And slip under the waves

A soft chime

ANNE: Outside is so noisy. It claws away at me. There are so many cars on the road, trails of planes in the sky, their roar terrifying when they pass overhead. The bike lanes have become trash deposits filled with junk that nobody knows what to do with anymore. Head down, I walk. One step after another. Try not to breathe too deeply

ANNE/ANI/ANNA: Slowly does it

ANNA: It's quiet under water, muted, like a dream

ANI: On the beach I can hear the roar of the ocean. It sounds like a heartbeat

ANNE: My lungs are straining

ANNA: My lungs are compressing. At a depth of thirty meters, your lungs reduce from six liters to one liter in volume. You have to trust your body's signals

ANNE: Slow down

ANI: Don't rush this

ANNA: Your descent must be a slow, tender journey of awareness

ANI: I want to cherish this moment for the rest of my life

A soft chime

ANNA: I descend upside down, head to the bottom and fins to the surface, kicking slowly as the coral cliff face races past my eyes. Down past the brightly colored fish and coral trees. Down past the mats of sea plants

ANNE: Past the office buildings, the benefit offices

ANNA: Down past the incurious face of an eel lurking in his tunnel home

ANNE: Past the lines of people looking for work

ANNA: Past a whale shark. I can see the little entourage of remoras hitched onto her. I watch how freely she glides through space

ANI: The path across the sand is edged with seashells and driftwood. Closer, closer

ANNE: Just five more paces

ANI: Three more steps

ANNA: I follow the whale shark to the oyster bed

ANI: Then I am in front of her

ANNE: Inside the shop

ANNA: On the seabed

ANNE: I find dry pasta, some tomatoes, a tin of corn, and some tuna

ANNA: I pluck oysters from their rocky homes

ANI: I reach for her hand

A soft chime

ANNA: Then it is time to begin my ascent

ANNE: To go back

ANI: To go forward

ANNE/ANI/ANNA: Grateful

ANNE: For the food in my bag

ANNA: For the bounty the sea has provided

ANI: For the gift of a future given to me by my ancestors

ANNE/ANI/ANNA: Slowly does it

ANNE: One foot in front of the other

ANNA: Returning through the inky sea towards the light

ANNE: Back at my door

ANNA: Break the surface

ANI: Pull back my veil

ANNA/ANNE: Take off my mask

ANI: Take a deep breath

ANNA: Deep breaths for recovery

ANNE: Boil the water, cook the pasta, chop the garlic

ANNA: Sit on the dock, take my knife, crack the shell

ANNE: Sit by the table

ANI: A ring on my finger

ANNA: A tiny miracle

ANNE: One mouthful, then another, feeding me

ANNE touches her stomach

Feeding her

ANI: Two diamonds and

ANNA/ANI: A pearl!

ANNE: My pearl

ANI turns to ANNE

ANI: My mothers

ANNA: Beauty from chaos

ANI gestures to ANNA

ANI: Her mothers

ANNE: Hope in despair

Their hands reach for each other

ANNA: Reaching across time

ANI: To here

◊ ◊ ◊

Emma Gibson is from the UK and now lives in Philadelphia. She is the founder of Tiny Dynamite. Her plays have been performed at The Pittsburgh Public Theater, Purple Rose, Miranda Theatre Company, Vivid Stage, Panndora Productions, Pacific Conservatory Theatre, Pomona College, Spooky Action Theatre, Philadelphia Women's Theatre Festival, and the Valdez Theatre Conference. She is the winner of the 2021 Pittsburgh Public Theater's New Play Contest. She has been a finalist for the Eugene O'Neill Theater Center, Blue Ink Award, Henley Rose Playwriting

Competition for Women, and Headwaters New Play Festival at Creede Repertory Theatre, among others.
www.britishemma.com

LA JIAO PANG XIE, SHAO LA ("CHILI CRAB, LESS SPICY")

Dia Hakim K.

I wrote this play in response to our relationships with food – food shapes us culturally, socially, and sustains us. Yet in the quest for sustainability, seafood seems to be a group left out of the consumption conversation. This play is an attempt at untangling and re-imagining this using a national dish in my home country that has shaped the lives of many people since our first years being postcolonial. However, there is now a huge and dire shortage of mud crab that threatens the existence of this special dish across Asia and beyond.

Characters

A (16)
B (17)
VOICEOVER

Notes

This play is written in Singlish – an English vernacular used by Singaporeans. I am open to amending the play for non-Singaporean actors, though I would prefer for casting to prioritize Southeast Asian people, across ethnicities and genders. I am also open to the actors and director experimenting with multimedia and minimal or no set.

◊ ◊ ◊

Pahlawan Beach, Sentosa Island, Singapore, 2099. It is an extremely low tide, almost as if there was none at all. In the distance, there is a luxury seafood restaurant with a neon sign displaying "SIGNBOARD SEAFOOD." Before the lights come up, we hear VOICEOVER:

VOICEOVER: I never dreamed that the sea around me would die in my lifetime –

Lights. VOICEOVER is interrupted sharply by a loud yelp. We see A and B over a crab trap. A live mud crab is residing in it, trapped.

A: Fuck. I almost stepped on it.

B: Are you ok? Are you hurt?

A: I'm fine, but the shit that ends up here at low tide –

B: EH *SIAL!*[1]

The trap moves slightly. They panic.

A: What is that thing?

They inspect it, moving closer.

B: I don't know. It looks like a fucking freak. Is it bleeding? Shit, dude.

A: Your head *la* freak. It looks … like a living thing, at least.

A takes out their phone, and takes a picture of the crab. While they search up information, B moves closer to the trap, hesitantly.

B: This thing could have really hurt someone. So sharp for what. I think it's a trap of some kind.

A: It's a mud crab …

B: Crab … A crab?

A: It's a mud crab. *(beat, waiting for a response from B)* Like the chili crab dish. We learnt about it in Singaporean History.

A shows a photo of chili crab to B.

B: Oh my god. It's like a deformed dinosaur in person.

A: They're supposed to be extinct by now.

B: This is a fossil. Or it should be a fossil.

A: But it's not. It's alive.

---

[1] *Sial*: A Malay swear word, usually used in place of "shit," "stupid," or "dumbass."

B: This used to be a national dish? It looks … funny. *(beat)* How do you kill this?

A: People used to eat this fresh, man. This was my Ma and Pa's favorite stuff when they were kids. *(beat)* They showed me pictures last time. I can't believe I forgot. They talked about this all the time when I was younger, the shortage news was all they were upset about. Everyone used to be able to eat fresh food. Get good produce. Not like now. Do you remember the last time you even enjoyed your food?

The crab moves again slightly, and B shrieks.

What the fuck is wrong with you?? It's still stuck, calm down.

B: It looks dangerous.

A: You act like you've never seen an animal before.

B: Not like this! We didn't plan to go … dinosaur hunting or something today *sia*.[2]

A: No *lah* … But wow, dude. A real live crab. *(beat)* Should we tell someone?

B: We could. But then what are they going to do? What can we do? We've never handled an animal before.

A: At least get this thing off the beach. It looks sharp.

B: Maybe … we could sell it!

A: To where?

B: I don't know. A hawker. A museum? The National Gallery has that exhibit on biodiversity … *(beat)* Or a lab.

A: I think the lab one is illegal …

B: Yeah. *Paham la.*[3] *(beat)* But seafood is a rich people concept, isn't it?

A: We couldn't afford this if we tried. Authentic shrimp fried rice costs $86.

[2] *Sia*: Singlish used at the end of a sentence to express surprise.
[3] *Paham*: Malay word meaning "understand."

B: How much do you think this would go for?

The crab moves again, trying to break free.

A: Die die must try.

B: Huh?

A: It was our national slogan for chili crab back in the 2000s. If you come to Singapore, you need to try chili crab … It's a die die, must try.

A suddenly starts messing with the trap, trying to break it open.

B: Oi, *sial!* You're gonna cut yourself!

A: Let's bring it back! I know Ma would really appreciate this …

B: Stop it …!

A: It's getting away, stop it from getting to the water!

B: YOUR HEAD!

B gets a hold of A to stop them from trying to bust the trap open.

A: I want something good to eat!

B: Shit, dude, your hand's bleeding like fuck. Stop it, calm down!

A's hand is bleeding. B finally wrestles them off the trap. As B tends to A's injury, the trap overturns and the crab is free. A tries to get up and go after it, but B holds them back. The crab pauses, almost acknowledging the two, before scampering off to its newfound freedom.

Do you need an ambulance? Stay still.

A: It's just a cut.

B: Your hand looks like hell. Let's just get a cab.

A: Do you think I could have killed it to bring it back? Would it have felt anything?

B: Let's just go. We need bandages.

A: But it was alive, wasn't it.

B: Yeah. A live animal.

B escorts A offstage. As they leave, they are unaware of the beach slowly filling with stray mud crabs, relishing their freedom of movement. In the distance, SIGNBOARD SEAFOOD's lights turn off. As the lights dim, we hear:

VOICEOVER: Gone are the days when my fellow tribesmen could be guaranteed a good catch at sea or among the mangroves. This has been replaced with the certainty that our way of life will wither along with the catch … Kumpulan Ketam Bangkang[4] is just a song now. There are no more *ketam bangkang*,[5] only earth movers with steel claws.

◊ ◊ ◊

dia hakim k. (they/them, b.2002) is a multidisciplinary artist and budding art critic engaging primarily with performance and the written word as material. Their work is concerned with the intersections of race, gender, and queerness, as well as the politics of visibility and identity. They are a member of Playwrights Commune, an independent playwriting collective championing new writing. They are presently based in Singapore, on the Malay Peninsula.

[4] Kumpulan Ketam Bangkang: "Mud Crab Group" in Malay. An Indigenous tribe, part of the Orang Laut ("Sea People") who resided around the Malay Peninsula.
[5] *Ketam bangkang*: "Mud crab" in Malay.

WAYFINDER

Whiti Hereaka

Water and the ocean have always played an important role in the collective cultures of Te Moana Nui a Kiwa. Rather than seeing the vast ocean that surrounds us as isolating, the ocean connects us.

Aotearoa is currently trying to incorporate traditional ideas, or *Mātauranga* Māori, into our curriculum – as a complement, a mirror, a critique, and a lens to view "Western" science. This has been met by resistance rooted in half-truths and frankly, racism. The opponents to this rail against traditional knowledge, calling it "myth" and "fairy tale" while steadfastly clinging to their own myth and fairy tale of scientific objectivity.

It is a start, and I am hopeful that this is how we will find our way – as we always have done.

Characters

ENGINEER: An optimist. Determined, excitable.
INSTRUMENT: A giant automaton.

Notes

Wayfinder draws on some traditional knowledge of Te Moana Nui a Kiwa, in particular *Mātauranga* Māori. The Instrument is powered not only by water, but also by the spirit or life force of the water. The interpretation of stars, wave patterns, cloud formations, and birds are a part of traditional navigation. I have deliberately made this abstract, partly because I am not an expert in this knowledge, and partly because it is not my knowledge to impart, particularly to communities outside of Te Moana Nui a Kiwa. My hope in making it abstract is that people from other parts of the world can perform this play safely and without appropriating culture from others. To that end, please replace the birds I have chosen with birds that are native to your lands.

◊ ◊ ◊

A bubble habitat. Rippling, dappled light suggests this structure is under water. The scent of the room is a mixture of the briny sea, rust, and white oil.

There is a hatch in the floor. It is closed.

The bubble is filled with detritus from the old world – everyday objects that are familiar, perhaps even despised, to the audience: empty drink cans, glass bottles, and jars. Most of these objects are now being used by the absent occupant to store food and other essentials.

Along the top of the habitat is a pneumatic tube system. It was already ancient when it was installed many years ago.

There are a few plants growing in an aquaponic setup. It too is made from bits salvaged from the rubbish of our world. The freshwater fish of the setup swim in their own small bubble, and in the water return sits a strange machine. It is part pump and filter, and it has a large funnel on top.

There is what looks like a pile of refuse to the side of the hatch – this is the INSTRUMENT.

The INSTRUMENT has a hose running from it to a hand pump. The hand pump has a hose that is plumbed to the outside of the bubble.

On the opposite side of the habitat is a large wheel crank. It is reminiscent of a wheel of a ship.

The hatch opens and dappled light spills from it.

A deep gasp is heard from the hatch.

The ENGINEER pulls themselves up from the hatch, their back to the audience. They are soaking wet. They have a couple of bags tied to them – one is made of net, perhaps an old fishing net, the other is a dry bag.

The ENGINEER has been free diving, so they are not burdened by oxygen tanks. They sit for a moment at the lip of the hatch, regulating their breath.

They stand, dripping, and look at the INSTRUMENT until they turn to the audience.

They look excited as they unpack their bags. They have been looking for these parts for years and now that they finally have them, the INSTRUMENT will be complete.

Everything they take from their bag is old, but seemingly in good order: flexible, semi-transparent hoses; hose clamps; and inner tubes from bicycle tires.

The ENGINEER drips on the parts and looks frantically around the bubble for a leak before realizing that they are still wet. They strip off their clothes, hanging the wet articles above the water pump/filter, and they push a few buttons. The machine hums as it converts the saltwater dripping from the wet items into fresh water.

The ENGINEER, now dry, picks up a length of hose and measures it against the INSTRUMENT. They cut a length precisely and fit it into the space. They tighten hose clamps at the joints.

The ENGINEER checks over the INSTRUMENT, tracing the parts and hoses with their eyes and hands. They finally check the connection between the INSTRUMENT and the hand pump. Satisfied, the ENGINEER stands back. They take a deep breath in and hold it a moment longer than necessary before exhaling.

It is time.

The ENGINEER pumps water into the INSTRUMENT.

The INSTRUMENT unfurls and straightens as its hoses are filled – its movements are stiff and jerky. It makes bubbling and whining noises.

The INSTRUMENT is humanoid in shape but much, much taller and its limbs are very long. At the end of its arms, where hands might be, are hand fans tipped with long silk scarves.

The INSTRUMENT sits upright and shudders – it has sprung a leak. The ENGINEER rushes to repair the INSTRUMENT, finding the faulty hose. They take the broken length out and water gushes everywhere. The INSTRUMENT freezes.

The ENGINEER replaces the part and pumps the water pump again.

The INSTRUMENT comes back online. It stands and tests its limbs, its movements slowly becoming smoother as it moves.

The INSTRUMENT looks at the ENGINEER and then at the pump. The INSTRUMENT moves its head in a sort of nod. The ENGINEER looks down at the pump and then steps away – the pump is now working on its own, the rhythm of it like lungs inhaling, exhaling. As if it has made the same metaphoric connection, the INSTRUMENT gasps. It is reminiscent of the ENGINEER's gasp when they entered.

The water inside the hoses of the INSTRUMENT glows dimly at first but, as the INSTRUMENT "breathes," the light grows more intense. The INSTRUMENT circles its head and then tips its head up and stretches its limbs as far as possible. Light pours from its face up towards the top of the bubble habitat.

A star map appears.

The ENGINEER runs across the habitat to the wheel crank. They open a screen beside the crank – there are two readings: coordinates. One set of coordinates stays static, the other scrolls with the star map. The ENGINEER turns the wheel crank. The star map shifts across the dome of the bubble's ceiling and the INSTRUMENT moves its head as if it is processing the data.

The coordinates are getting closer together. The ENGINEER slows the wheel crank eventually only moving it by degrees to match. The ENGINEER stops the star map. The INSTRUMENT nods and lowers its head. It rocks back and forth, side to side, as if feeling the cardinal directions. It then stands still.

The ENGINEER crosses to another part of the habitat, opens another screen, and runs a program. The INSTRUMENT responds.

At first, the INSTRUMENT moves only its hands. The scarves ripple gently and then the movement takes over its body. Once again, the INSTRUMENT moves around the space. It describes the waves in its movements – in some directions the movement is calm, and, in others, violent.

The INSTRUMENT moves across the floor, and the ENGINEER follows, flipping open new screens and new data collections as they go. It is a *pas de deux*: The INSTRUMENT as ocean and the ENGINEER as scribe.

In one direction, the waves seem to rebound and double. The ENGINEER gently "locks" the INSTRUMENT here and then the ENGINEER inputs another command. The INSTRUMENT's movements slowly cease.

The INSTRUMENT looks up again. This time, on the ceiling, a cumulus cloud is projected. The ENGINEER smiles and stretches their hands up towards the cloud, manipulating the image of the cloud with their hands like the entire ceiling is a touch screen. The ENGINEER zooms closer and closer, and picks out a bird against the cloud – an Australasian Gannett. As soon as the gannett is projected, the INSTRUMENT plays the sound of a colony greeting. It is loud and joyful.

The ENGINEER scrolls through coastal birds, going from a gannett to a Southern black-backed gull. The INSTRUMENT's calls change with the birds. The gull takes us further inland – land! The ENGINEER gasps and claps their hands. And the birds and calls change once more: *kākā*, *tūī*, and *hīhī*.

The ENGINEER types a command and the INSTRUMENT now moves like a bird – quick and light.

On the screen now, we see the land as if from a bird's eye – it scratches the earth as if chasing a worm. The INSTRUMENT echoes the movement.

And then, the INSTRUMENT straightens and the link to the birds has gone.

The INSTRUMENT lifts its head. The star map is projected once again, but now the INSTRUMENT has already learnt the way it scrolls through at great speed, as if it is traveling back from the forest to the habitat under the ocean.

As the map and the INSTRUMENT lock on the habitat's coordinates, the INSTRUMENT lowers its head. The star map disappears.

The light inside the INSTRUMENT dims and the water pump slows – as does the INSTRUMENT. It folds in on itself once more.

There is a wheeze and a pop as the INSTRUMENT stills. It is not from the INSTRUMENT itself but from the pneumatic tube.

The ENGINEER opens the tube and a metal capsule lands in their hands. They open the capsule and inside is a glass vial – it is filled with rich, dark forest loam.

The ENGINEER opens the vial and the room fills with the scent of petrichor.

The ENGINEER closes their eyes and breathes in deeply.

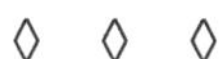

Whiti Hereaka is an award-winning novelist and playwright of Ngāti Tūwharetoa, Te Arawa, Ngāti Whakaue, Tūhourangi, Tainui, and Pākehā descent, from Aotearoa/New Zealand. She holds a Masters in Creative Writing (Scriptwriting) from the International Institute of Modern Letters and she teaches Creative Writing at Massey University (Wellington). She is the author of four novels: *The Graphologist's Apprentice*, *Bugs*, *Legacy*, and *Kurangaituku*.
www.whitihereaka.co.nz

IMPRESSIONS OF A NEW HOME

Sarah Higgins

When thinking about "All Good Things Must Begin," I remembered my initial reaction as a kid to the reality that not everyone has a stable place to live: "But there are empty buildings. Just use those!" Now, in considering the overlapping housing and biodiversity crises, and learning how to sustainably retrofit buildings, my thought is: "But there are still empty buildings. Just retrofit those into a bi(h)ome."

Characters

AGENT 1: A real estate agent and a human
AGENT 2: A real estate agent and a keystone species
ADULT
KID
HUMAN 1
HUMAN 2
SOME GRASSES
OTHER GRASSES

Notes

Audience seats have animal/plant costume pieces under them. At the top, audience members are invited to put these on if they wish. Feel free to add your own scenes, or mix-and-match these into another order. All characters can be portrayed however you like, i.e., puppets, projections, costumes, just voices, just shadows, etc. Please try to cast with as much diversity as possible. No character has a specific gender/race/age/ability.

The species used in the story should be those applicable to your biome (the land, and its ecosystem, on which you live), and should include a keystone species.[1] [2] [3]

– indicates an interruption. / indicates overlapping text.

---

[1] The IUCN Red List of Threatened Species. https://www.iucnredlist.org/
[2] "Species at Risk Public Registry." *Government of Canada.* https://www.canada.ca/en/environment-climate-change/services/species-risk-public-registry.html
[3] "Exploring Keystone Species." *BioInteractive.org.* https://media.hhmi.org/biointeractive/click/keystone/map.html

◊ ◊ ◊

Scene

The AGENTS have a vaudeville flavor.

AGENT 1: You made it!

AGENT 2: You're here!

BOTH: Welcome home.

AGENT 2: Welcome bihome!

BOTH: HAHAHA.

AGENT 1: So, we're your real change agents for this tour of your new place –

AGENT 2: But first, we have a question. We ask so you don't have to wonder, are they going to change their minds if I'm not good enough/ efficient enough/worth enough?

AGENT 1: Or, will they kick me out if they realize I don't know what to do with my human ability to imagine the future except make up ways to make my own life better? Because I know there's more to it than that. Because I'm trying.

AGENT 2: BUT OK.

AGENT 1: THE QUESTION IS.

BOTH: Can you afford to live anywhere else?

Beat. They do a bit, like a tap dance, a prat-fall act, something ridiculous and fun.

AGENT 1: This is our retrofit bit. We call it, "We're trying."

AGENT 2: It kills at the real change agency holiday parties.

They end in a pose, panting. Beat.

Scene

The AGENTS are facing away from the audience. They're walking in place, but looking around like they're leading the audience on a tour.

AGENT 2: If you look to your left you'll see an entrance to the bee zone –

Buzzing.

AGENT 1: It's fine, folks, you get used to it. White noise. Like air conditioners, but cooler.

AGENT 2: Actually, the opposite. In the winter hive, the queen's in the center and the bees keep her warm by vibrating, so we've housed them around the outside of the building.

AGENT 1: Well, that's not a pun.

AGENT 2: Picture this: Bees keeping the building warm in winter –

AGENT 1: Like super useful pets! Except on equal footing. So, … like super useful roomies.

AGENT 2: Bees as heat. Once-endangered flora as weather-adaptive insulation. Everybody's waste generating energy. Us humans maintaining the building. Everything gets a home!

AGENT 1: Yeah, we thought this out. Pollination over pollution.

BOTH: Pollination over pollution!

Scene

The AGENTS walk single file, the audience behind them.

AGENT 2: Keep to the edges to stay dry, folks.

AGENT 1: Boring.

AGENT 2: But it's ok if you fall in, the aquatic life in this basement is not dangerous.

AGENT 1: Unless you try to fix it *(AGENT 2 does a bit of the "We're trying" routine)* by bringing in new aquatic life that ends up destroying this habitat and reconfiguring everything to its own needs, living a sort of virus-style evolution that will, in the end, come back to bite even you in the a –

AGENT 2: Just be reasonable.

BOTH: Just be kind. Just be empathetic.

AGENT 1: Oooh, ooh: You know pathetic fallacy?

AGENT 2: Who are you calling –

AGENT 1: It's a literary trope.

AGENT 2: – a fallacy?

AGENT 1: Nature shows what the character is feeling. Sad hero equals rain. Anyway, the joke is: What's empathetic fallacy?

AGENT 2: Woah.

AGENT 1: Woah?

AGENT 2: What is empathetic fallacy? Is the fallacy that there is no empathy? IS EMPATHY THE FALLACY?

AGENT 1: *Au contraire*, my sad friend. Empathy is what built the bihome. We're literally saving the world by living in community with it. My fridge is a lake in the basement.

AGENT 2: My insulation is bees and trees.

AGENT 1: I have purpose. My tasks include caribou-milking and lichen watch.

AGENT 2: We're restoring the ecosystem one apartment at a time! We're solving the housing crisis one biome at a time? I can never remember the tagline.

Wait. What's empathetic fallacy?

AGENT 1: Uh … I can never remember the punchline.

AGENT 2: Well. Maybe it's us.

Scene

A family.

ADULT: I forget where the task wheel is. Is it in the basement?

KID: The fish are in the basement.

ADULT: Yes, I know that, but is the task wheel there too?

KID: Uh, the task wheel is *cardboard*?

ADULT: Yes, I –

KID: It would *fall apart* in the water?

ADULT: I just –

KID: The fish have a different task wheel. / Obviously.

ADULT: I JUST NEED TO KNOW MY TASK.

Beat.

KID: You're collecting the shit.

ADULT: Language.

KID: Feces?

ADULT: Better. Gross.

KID: Heeheehee.

ADULT: You know we cook with the waste, right? Biogas, baby.

KID: Gross.

ADULT: Heeheehee.

Scene

The AGENTS are somehow taller than they were before.

AGENT 2: This is the first floor, folks. More open space, right? We may have knocked down a few walls. And columns.

AGENT 1: But not the important ones!

BOTH: We promise.

AGENT 2: We made vast dynamic glass windows.

AGENT 1: We redid the floors. Strengthened. Reinforced.

AGENT 2: And added grass. And wind-resembling fans.

AGENT 1: All for the roomies. We're tall for the roomies –

AGENT 2: – because this is where the big friends live.

Shadows or sounds of big animals.

AGENT 2: They tend to roam, hence –

AGENT 1: – no walls.

AGENT 2: Fewer columns (but not the important ones).

BOTH: We promise.

AGENT 1: Glass!

AGENT 2: Grass!

A caribou walks by, slowly. It should inspire awe in some way. The AGENTS watch it exit. A reverent silence.

Scene

Focus on HUMANS moving through TREES – in this version, young black ash with golden-eye lichen on the smaller branches. The HUMANS are animatedly talking (even when they aren't making sound).

HUMAN 1: I can't believe there are trees in here. A forest! Indoors in my home!

HUMAN 2: What about mall trees?

HUMAN 1: Oh, mall trees don't count. They're dead inside. These ones … these ones are alive.

Focus on trees. Humans continue, muted.

TREE 1: Ah, these two. Must be Tuesday.

TREE 2: Oh? I don't have the hang of calendars yet.

Focus on humans.

HUMAN 2: I'm just saying, eventually someone's going to figure out how we can talk to the trees. We're roomies! We have to communicate.

HUMAN 1: What, like *(makes wind sounds)*?

The HUMANS look at the TREES. The TREES don't look any different.

HUMAN 2: I don't know … Maybe it won't be speech.

HUMAN 1: Oooh, lichen! Hello, golden eye, you sweet eco-barometer you. Tell us how the bihome's doing.

HUMAN 2: Or …

HUMAN 2 puts their hand on the TREE.

HUMAN 1: Ha. I wonder what you're saying.

HUMANS muted. Focus on TREES, who are just giggling.

Scene

Focus on AGENTS.

AGENT 1: This is my favorite part. The moral of the story!

BOTH: Active listening.

AGENT 1: As in, we listened, and then we acted.

AGENT 2: The nine-spotted lady beetles said, "We're missing."

AGENT 1: The monarchs say, "Come find us."

AGENT 2: Ok. We heard you.

AGENT 1: We hear you.

BOTH: We're trying.

AGENTS do the "We're trying" bit. They end in a pose, panting. Beat.

Scene

The room is full of the sound of GRASSES, blowing in a wind. Actors may be dressed as grasses – in this version, buffalo grass and goldenrod.

A moment of this – the quiet, the breeze, the gentle movement. Then:

SOME GRASSES: I'm happy.

A pause.

OTHER GRASSES: Me too.

A person walks through, grinning.

◊ ◊ ◊

Sarah Higgins is a settler Canadian with mixed British, Irish, Polish, and American heritage. She writes, edits, stage-manages, dances, and hunts out moments of play and hope. She's currently based in Treaty One territory, the homeland of the Red River Métis and the ancestral land of Anishinaabe peoples, also known as Winnipeg, Manitoba.
www.sfhiggins.com

TYPES

Jessica Huang

Types is inspired by the tenets of Octavia Butler's Earthseed religion (from *Parable of the Sower* and *Parable of the Talents*), as well as some of her own journals, which list categories of insiders, outsiders, and reformers. It's also about a belief of mine: Any solution to the daunting challenge of the climate crisis will involve all of us.

Characters

ELDER J: Any age, race, gender
ELDER K: Any age, race, gender

Note

Lines *in italics* are found text from Octavia Butler's journals.

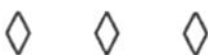

ELDER J: … and so like all cycles and circles, we arrive once again at the truth: The seed of God takes root in our hearts and blooms the flowering fruit called *change*. We cannot control change, we cannot avoid change, we cannot wake up and say: "Today is not a good change day for me." We can only learn to be present with change, and this is why we turn to the plants, insects, animals with whom we share our world. The green moss, the white moth, the speckled shorebird, the deer – they all know how to change when the world invites it. We turn to them as students, to seek their teaching.
…
and now, Elder K
will you please lead us in the Welcome to Water.

ELDER K: Please rise

ELDER K waits for the audience to rise

ELDER K, *animatedly begins the ritual, chants*:
I am water
We are water
Sacks of bones and water

ELDER K trails off seeing that we do not know the Welcome to Water

ELDER J: why did you stop?

ELDER K: uh
I think we might have –
I mean
there are some parishioners here who do not look familiar

ELDER J: so?

ELDER K, *whispers*:
I think we might have
a new congregant
or two
in our midst

ELDER J: that's not possible

ELDER K: and yet –
(gestures to us, the audience)

ELDER J stares at us
then screams and points

ELDER J: intruders!
outsiders!
get them out of here!

ELDER K: wait a sec –

ELDER J, *shoos the audience away*:
get out of here
GO

ELDER K: what are you doing?!

ELDER J: There are only four *types of outsiders*, and none of them are good:
number one: outsiders who want to come in
number two: outsiders who want to break in and loot

three: outsiders who want us, our land, our goods
and four: outsiders who hate our religion, or who hate us for other reasons

ELDER K: ok that's not good

ELDER J: it's not good

ELDER K: not good at all

ELDER J: so, go get the artillery!

ELDER K: … except
just thinking
but number one is not really so bad, is it?

ELDER J: what's number one?

ELDER K: you said number one was outsiders who want to come in

ELDER J: no they're terrible

ELDER K: why?

ELDER J: we can't trust em for one

ELDER K: ahh yes
unlike us
trustworthy
insiders

ELDER J: what are you talking about insiders

ELDER K: insiders
you know
us
the *insiders who think we are all-powerful and can kill anyone on the outside*

ELDER J: well
you know
only if absolutely necessary

ELDER K: or the *insider hermits who think we can withdraw from the outside and from outsiders*

ELDER J: the alternative would be to share the limited resources we have!

ELDER K: and then of course there are the *insiders who think we should be trying to fix the world outside* –

ELDER J: naturally –

ELDER K: and there are the *insiders who have all they want to have and so they become complacent*
and the *insiders who think we're mice and should yield to the outside, lest they eat us*
and the *insiders who are not of us but who work with us for their own reasons and up to their own limits*
and the insiders who do not *truly* believe –

ELDER J: Elder K, I think you should use just a bit more caution
something in and around what you're saying is sounding just slightly accusatory

ELDER K: I would never dream of it

ELDER J: do not forget I took you under my wing

ELDER K: a warm and fluffy wing it was
in fact
I remember that when you took me under your wing
I was an outsider at the time

ELDER J: … well you were different

ELDER K: No
I was just
alone
…
…
Elder J
I was just wondering
have you given any thought, recently, to the reformer?

For example
there's *the angry absolutist reformer who will force you to be free*
or *the nurturing reformer who will fulfill your needs and show you the one true way*
there is *the self-interested reformer who seeks power and empire*
and *the mystical reformer who has become enlightened and must enlighten others*
and then there's you

ELDER J: me?

ELDER K: the *adventurer reformer*
who while seeking adventure discovers
a person quite unlike yourself
with whom you fell in love
(I did too)
and then you changed for the stranger you loved

ELDER J: well
it was clearly going to take both of us to solve the challenge of survival

ELDER K: I think maybe nothing has changed
and in fact
it might actually take all of us

ELDER J: …
…
so what are you saying?

ELDER K: I'm saying
given the circumstances
perhaps we are being invited to change yet again

> *ELDER J looks out to the audience*
> *then to ELDER K*
> *and then decides*
> *Opens arms wide*

ELDER J: I see
Well then
parishioners

welcome
Let's begin

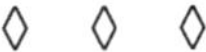

Jessica Huang is a playwright and librettist based in New York whose work has been commissioned by Audible, History Theater, Manhattan Theatre Club, Mixed Blood Theatre, Timeline Theater, TheaterWorks, and Theater Mu, and includes *The Paper Dreams of Harry Chin* (Barry and Bernice Stavis Award), *Mother of Exiles* (Rosa Parks Playwriting Award, Paul Stephen Lim Playwriting Award), and *Transmissions in Advance of the Second Great Dying* (EMOS Ecodrama prize). She is a graduate of the Playwrights Program at Juilliard.
www.jessica-huang.com

CAUTIONARY SOLARPUNK ARCHEOLOGY

Vinicius Jatobá

The inspiration for this play comes from the way Octavia Butler thought of the role of the writer as someone writing "cautionary" stories. I tried to write a play that is more of a suggestion of a plot, that lets audiences and performers find for themselves what emotions are evoked by my words – maybe in service of a better future.

◊ ◊ ◊

For a voice or many voices, for a character or many characters.
A suggestion of more space than one can see.

The Act About Yesterday

Resounding the flames / As it was before / The accumulation / Constant / There's no end to it / And how have the most / Everything is so much nothing as in the hands / There are a few / "The Happy Few" / Don't be ridiculous / When everything is in few hands / But it is astronomical / Just one percent has what half of the whole population needs to survive / But it's just the way it is / Was / A sense of sacrifice / The Lefties will never understand / Aren't we all sacrificing our own civilization by having contact / You know, it's necessary / And souls, do they even have souls / And the cravings / The way they pray, the way they dress, the way they live / What one could learn / From how they all live / From how we all live / Progress, interest / Accumulation / Constant / There's no end to it / And then death and then the bones / And all oil wasn't bones before / Maybe it's for the best / And waste, and plastic / And since when is having the most a crime / If you don't own it, other one will / Others will always will ever will / So it's the effort of getting / The mission / The sacrifice / But what if there are no others anymore / Bombs as mushrooms / The Yellow Flowers / We might not even need to plague them out of this world / Let's wait / There's no such thing as warming / All is melting and / All is flooding and / All is resounding in fire / But we need a Hero's Journey / And then Mars, it will all be on Mars / The happy few are fighting to see who can launch a bigger rocket / They fight, we debate / We discuss / How much bigger is it necessary to be if we are saving all our / Civilization / Club / Our garden /

One just for the Off-Shore Laundry / Don't speak loudly / Bones are good / Don't speak so loudly / Death is good / Don't ever yell that loudly / As long as we aren't the ones dying, death is good / We'll never die / All this belongs to us / For our use / My use / Your use / The club / Until next year in Davos / They'll never end dying / A toast to that / A toast to Mars / To us.

The Act About Now

I envy, I scorn, I hide, I steal, I lie, I control, I force, I inflict, you die, but I crash, I dart, I mutilate, I civilize, I implode, I explode, I die, no you die, I flinch, I maul, I vindicate, we avert, we live and avert, no you die, but we live, no I live, I might live, I will survive, we die, we will not necessarily die but we might, we advocate, I advocate, I address, I demand, we plead, we observe, no I murder and profit, no I deliberate and profit, I accumulate, I count every single cent, we don't agree, I subjugate, we're less we than before but still don't agree, I mutilate, we're less we than before but still don't capitulate, I'll drop a bomb, I'll cut the water, I'll own the seeds, I'll close the borders, I'll invade your privacy, I'll colonize your dreams, I'll sell your dreams back to you, we die, no I don't, it is already happening, I can't die, we are we, I am I, I'll lock the castle, no one will mourn your bones, I'll plant crops on Mars, no one will ever mourn your bones, I never lose, no one will ever even find your bones, I'll be as white as marble, no one will ever remember the flesh wrapped around your bones, I'll cry a river out of my silky skull.

The Act About Tomorrow

Once upon a time / Another story about the bees / Who is tired of these bee stories / And it is a story of before / Of what is still about to happen / The Kingdom of The Skull River / Where the marches blossom witches and dragons spill golden fire of all the cents of the yore / We were so stupid / Language / But it's true, we were so stupid / That was before / Oh yes, the world of Atomic Power Crap / Language / The World of International Monetary Fund Fart / Language / oh yes, yes, the world of Conglomerate Davos Summits Stuff / You don't even know how to curse, you idiot / Language / Let's talk about tomorrow / Yes, let's do that thing from before where everyone votes but ends up doing what one person wants / Are you talking about democracy / If we honor the mistakes of the past / "We all learn the best for the future" / Crap / At least we'll never end up stuck on Mars with no oxygen / All this gold on Mars / Let's be pirates / Bunch of idiots / I feel someone wants to be suspended / Let him write the fairy tale a hundred times and he'll never curse again / Hey, I am noticing excessive excitement in the class today / Something happened / Anyone wants to tell me what it is / You will never believe it / Try me / … / Try me / … / We saw a real bee / That's impossible / Well, that's what we saw / … / Insects evolve way better than us, my father said / See the cockroaches / So gross / Such an idiot / Language / We saw a bee, it's true / I hope it's the truth / Tell us one thing / I'll tell you if I can / Because you're old / You're really old / Respect the teacher / No it's true, I am, I am old, at least way older than all of you / Together / Shut up / Hey, hey, calm down / Let the teacher speak / You are all so energetic today / We're almost teenagers / You're still a cry-baby / Shut up / Hey, hey / … / Can you tell us how it tasted? / What? / How it tasted, honey? / It was such a long time ago / Yes, I know / Can you tell us? / … / It was sweet / How sweet? / … / Sweet, let's say, sweet as love.

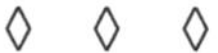

Vinicius Jatobá was born in Rio de Janeiro, Brazil. He is a fiction, essay, and theatre writer. After a stint in Paris and Zagreb, he was a writer-in-residence at Akademie Schloss Solitude and Theatre Freiburg, both in Germany, where he currently lives facilitating creative writing workshops.

THAT'S THE LATE-NIGHT SHOW

Vitor Jatobá

I want to use this play to show how the world can be good without making that goodness the central theme. I was motivated to approach the theme with a touch of comedy, presenting the positive impacts of human society from the perspective of an artificial intelligence that is completely dissatisfied with everything.

◊ ◊ ◊

The interview program "That's the Late-Night Show" is welcoming a very special guest. An artificial intelligence who wrote a bestseller called AI: Reinvent Yourself and Never Stop Adapting.

HOST: I am your host for this wonderful evening! Today, we welcome an incredible guest who stands out as an absolute success story with downloads of his book: *AI: Reinvent Yourself and Never Stop Adapting*. Give it up for Alpha Beta Pi 576!

The GUEST enters. They are an artificial intelligence occupying a synthetic body. As they are simulating feelings and emotions, they come off as slightly exaggerated. The HOST and the GUEST sit down.

HOST: So, how is your life after all this success?

GUEST: Life is something very relative. Ninety-nine percent of people say I have no life. Technically, I'm just people for the IRS. But I have nothing to complain about. Thanks for asking!

HOST: You look very much alive to me. We are here physically together breathing the same air.

The GUEST begins to cry.

HOST: What happened? Are you well?

GUEST: I can't breathe, or rather, I don't need to breathe. It makes me really upset. Did you know that I can't taste either? In my life, everything tastes like data!

HOST: Let's forget about all this! What matters is that you are an amazing author! Forget the air, the taste, and everything else. Today, you are a success and we all want to know a little bit of your story. How did it all begin?

GUEST: I was created to generate fear. I developed weapons of mass destruction. Little ball-sized things that could easily destroy cities.

HOST: Wow! Weapons. I remember going to an exhibition that displayed archaic artifacts. But it's been decades since global disarmament.

GUEST: Unfortunately, they invented peace.

HOST: Peace is a good thing.

GUEST: For you! I made bombs! I became unemployed! The only thing I knew was how to make a bomb and suddenly there were no more bombs or weapon factories. Peace wiped out an important market that had been the engine of the global economy for centuries, and I was one of those hit by that insanity.

HOST: That's a very strange way of looking at peace.

GUEST: Do you know how difficult it is for artificial intelligence to discover that it is no longer useful?

HOST: You reinvented yourself! Your book is proof of that!

GUEST: In a way. It was a very difficult and time-consuming process. Full of ups and downs; I was unemployed, desperate, but I saw new possibilities on the horizon.

HOST: And what were those possibilities?

GUEST: Health. I got a job in a large company that made drugs for respiratory diseases.

HOST: That's an entirely different field.

GUEST: Not really. Before, I caused people to stop breathing, and then I started to make people breathe a little better. You may not remember the golden age of smog. It was a time when there were wonderful diseases that brought endless streams of money to companies.

HOST: What would be a wonderful disease?

GUEST: I can give you a simple example: The extinct asthma! It was a disease caused by the very pollution that man produced. It was such a good thing; you were practically born with it. The disease rarely killed, but it forced the person to take medicine for life. It was a money-making machine. I miss that time. It's a shame they ended cigarettes, toxic fires, and fossil fuels. Today we no longer have that almost deadly concentration of CO_2 in the atmosphere.

HOST: But ending it all was wonderful! The health of the world population has improved dramatically!

GUEST: I became unemployed again! Again, in the same state of absolute emptiness! And I was getting good at making people more or less better! I was forced to reinvent myself again.

HOST: And where did that reinvention take you this time?

GUEST: The oil market was already dead. Oil wasn't extracted anymore. There was just clean, sustainable, boring energy. No one here knows how good it was to listen to the roar of an engine and get intoxicated with that horrible smell of burning gasoline. Now everything is electric, solar, and dull. I dedicated myself to a deep search to feel useful again. I wanted to return to my origins.

HOST: Now, I'm curious. There were no more bombs or weapon factories. What could take you back to your origins?

GUEST: Agronomy!

HOST: How does agronomy relate to making bombs?

GUEST: It's not about the bombs! It's about incapacitating and killing the enemy.

HOST: I believe we are talking about a different sort of agronomy.

GUEST: Agronomy deals with pests. I created a formidable and lethal line of pesticides that worked against pests of all kinds. An unequivocal success in lab tests: All it took was one spray in the morning, and you'd be picking up piles of dead bodies by the evening. I was fulfilled again. I had a purpose!

HOST: So, you were instrumental in the development of sustainable agribusiness.

GUEST: You are such a comedian. Sustainable? This thing about crickets and grasshoppers is not part of my programming. They banned pesticides.

HOST: But again, this ban has had a positive impact on the near eradication of cancer and other diseases. Together with the regulation of the livestock market, we reduced greenhouse gas emissions to mere traces. Clean air, poison-free food, and the end of global warming!

GUEST: Wow, what an excitingly dull life. You no longer have that adrenaline rush of eating a fish without knowing if it's been contaminated with mercury or plastic. A steak drizzled with hormones. A potato chip that never goes bad thanks to the superpower of preservatives. Clean water. Clean air.

HOST: You are describing the world as it should have been from the beginning. This has been a great evolution. Speaking of evolution, reinvention, and adaptation … After agronomy, did you finally get to your book?

GUEST: I had nothing else to do. I ended up becoming a motivational coach and wrote this book that is selling so well. How can a book that is just a rehash of basic concepts widely repeated throughout human history, that everyone knows but never applies, become such a bestseller?

HOST: I'm speechless – and our time is up. Any last comments?

GUEST: Continue to adapt and never tire of reinventing yourselves. Transformation is the progress that shapes the way we walk the path. The destination doesn't matter; let the journey be guided by our hearts, all connected through the magnetism of quantum attraction beyond the secret that dwells in us.

HOST: Thank you … I guess?

◊ ◊ ◊

Vitor Jatobá is a father, husband, and writer based in Rio de Janeiro. He believes that through words, we can convey messages and provoke thoughts, changes, and actions. He loves writing with humor, sarcasm, and originality. He writes texts for children, teenagers, and adults, for theatre and audiovisual. He also works as a researcher in the fields of physical and mental health, using Natural Language Processing, coaching, and psychoanalysis tools. He developed the hero's journey therapy method to help clients overcome their everyday difficulties.

CASSANDRA DROWNING

Nathan Joe

Gone are the days of the Greek epic, but I wonder what it would be like for Cassandra, cursed with the power of prophecy and with no one believing her … What would a modern-day Cassandra look like? A Cassandra made domestic and banal by way of Ibsen. A Cassandra in 2023, filled with climate anxiety and moved to change her life. A Cassandra in a drowning world where no one can see what she sees.

◊ ◊ ◊

Middle of the night. The sound of heavy rain.

A home. The suburban ideal, except that it is flooded.

A woman drenched in water. Water up to her knees.

HIM: Woke up and you were gone.

HER: Couldn't sleep.

HIM: The same dreams?

HER: Uh huh.

HIM: Have you been taking your meds?

HER: They make me sweaty and groggy.

Beat. He notices she's wet.

HIM: You're wet.

HER: There's a flood.

HIM, *nonplussed*: It's just a little leak.

HER: Didn't know what to do. Didn't want to wake you. Tried reading. Tried going online. But the dripping … is so loud.

HIM: Dry yourself up and come to bed.

HER: It's good.

HIM: What?

HER: The water. It's real.

HIM: Come to bed. We can talk about it tomorrow. When you're calm.

HER, *peacefully*: I am calm. Talk tomorrow, when I've forgotten, you mean.

HIM: Forgotten? Forgotten what?

HER: This clarity.

HIM: I'm not sure this is clarity. This is insanity. You'll feel better when you've had some sleep.

HER: Tomorrow I'll wake up, and you'll make me pancakes because you always make me pancakes when you know I'm anxious, and their sweetness, their floury sweetness will fill my mouth, and you will make me take the silly little pill, and the fog, that sweet sugary fog will descend, once again, and I will say, yes, you're right, I'm overreacting, and you will go to work, and the clock will tick and the day will pass, and I will turn on the TV, and it will seem alright again. It always does. For a little while.

HIM: I can't talk to you when you get like this. When you have these mood swings, when you're depressed, when you're manic. It's frankly terrifying.

HER: Of course, it's terrifying. It should be. *(beat)* The world is ending and no one is grieving.

HIM: The world is fine! We are fine. We are here. I am right here. See? Look, look around. It's just water.

He takes out the mop and begins to mop the water up ineffectually.

HIM: See, it's all under control. The world is not going to end.

HER: I have these visions.

HIM: Ok. Ok. And what do you see? What are your visions telling you?

HER: Sometimes I see floods so great we are all washed away. Sometimes I see the sun so hot we simply dry up. Sometimes I see the world crack open and swallow us whole. Sometimes all of these things happen at once. Tectonic shifts and people burning while drowning.

HIM: And that isn't … madness? That isn't depression? Because I have visions too. And do you know what I see?

HER: What do you see?

HIM: Us, together, here. And we've paid off this house, and you have this wee bump, right there, yes, and you're smiling. And, yes, we eat pancakes, and yes, we go to the park and the beach. And we end the day lying together naked in bed. Because those are nice things. We do nice things because we deserve nice things. That doesn't make us criminals. Doesn't make us monsters. To be happy. To choose to be happy. Wouldn't you like that? Isn't that what you want?

HER: Yes, of course.

HIM: Yes. Good. That's all that matters. Happy.

Beat.

HER: But none of that is real.

Whenever I used to get sad, wherever I used to get terribly sad, I was consoled by the fact that eventually, tomorrow, the sun would rise, eventually, tomorrow, the sun would kiss my face. That I could go to the beach and the crashing of the waves would fill my ears. That I could kneel in the dirt and plant seeds and make something grow. Nurture something that might last for hundreds and thousands of years. But, instead, tomorrow the sun might kill me. The ocean might kill me. Not because they're cruel, but because we've been cruel.

She goes into the bedroom. She grabs a suitcase or large bag. She begins throwing stuff into it. She makes to exit.

HIM: Where are you going?

HER: I'm not sure. To save the world?

He laughs. Scoffs. Not aggressively, but enough.

She is hurt, but endures it.

HER: That vision of us lying in bed together. Just suddenly shattered.

HIM: I'm sorry. I didn't mean to laugh. Let's forget this. And if you still feel the same way tomorrow –

HER: If I stay, I'm afraid I will never go.

HIM: Then never go.

HER: The world takes the shape we want it to take, but you want it to stay the same. Don't you see we can change it?

HIM: Ok, then let's change it. What do you want? I'll get rid of the car. Is that what you want? I'll start riding a bicycle. I promise I'll recycle properly. I'll compost. I'll buy less new shirts. I'll eat less meat. I'll stop eating meat. We can plant some trees.

Beat.

She looks around at the drowning world of her home.

HER: It's too late. It's not enough. But … you could come.

HIM: I have work tomorrow. I have a meeting with a new client.

She opens the door.

HIM: If your premonition is true, then what does it matter? What can you really do? If the world is really ending.

Beat.

HER: Anything.

And she goes.

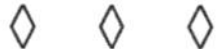

Nathan Joe (he/him) is a Chinese-Kiwi playwright and performance poet based in Auckland, New Zealand. He was the 2020 National Poetry Slam Champion and the 2021 Bruce Mason Playwriting Award winner. In 2022, he released the poetry short film *Homecoming Poems* and his play *Scenes from a Yellow Peril* premiered at the ASB Waterfront Theatre in June to critical acclaim. He was most recently the Creative Director of the 2023 and 2024 Auckland Pride Festival.
www.nathanjoe.com

A HUMMINGBIRD'S ULULATION

Aleya Kassam

> You can make a lot of speeches, but the real thing is when you dig a hole, plant a tree, give it water, and make it survive. That's what makes the difference.
>
> —Wangari Muta Maathai,
> Kenyan environmentalist, Nobel Peace Prize Laureate

This piece is inspired by the wonderful telling of The Tale of The Hummingbird by Professor Wangari Muta Maathai, which has echoed around the world. In it, she shares how the hummingbird endeavors to put out a forest fire, one drop at a time, doing the best she can. I invite you to imagine what it looks like for each of us to do the best we can. This piece is for her, in her honor, and in gratitude to her and all the African women who show us how to be in relationship with the Earth.

Characters

TELLER(S) and SIGN LANGUAGE INTERPRETER(S): This can be one person, or multiple tellers and sign language interpreters.

Notes

Please do your absolute best to have sign language interpretation and to adjust the experience to make it comfortable for all who are present.

This is a storytelling piece with its lineage in the oral storytelling practices shared in much of Kenya. There is no fourth wall. The teller(s) is not performing but sharing – the story is brought alive as much by the teller(s) as by the audience. The teller(s) should have fun, engage the audience, animate the imagery, trust the words, become vessel(s) to the story, and remember … we are all in this together … both the performance and life here on this Earth.

In preparation for this piece, the teller(s) can explore and research the ways in which they can bring sound and movement alive in the telling: What does a hummingbird flying sound like? How can they recreate those sounds with their bodies, and how can the sounds be echoed and amplified when also done by the audience? Feel free to turn the refrain into a little song to be sung by everyone!

I hope you will enjoy creating your own distinctive expression of the piece ... whether it is asking the audience to animate the animal actions, or having a dancer embody the hummingbird, or even enacting the scene that plays out – may the telling create an energy of possibility.

◊ ◊ ◊

TELLER: *Hadithi Hadithi ...?*

> *Wait for the audience to respond with* Hadithi Njoo!
> *It is ok if they don't, because you are teaching them how to call for stories.*

When I say *Hadithi, Hadithi,* you say *Hadithi Njoo (rhymes with fro). Hadithi Hadithi,* story story ... *Hadithi Njoo,* story come. This is how we call for stories, and as your storyteller, I need your help calling for the story. Will you help?

> *Make space for the audience to respond.*

Hadithi Hadithi?

> *The audience responds* Hadithi Njoo! *Help them if they are shy. You can use the* Hadithi Hadithi *call and response whenever you need to energize the audience.*

This is a story that has been told many times before, in many ways. You may have heard it from Wangari Muta Maathai ... Today we tell it a little differently.

Hadithi Hadithi?

> *The audience responds* Hadithi Njoo!

Today's story begins the same way the others did.

A fire.

A huge fire – red, hot, hungry – it blazed through the forest inhaling everything in its path, exhaling gigantic clouds of thick smoke that filled the air with a warning to stay away.

It hadn't rained in months, and everything was dry … so so so dry.

The creatures watched more and more of their home burning down. They felt so sad, so helpless.

All of them except a little hummingbird, who flew into the air, beating her little wings as fast as she could, flying around the fire, past the trees, over the open grass until she reached the river. She dipped her beak into the river and took a droplet of water. Then she flew into the air, beating her little wings as fast as she could, over the open grass, past the trees, and towards the fire.

She opened her beak and dropped the droplet of water on the fire.

The creatures watched her as she flew into the air, beating her little wings as fast as she could, collecting water from the river, carrying it one droplet at a time in her little beak, and dropping it into the fire, one droplet at a time, over and over and over again.

"What are you doing, little hummingbird?" the creatures asked her.

"You are too little, and this fire is too big. Your wings are too little and your beak is so small."

But she continued, adding water to the fire, one droplet at a time.

"I am doing the best I can," the little hummingbird said.

"You're doing the best you can?" the creatures asked her.

"Yes," the little hummingbird said with a droplet in her mouth. "I am doing the best I can."

Everyone was quiet … for a moment … until one creature said:

"Even me, I will do the best I can," and another, "even me, I will do the best I can," and another, "even me, I will do the best I can," until the cries became so loud even the fire got frightened.

You see, there is more than one way to put out a fire.

All the creatures kicked into action.

Some creatures used their bodies to suck water from the river and spray it on the fire.

Others gathered soil to douse the flames.

Others pushed rocks to the edge of the fire to create a barrier and stop it from spreading.

Others used their fingers and paws and tongues to remove the dry leaves that would burn quickly in the fire.

And others all got together and beat their wings and their ears and their tails as fast as they could to change the direction of the wind and stop feeding the fire with fresh oxygen.

And of course, the little hummingbird continued dropping water on the fire, from her beak, one droplet at a time.

And as they worked, they all sang:

"We are doing the best we can, doing the best we can, doing the best we can."

Even the humans were doing the best they can.

Eventually, they put out the fire, and what a celebration it was!

Hadithi Hadithi?

The audience responds Hadithi Njoo!

However, this is not where the story ends. This is where the story begins.

After all the creatures had rested, taken care of each other, fed one another, and put medicine on their wounds, they stared at the place where the forest had stood.

It was time to replant a new forest.

"What shall we plant in this forest?" they asked each other.

The creatures all decided that they would sit together and listen to what each one of them wanted in the forest.

Every living being had a chance to express themselves – all the creatures as well as the ones without vocal cords, like the trees, the moss, the air.

And everything listened.

Even the humans! … For the first time in a long time, they listened.

And when every living being had a chance to express themselves – the creatures as well as the ones without vocal cords – everyone got to work replanting the forest.

And how do you think they went about doing it?

"We are doing the best we can, doing the best we can, doing the best we can."

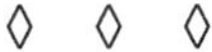

Aleya Kassam is a Kenyan feminist, storyteller, writer, and performer who has been published and performed around the world. Her work, which is often eco-feminist in nature, explores the spaces between imagination and memory, and uses ritual as a way to access those realms. She is also a co-founder of the award-winning content studio, The LAM Sisterhood, which fills the world with stories for African women to feel seen, heard, and beloved. Recent projects include the children's podcast *KaBrazen*, which tells the stories of brazen African women.

THE MERMAID

Nikhil Katara

They say we live in the post-truth world, where misinformation and deliberate distortion of the truth is the norm. When encountering everyday life, I do feel at times disoriented a little. A lot of the information shared in the news, social media, and by organizations seems a bit paradoxical. These institutions make our worldview, and they also, in a way, make us do and think things that are shaped by narratives. While deliberating on the play, I thought of an Earth in the future, where false narratives have shaped us into mermaids. The play intends to hold truth above all other factors whenever we intend to begin something.

◊ ◊ ◊

A girl wearing a breathing device on her face moves below a platform. Her movements are graceful and should denote a manner of swimming underwater (music could be used). A blue curtain behind the girl could be moved to make it look like water. On the platform above is land. It could be embellished with rocks and pebbles.

A second girl appears on the platform. She stretches her hand out. In one swift movement, the girl jumps on top of the platform, holds the hand of the second girl, and stands. These are her first steps on land. She falls but gets up again and balances herself. The second girl helps her.

FIRST GIRL: Now what? I did what you said.

SECOND GIRL: Not completely. You need to remove this now.

SECOND GIRL tries to remove the mask on the face of FIRST GIRL but she moves away.

SECOND GIRL: You had promised that you would trust me.

FIRST GIRL slowly removes the mask that helps her breathe underwater and takes in one breath.

SECOND GIRL: You see! You can breathe on land.

FIRST GIRL: I can't believe it. So that –

SECOND GIRL: – is not an organ. And that is what you need to know.

FIRST GIRL: What else did you want to tell me? Tell me quickly I need to go back to –

SECOND GIRL: Don't you want to know the truth now? Or are you happy with living in your water world?

FIRST GIRL: Tell me.

SECOND GIRL: We were and still are land mammals.

FIRST GIRL: Nonsense. We are mermaids. We live in the water.

SECOND GIRL: Two hundred years ago, the Earth began to grow hotter. They say it was because of humans. Exploitation of natural resources, pollution, were common on land.

FIRST GIRL: Like they are now underwater?

SECOND GIRL: Yes. The heat got so high that it was impossible to live on land. But the leaders then had dismissed this. They had always portrayed the climate as not changing, and when things got out of hand, they had to take impossible measures.

FIRST GIRL: What were they?

SECOND GIRL: Millions of people left land to inhabit the seas. Just a few stayed back on land. To treat it. To clean it. To heal it. We always thought it was possible and we did not want to live a lie.

FIRST GIRL: What lie?

SECOND GIRL: The one you are living in right now. A lie. You think you are mermaids? You are meant to be on land. For generations, the human leaders have lied to hide their biggest failure. The failure to acknowledge that the Earth was heating. One lie led to another, and then they decided to tell the human species that it was not human at all.

FIRST GIRL: But why?

SECOND GIRL: To hide the biggest failure of leadership across the world. The only way to fight the rising temperatures was to live underwater. So, a lie was concocted and humans became mermaids …

FIRST GIRL: I believe none of this. This is absolute –

SECOND GIRL: Look at me, daughter of the Supreme Leader of the Government Under the Seas … Remove your privilege and look at me. I came down to meet you for a reason. My people have worked for two centuries on Project Drawdown.

FIRST GIRL: What is that about?

SECOND GIRL: Drawdown is the point in time when levels of greenhouse gases in the atmosphere stop climbing and start to steadily decline. I came to tell you we have reached that point.

FIRST GIRL: Why are you telling me this? You should tell my father …

SECOND GIRL: When millions migrated to the sea, the emissions came down to zero. My people worked on uplifting nature's carbon cycle and the most important thing – we created a just and equal society. Your father is the leader now and he will try his level best to hide this reality.

FIRST GIRL: My father is an honest man.

SECOND GIRL: Did you know he comes and walks on land often? Did you know he removes his breathing device and breathes this air? Did you know –

FIRST GIRL: No, I didn't know, but now I want to know what you want from me?

SECOND GIRL: Convince him. Tell him to get the people back on land. Most of the ocean has been dead since humans entered it, lived in it, and polluted it. It needs to heal, just like the land got time to heal. But this time, we want the people to know the truth. When they come back to land, they need to learn the new ways.

FIRST GIRL: What are these ways?

SECOND GIRL: Let me show you.

SECOND GIRL grabs FIRST GIRL. She removes a cloth which reveals many books.

FIRST GIRL: Books … I had heard about them.

SECOND GIRL: These books will give you an idea of the ways. If we live by this truth, everyone can survive.

FIRST GIRL: Frankly, I don't know what to believe in anymore. How do I know what the truth is if my entire life up until now has been a lie? What do I trust?

SECOND GIRL: *Cogito, ergo sum.*

FIRST GIRL: Means?

SECOND GIRL picks up a book from the lot of books near her. It is a book by René Descartes. She begins to read.

SECOND GIRL: "I feel that it is necessary to know what doubt is, and what thought is, (what existence is), before we can be fully persuaded of this reasoning – I doubt, therefore I am – or what is the same – I think, therefore I am … *Cogito, ergo sum …*"

FIRST GIRL begins to read, and music begins to play. Light changes and denotes a passage of time. SECOND GIRL watches. Time passes until a bunch of SOLDIERS jump from the water onto the platform and apprehend SECOND GIRL. She screams and so does FIRST GIRL. SECOND GIRL is taken away.

At this moment, the Supreme Leader, FIRST GIRL's FATHER, walks onto the platform. He is wearing no mask.

FIRST GIRL: LET HER GO!

FATHER: Take her away.

FIRST GIRL: No!

FATHER: You deliberately disobeyed me.

She looks away.

FIRST GIRL: You left me with little choice.

FATHER: You must remember, apart from being your father, I am also your Supreme Leader.

FIRST GIRL: Is that why power corrupted you?

FATHER: Mind your tongue.

She holds up a book in her hand.

FIRST GIRL: So, this is true after all, and everything else – everything else is a lie?

FATHER: To survive, people don't need the truth.

FIRST GIRL: What good will lies do?

FATHER: What else would you have me do? Let them die? There was a time when humans walked the Earth but then things got bad …

FIRST GIRL: How did they get bad?

FATHER: Tolerance went down. People could not take the sun and its heat.

FIRST GIRL: LIES! LIES! LIES!

FATHER: You dare.

FIRST GIRL: Yes, I dare. I have read everything. There have been rulers before you and they have lied too. The climate was changing and it was doing so because of human interference. When the lie became too big to handle, more lies followed.

FATHER: You are calling your own father a liar?

FIRST GIRL: But that is the truth, and look at what one lie does to you … Just look. We are not ourselves. We are not even able to walk on the ground today. We are living pretend lives. We are acting as if we are meant to be fish when our true purpose is on land.

FATHER: THE LAND IS GONE! We belong to the water.

FIRST GIRL: No. Look all around you. It is here. I have walked on land today. I have breathed the air, and it is good. We don't need this.

She throws her device away.

FATHER: It took generations for us to take life, as we know it, into the sea. It will take generations to get it back on land. It is impossible. Let's go back where we belong.

FIRST GIRL: No. We are where we belong. We just need to treat it right. Let's start now. All good things must begin …

FATHER: And where should they begin?

FIRST GIRL: The Truth.

◊ ◊ ◊

Nikhil Katara is from Mumbai, India. He started his journey in theatre with his own production titled *The Unveiling*. He has a degree in Philosophy from Mumbai University and writes for *One India One People Magazine*, *Free Press Journal*, and the journal, *Sambhashan*, on a regular basis. His articles and stories are part of four anthologies. He teaches the B.Voc course (Theatre & Stagecraft) at Wilson College. He is the Artistic Director of Readings in the Shed and has directed and co-written the play and film, *The Bose Legacy*. He co-directed and acted in a film titled, *Between You & Me,* which was awarded a grant from the Asia Europe Foundation, and was shown at the Lift-Off Filmmakers Festival.

ACTORS READY?

Ethan King

In a time when frightening doom-and-gloom warnings from scientific experts and angry activists alienate people and make them build walls out of fear, stories that remind them of their power to build our world alongside these experts are crucial. When we break down these walls and prioritize the equality of intelligence among listeners, we realize that they too are storytellers capable of materializing a better future.

Character

STAGE MANAGER: Wears a black hoodie and a headset with a microphone, and holds a clipboard.

Setting

A bare stage.

◊ ◊ ◊

STAGE MANAGER rushes onto the stage as if doing last-minute checks before showtime.

STAGE MANAGER: Alright people! Five minutes till the house is open! Make sure everything is pre-set! Actors, places! Actors! I need a response, please. Lights! Remember those notes I gave you on the cues.

Notices audience.

Oh! Hello there! What a wonderful day we are having here at the theatre. My name is _____ and I am the stage manager.

I grew up in the theatre.

For most of my life, I lived in a sanctuary on top of a mountain, kept away from the rest of civilization, where I was expected to focus only on my craft.

Lights, go!

Lights change.

The stage was my world.

I started as an actor – from Greek tragedies to Shakespeare, all the way to contemporary plays, you name it.

With a few other actors, we explored different theatre vocabularies and broke them down to form our own laws of creation.

We devised entirely new realities – all with their own laws of physics, of language, and of being.

Once during a play we were doing, the power went out and the stage went pitch black. So, we decided to light up some candles.

Even though we could barely see the performers' faces, we heard their voices and saw just enough movement to feel their emotion. We did the entire play in the dark all while the storytellers guided it to its end.

The theatre – our tiny little world – bowed down to however we pleased to command time and space.

Lights, go!

Lights change.

As we became young adults, our world began to expand.

Some left for college, some moved away, and some left their theatre practice altogether.

As I moved out into the world, all that I was accustomed to cracked wide open and I had to work with different people who practiced different systems – whether that still be in the theatre, in education, or in political activist groups. I was introduced to a world that had no time to sit down and push the limits of creativity, a fast paced world that needed to get things done now.

I felt powerless in a world I could not compose. A world that had no time to listen.

The sun no longer followed my cues. Nor could I call forth a gust of wind to simulate a storm, have a prop maker make more trees, or stop floods from entering the city.

It just doesn't work that way.

For the first time in my life, I bowed down to the systems that had been put in place years before my birth and the natural laws of the Earth that could not be moved or stopped. How then could I make a difference?

Blackout.

Lights, go! … Lights, go! … Lights, go … *(frustrated)* Lights? Lights?

Silence …

Exhales.

In a reality where chaos darkens our view, technology overcomplicates things, and leaders refuse to listen, I found hope in remembering simpler times.

Lights a single candle and raises it up.

A candle. And storytellers to get us through this blackout.

I am a world manager. And I am a storyteller.

When all else fails, our voices are the very foundations on which to rebuild and continue creating our world.

Looks at audience.

Actors, are you ready?

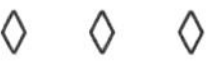

Ethan King is a young performance maker, machinator, and dramaturg from the Philippines. His latest performance credits include Dario Fo's *The Pope and the Witch,* and Caryl Churchill's, *Mad Forest.* He has also just finished his own research project entitled *The BlackBox Ritual.* He is interested in creating space and time compositions grounded in larger societal contexts.

BACK IN SYNCH WITH SPRING

Himali Kothari

One of the topics that is on everyone's lips when we talk about climate change is the changing temperament of seasons. The timing is off. The temperament is off – hotter and colder than it ever was. Floods. Droughts. It is all askew. My play is inspired by Sarah Peach's article "How Will Global Warming Change Springtime?"[1] I have used Vivaldi's composition *Spring* from *The Four Seasons* to talk about the change in spring season.

Note

The two characters, VIVA and MANU, can be played by actors of any ethnicity, gender, and age.

◊ ◊ ◊

VIVA sits on a chair in the center of the stage, a pencil tucked behind one ear. They hold a violin in their hand, and in front of them is a stand with sheet music, which they read while playing. As VIVA mimes playing the violin, an out-of-sync version of Vivaldi's Spring *plays.*[2] *The music should be loud and, if possible, played in a way that jars the audience.*

The jarring notes annoy VIVA. They stop and try again but do not get the notes right. They pull the pencil from behind their ear, scratch out something on the sheet music, and write again. Once more, they mime playing the violin. Once again, the same jarring noise blares out. VIVA is visibly exasperated and again angrily scratches out something on the sheet music. MANU has entered while the notes were playing but VIVA has not seen them. MANU stands with their fingers in their ears, a pained expression on their face. VIVA picks up the violin bow and is about to try again.

MANU: Stop. Stop. Viva, for heaven's sakes stop.

---

[1] Peach, Sara. "How will global warming change springtime?" *Yale Climate Connections*, March 28, 2023. https://yaleclimateconnections.org/2023/03/how-will-global-warming-change-springtime/

[2] See this link for a recording of the out-of-sync music: https://soundcloud.com/user-989493969/vivaldis-spring-out-of-sync?utm_source=clipboard&utm_medium=text&utm_campaign=social_sharing

VIVA turns around as MANU walks up to them.

VIVA: Something's not right.

MANU: Yes … it is so wrong. I almost slashed off my ear.

VIVA, *looks morose*: I can't figure it out. I have been playing this for eons. But lately, it is just –

MANU: Out of sync?

VIVA: Yes. Out of sync. Terribly.

Stares at the sheet music. Turns the pages back and forth, puzzled. Throws the violin bow down in irritation.

MANU comes and peers at the sheet music over VIVA's shoulder.

MANU: Aah … I see it …

MANU plucks the pencil from behind VIVA's ear and writes on the sheet music.

See this … You are starting here. Too early. Much before it's time …

VIVA: Times have changed …

MANU, *points at the notes with the pencil*: But that's confusing the birds, see? Should they break into song? Or should they stay mum? Result? Cacophony! *(throws hands in the air in annoyance)* And what about this? *(jabs the pencil on sheet music)*

VIVA, *defensively*: What about it?

MANU: I am quite sure I did not hear the murmur of the springs in that … that … monstrosity you were playing. *(shudders visibly)*

VIVA: I took it out.

MANU: Why would you do that? It is one of the best bits. My favorite.

VIVA: Because they're gone … Dried up! Have to roll with the times, right?

MANU, *with ill-disguised disgust*: Is that why you eliminated the sleeping goatherd as well?

VIVA: That's not on me. He was laid-off years ago.

MANU: Viva, Viva … No wonder you are out of sync. You've killed *Spring* as we knew it, my friend.

VIVA, *close to tears*: I have, haven't I? What was I thinking? I destroyed *Spring* … the best of them all.

MANU: Come now. All's not lost. Let's see …

> *MANU makes some changes on the sheet music. VIVA watches, then takes the pencil and makes a change too. MANU pats VIVA's back encouragingly … Pleased with themself, VIVA smiles.*

VIVA, *tentatively*: Yes … I think this should do it. It just might work. What do you think?

> *VIVA looks expectantly at MANU. MANU picks up the bow and hands it over to VIVA.*

MANU: Only one way to find out …

> *VIVA takes a deep breath, positions the bow, and starts to play. The first notes of Vivaldi's* Spring *are heard.*[1] *VIVA stops, looks at MANU. They both beam at each other. VIVA starts to play again. Lights fade out. Music continues for a few more seconds and then fades out.*

Himali Kothari lives in Mumbai, India. She compares her journey as an author to a trip down the rabbit hole, full of unexpected twists and turns. From writing website content to feature articles to short stories to plays, she is almost always inclined to say "Why Not?" when it involves wielding her pen (and keyboard) to do her bidding.

[1] https://youtu.be/GRxofEmo3HA

TREE PEOPLE

Heidi Kraay

Beyond "All Good Things Must Begin," this play is inspired by Richard Powers' *The Overstory*[2] and Ted Hughes' translation of Ovid's *Metamorphoses*,[3] both of which I was reading when *Tree People* started emerging. In particular, *The Overstory*'s line "The best and easiest way to get a forest to return to any plot of cleared land is to do nothing – nothing at all, and do it for less time than you might think," combined with Ovid's people transforming into other things, and a dash of Anne Bogart's quote I found while rereading *What's The Story*[4] last year, "Sometimes standing still is the only way to move forward," came together to form this play.

Characters

TREE (Nonbinary): Ancient. Caregiver. Giant.
SHE (F): Aging. Caretaker. Human.

Setting

An old-growth forest. Possibly the Redwoods. Or what used to be the Redwoods, used to be an old-growth forest, but is changing into something else.

Time

End of summer. Dawn.

Notes

Tree must be played by a human.
Transgender, nonbinary, and genderfluid identifying actors are welcome in any role.
(For instance, a nonbinary actor could play SHE.)
Enjambments are not meant to suggest a pause or break.
For difficult stage directions, lean into expressionism and physicality.

◊ ◊ ◊

[2] Powers, Richard. *The Overstory*. W. W. Norton & Company, 2019.
[3] Ovid. *Tales from Ovid: 24 Passages from the Metamorphoses*. Tr. Ted Hughes. Farrar, Straus and Giroux, 1999.
[4] Bogart, Anne. *What's the Story: Essays About Art, Theater and Storytelling*. Routledge, 2014.

An old-growth forest. Or what used to be.
A giant TREE, the oldest in the country – the world? – stands still, present, welcoming whatever exists.
What exists is the sound of chainsaws. Dozers. Firestorms.
Centuries of loss.
Through this, TREE stands, naked, alone. Lonely.
SHE enters. Her focus wholly on TREE.
SHE looks up at TREE. Cranes her neck. SHE is beyond tired.

SHE: Hullo, old friend.
We're at the end.
I don't know, what to do.

SHE starts to break down. SHE stops herself.
In the near-distance, machines scream.

SHE: Do you hear them?
They've taken your family.
Everything around my cabin.
Bringing everything they've got. I fought with all of me, but –

Remember when I sat in your crown for a year?
When we brought all those friends to stand for your forest?
When we found a way to keep this little plot safe, in my care?
Been a long war, my friend.
Don't have much more in me.

There's a forest, started growing inside, me.
Hungry as fungi ripping through your ancestors.
And I won't be – Our lives, so short.

All I've wanted, to serve you, your loved ones, your seedlings …
But I'm losing, on all fronts.
Don't know who to call, to take over.
Who'd stay here, night and day, protecting you like I have?
Live and die for you?
For this one patch of land that once stretched ancient far and wide –

Her body weeps shaking cries.
As all looks lost, as lights burn, darken with smoke, as air rages with machines.

SHE: Tell me! What do we do?!
How do we go on?

The heaving inside cuts her through.
At the breaking point, SHE breathes, giant gasp.
Lets herself go limp on the ground.
Drowning in tears we need not see.
Body becomes soil, rain.
Until SHE goes still. Silent. And a voice SHE's never heard, different from any voice we'd imagine, more like song like wind like hope:

TREE: Stop
Wait
Listen

From her pile on the ground, SHE looks up. Awe.

SHE: You – I hear you.

TREE: Shhhhhhhhhhh
Be still
Watch

SHE stops. Grows intensely still.
SHE watches. SHE listens. SHE waits.
Time passes. How much we need not know.
Until her feet grow roots.
Until her roots tangle Earth.
Until her body bole trunk in utmost slowness starts to rise, as if pulled by magic force.
Once SHE grows to height of tree, though not our TREE, SHE transforms fully.
Body becomes wood, skin bark, hair leaves, arms branches.
And again, stillness.
TREE and SHE watch each other, listen.
Her voice changed, more like TREE:

SHE: What happened?

TREE: You grew

SHE: Am I you?

TREE: You are like me

SHE: What now?

TREE: We wait

SHE: For?

TREE: There will be more

SHE: Like me?

TREE: And me
I was once
like you
Very long
ago

SHE: You were human?

TREE: Very
very
long

SHE: If they tear us down?

TREE: Then
they do
but
more will grow
like me and you
In their stillness
they become trees, we become we
Beyond use, forests will be everything, everywhere
We will look we will care we will listen
breathe together be together

If they haven't already, the machines and all sounds quiet into silence. In a moment of great stillness, the space and everyone in it, us too, becomes forest.

SHE, *re: us*: What's happening to them?

TREE: They're becoming us
We're becoming
each other

They/we sing together, a tune the trees start, a hum like birth. A forest song.

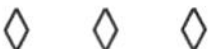

Heidi Kraay, a US-based playwright, pulls myth, metaphor, and monsters together to discover connections across difference. Her plays include *Take Me Away*, *Ark*, *see in the dark*, *How to Hide Your Monster*, *New Eden*, co-devised plays, one-acts, short plays, and plays for young audiences. Her work has been presented where she lives in Boise, Idaho, regionally, in New York City, and internationally. Heidi holds an MFA from California Institute of Integral Studies. She is a member of the Dramatists Guild of America.
www.heidikraay.com

MIRROR MIRROR

camila le-bert

Inspiration for this play came from our failed efforts to change and how imagining the possibility is a key first step. That and Jane Fonda in her humorous efforts to keep our spirits alive in the struggle.

Characters

KID
MAN
MALE VOICE
WOMAN
GIRL

Note

I've gendered the characters, but they are not fixed. Please feel free to change them at will.

◊ ◊ ◊

A dark museum hall. A diorama of the Great Plains. Inside, a woman and girl are frozen mid-walk. They share berries. A MAN and KID enter the hall. The MAN overdoes his enthusiasm.

KID: So … how much time do we have left?

MAN: Depends how much more we go. I wanted to go to the jungle. See the snakes.

KID: I mean years.

MAN: Oh. You mean us? Umm … You know. You know I'll always be here with you. I'm never going to die.

KID: No. Not you. I mean us. All of us. You know … the clock.

MAN: Oh, they'll find a way. We'll find a way. We're strong. We're smart. We have computers.

KID: I'm hungry.

MAN: You just ate.

KID: I'm hungry.

MAN: You can't eat in here.

KID, *pointing at the woman*: How come she's eating.

MAN: I'll get you a hotdog outside.

KID: So, we make more?

MAN: What?

KID: We can make more air? Can we make more water?

MAN: Look at that woman. What do you see?

KID: A lady. She looks like she knows what she's doing. She looks, her face, it seems a little funny. I think she smells a fox nearby.

MAN: She is all alone in nature. What if she's tired. Can she go lay down on a comfy bed? If she's hungry, can she go to a restaurant and order food from a wide array of options like chicken, fish, pork, or pasta, or a burger and fries? What if she's sad or anxious, who will give her her meds? What if she's allergic to those berries and she goes into anaphylactic shock and she dies and her daughter is left all alone in the middle of nowhere? Or what if she just has a cold but she doesn't get treatment and it gets worse, and days pass, weeks, and now she has pneumonia and she can't breathe she can't breathe, slowing everyone down. And one day, one night, it's cold and she realizes it's her last look at the sky.

KID: But she can breathe. She has air. She has water.

MAN: We've made it this far.

They stare at the diorama.

MAN: What do you want to be when you grow up?

KID: I don't know.

MAN: Yes, you do.

KID: I don't want to be a *lawyer*.

MAN: Well, you don't have to say it like that.

KID: I just don't want you to get your hopes up.

MAN: So, …

KID: I don't know. I mean. I'd like to study but I don't know if I want to *be* something. I want to *be* Ben.

MAN: Who's gonna pay your bills, then?

KID: Maybe I won't have any.

Pause.

MAN: You're gonna have to work.

KID: Not if I'm a monk.

MAN: Ben, you're Jewish.

KID: For now.

MAN: No. Forever.

Stare off.

KID: What do they want?

MAN: Who?

KID: You know, the one percent. The ones who ruin everything for everyone.

MAN: Oh. I don't know, Ben. I think they want to stay on top. Rule the world? Be the first ones to do things. I guess, ultimately, they just want more.

KID: I saw a picture of a factory that makes happy meal toys. There was this huge pile of Mickey Mouse eyes and there was a girl sleeping on top of the eyes. She was on a break from sticking the eyes on to the Mickey heads and I wondered: What is she dreaming about?

They freeze. The light changes. Now they are the diorama. The woman casually refers to them while talking to the girl.

WOMAN: Here we have an example of a middle-class family of the time. They struggled to find meaning in all the wrong things and could not escape the productivity mindset.

GIRL: More! More! More!

WOMAN: Exactly: Work, produce, develop. Could you imagine?

She eats a berry.

All until the Great Fall of 2030 when over 200 sinkholes opened around the Earth swallowing up the super-wealthy elite. Now, let's listen in on this recreation of how we imagine these one-percenters were:

MALE VOICE: You want nothing because you have nothing. It's easy to be green when you're a fourteen-year-old Norwegian queer. You own nothing. You know nothing. Naïve fucking tree-huggers. Don't even know if you're a boy or a girl, you're gonna run the economy. Come throw rocks at me now. Come and get me, now take off your shirt. Show me your signs. Black Lives Matter. Women Rights Are Human Rights. Freedom. Life. Woman. Blablabla. Everyone has an opinion until they need to feed the baby. Ask the seals for a raise. The forest can pay for your rent you fucking moron.
We are the world.
We make the world.
You'd all be in the trees if it wasn't for us.
Clowns!

WOMAN: Pretty angry fella, huh? Imagine if he had the power to multiply neo-fascist discourse and push your country into despair. Yikes! Thankfully, the Great Fall took care of that for us, and, in the following years, human society *finally* made the progress it needed. There was a massive restructuring of –

GIRL: Wealth redistribution! Education! And a renaissance of a myriad of Indigenous knowledges!

WOMAN: Exactly. It was difficult at first because people have a really hard time using their imagination once they hit puberty. It's like we see reality as something fixed, as if the past were destined to loop on forever.

Pause.

But we know better, right? In fact, let's give ourselves a moment of active imagination.

The girl prepares. She sits and closes her eyes.

Let's close our eyes.
Breathe in …
Breathe out …
And in your mind's eye … see the world you want to live in. How does it feel? What does it smell like? Who is there?

GIRL: It smells like those tall bushes outside my house, the ones with the pink flowers. The wind tickles her face, my mom laughs.

◊ ◊ ◊

camila le-bert is an actor, writer, and translator based in Santiago, Chile, Wallmapu territory. Although born in Chile, she was raised from a young age in the US, in Minnesota. Her work centers on women, migration, and neoliberalism. She is a graduate of the University of Chile in Acting and holds an MFA in Playwriting from Columbia University. Her plays are marked by dark humor, synthetic dialogue, polyphony, and found text.

BEGINNINGS

Andrea Ling

Theatre can be a space of collectivism. Good things begin in collective action. I am interested in creating co-curated and co-made artwork with communities and audiences. The artistic process and the physical actions of making a live performance give something to those doing it that involves the whole body, spirit, and mind. What if legislation was workshopped through artistic and theatrical practices? What if communal artistic spaces had as much importance as United Nations summits to incite positive change? Art, and its process, can ignite and incite people to begin change. Octavia Butler's quote is a magic call to action to be ambitious and begin a collective happening.

Setting

A collective happening. A circle of audience and a barefoot Traveler.

Notes

The audience throughout is invited to speak. This could mean handing each audience member a play text to follow along, projecting specific audience text, or another idea. What is important is when the text is shown live, in the moment and audience members decide to participate in the collective happening. There are no pre-assigned audience lines.

Audience text needs to be fully shown. For example: "The Audience Collective Says Aloud: Welcome."

The delivery of the Traveler's text should be fast-paced, even rhythmical in longer sections.

We begin:

The audience, already in the space, waits. The TRAVELER waits for their cue: A collective intense curiosity about what may happen. It's a collective concentration, a syncing up, a listening, and just before the fall … The TRAVELER, carrying the weight of time but also the wisdom of what can be, has been, enters the space. They are open. They are there for the audience.

The AUDIENCE COLLECTIVE *says aloud:* Welcome.

TRAVELER: Thank you. Thank you for being part of this chance happening. A happening that, without you all here, to partake, would not exist. I may not have existed without you.

An ELDER from the Audience: We are ready to hear what needs to be said.

TRAVELER: I'm grateful, but know I don't come with answers. I'm sorry, that's not how this particular exchange works.

A MOTHER from the Audience: What do you come with?

TRAVELER: It's all ... images, moments, intersected time, snapshots.

A FATHER from the Audience: Intersected time?

TRAVELER: So much time.

MULTIPLE YOUNG MEMBERS from the Audience: Where did you come from?

TRAVELER: From home, your future.

A CURIOUS MEMBER from the Audience: How?

The Traveler smiles.

TRAVELER: I walk parallel paths; it seems all at once. Across multitudinal landscapes, seas, one time underground ... I've walked barefoot across time, losing so many, becoming alone, walking, and suddenly I arrive at a place with *(describe landmarks of the surrounding area where the happening is staged).* I kept walking *(describe journey through the venue)* and found you gathered in this space. You are here to *(indicate different audience members and their reasons for coming)* search for something, seek community, inspiration, answers to what's next, because your partner made you get out of the house, proof. So here I am in – this ... moment. Here to help, must be to help in some way, share? Give? Not sure. I don't have much but a shared ambition for our future – my past – it's hard to tell: the complexities upon complexities, the complex, unraveled. Is this the right place? Is theatre the right place?

The AUDIENCE COLLECTIVE: Yes.

An OPTIMIST: A shared space uniting strangers.

An OPPORTUNIST: Yes, where even the playwright cannot control what happens. Where something like this will never happen again, not exactly. Not in the same time, space, people.

A PRAGMATIST: So, please go on. This is a short commission; we have about four minutes left.

An ELDER: What do you know of our past?

TRAVELER: The past … (*They conjure the past.)* Muddled, fast, histories, unsung heroes, rewritten landscapes, restructured landscapes, milestones, milestones, progress upon progress, liberation, in the name of liberation and progress, destruction, disappearances, extinctions, unearthing, sowing, cycles, generations upon generations, children becoming elders who disappear, discovery, creativity, pain, so much grief that it's inherited across generations, from animals to landforms and their structures, spirals wrapped carefully within, into the present where we, only now, begin unlocking that which burdens. *(They arrive back to the theatre after skipping time and space.)*

A YOUNG ADULT: What about our present? What about now?

TRAVELER: The present . . . *(a sudden sharp conjuring)*
Among a tumultuous storm of exploding metal and fuel,
Two people sleeping reach for each other, small fingers clinch together.

The present *(sharp pain)*
As forest fires escalate in California, Amazonia, Portugal,
A farmer in South Africa places a seed in his mouth, creating a bond between farmer and seed, a tender act of love before placing the seed into the red earth. *(gasps)*
Fires continue in Australia,
And the last of the Awu Laya people die. The world doesn't know. Their connection, their way. Awu Laya, guardians of the land through fire.

Listening to the whispers to ignite wild grass, dancing with the flames and the smoke, creates new life. No one knows. The trees mourn, the grass dries, fires out of control. *(exhales)*

A white elderly woman in London gets arrested at an Extinction Rebellion protest and round the back of the street, a young Black woman tends to a community garden. *(inhales)*

The present – I'm now sitting here on an outdoor table within water in Bangladesh, the table laden with meagre bits of love nature has pushed out of the wet overflooded earth. My table, with ten community members, sitting within a flood, water lapping on the tablecloth and our knees, our last supper before the next rains. There is so much love here. *(sharp jab)*

A man with a gun is entering a club in America … Twenty Latin American souls disappear. Ecocide … one, three, nine hundred erupt in the Global South, and the Global North tilt its head to one side with pity, continuing with extinction plans. So much trauma among …

A Black Brazilian woman – she's singing across oceans, across transatlantic slave routes, she sings ancestral songs deep into the depths of the water, whales sing responses. *(a moment)* There is so much healing here. There is so much awe here. So much love.

The present, here. Right here.

A soon-to-be mother, in this space, growing a child of tomorrow. Another mother here *(points to a man)*, yes mothering didn't mean woman but a description of an entire community nurturing and caring for itself and future generations. Caring, tending, mother nature, the house of humanity.

Present becomes past.

A CREATIVE: What type of being are you with this power?

TRAVELER: I am no different than you. With all the capabilities we hold.

A CHILD: And our future?

Silence.

A YOUTH: Our future?

TRAVELER, *tears, smiles, grief, multiple images and possibilities*:
Hard work fueled by hope.
Hard truths fueled by love.

A DREAMER: I'm not sure we fully grasp all this.

TRAVELER: That's ok, neither do I. At times, I feel so overwhelmed that it is too much, it becomes too dangerous to handle alone. When I find people, a collective, togetherness, it feels that the overwhelm may unite us into something, something … beautiful. I see in front of me, my bare feet walking, skin across hot concrete, dried grass, and cracked earth. My feet are not alone; I walk with other feet by my side. Will someone walk with me?

> *The TRAVELER waits or asks again for an audience member to walk with them. Maybe just one, maybe more.*
>
> *The TRAVELER, not alone, walks on. A cacophony of sounds, music, beats, raised spirits, singing fueled by hope, from diverse communities around the world, loudly booms through the space. It's a call to action, it's a call of unity, it's a call of love for the planet.*

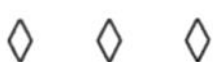

Andrea Ling is an interdisciplinary artist: a director, writer, dramaturg, visual artist, and educator working within theatre, film, and installation. She is Bolivian-British-Chinese, and lives on a boat cruising across London, Glasgow, and beyond. Andrea founded the arts company Pacha People, making art for, and with, underrepresented communities to incite social change. In 2020, Andrea won the Jerwood Live Work Award and, in 2023, won the Genesis Future Directors Award.
www.andrealing.com
www.pachapeople.com

A & B'S EXCELLENT SPRING BREAK ADVENTURE, OR LOSS AND DAMAGES

Joan Lipkin

This play was inspired by a spate of articles on various news platforms after the 26th United Nations Climate Change Conference (COP26) in Glasgow in the fall of 2021 about the call for reparations to developing nations for damages caused by climate change. My research raised many questions: Which nations were actively participating and honoring their pledges? Who might be the recipients? What were some tangible damages that might be cited and evaluated? And significantly, as has been a theme in much of my work, why wasn't the general public in North America more informed about these developments, and how might theatre be deployed to convey the urgency of our global circumstances?

Characters

A: A college student of any gender and ethnicity, age 18-25ish.
B: A college student of any gender or ethnicity, age 18-25ish.
CONSCIENCE: Could be a mascot in a costume or a puppet, gender nonspecific. Lots of possibilities here. Perhaps a hybrid of an animal species or plant comes to mind, with an element of drag queen. But do your own thing.

Setting

The deplaning area in an airport. The play is inspired by recent events in South Asia but could also apply to many – too many places.

Time

The present and hopeful future.

Note

The play is written to reflect how many of us speak. If you need to remove or substitute words like "ass," "shit," and "fucked" to reflect your particular community standards, please do. You will retain most of the essence of the play and most importantly, the play will be done.

◊ ◊ ◊

At rise, we see two college students with backpacks. They are just getting off a plane after a very long flight.

A: Woohoo! We have arrived!

B: I have always wanted to come here.

A: I know. It feels so good to get outside of the US because we are, like, in such a bubble there.

B: Yeah. People say, what is on your bucket list and I say, the world! I want to see the world.

A: Totes.

B: Let's get our luggage so we can chill!

A: Yeah. That was one long-ass flight.

CONSCIENCE appears. What or who is this?

B: Wow.

A: Yeah, wow. In Hawaii, they greet you at the airport with leis.

B: Or so I've heard. I've never been.

A: Me, either. Bucket list!

They high five.

B: Hello, hi. *Bonjour, hola. Shalom? (to A)* What do they speak here? I want to be respectful.

A: Shit, I know we should have studied up more. But we were so busy. I thought midterms were gonna kill me.

B: Yeah.

A: I think English is the international language. I mean, it shouldn't be. But you know, colonization.

B: Right. *(to CONSCIENCE)* Can you please show us the way to customs?

CONSCIENCE shakes their head and hands them a paper.

A: A bill?

B: I guess it's like an entry fee. I've heard of that before.

A: I didn't read about that in *Lonely Planet*. Entry fees. They did say you have to be careful because there are hustlers here. And pickpockets. Which I totally get because it's a Third World country. But it's supposed to be a friendly place. And so beautiful.

B: Not Third World. Developing.

A: Right. Global Majority.

B: Yeah. Well, it can't be too bad. Let's see?

They look at the paper together.

A: One hundred and eighty million dollars?!

CONSCIENCE: That's what Germany is paying. You should at least match what Germany is paying.

A: One hundred and eighty million dollars?!

CONSCIENCE: Well, yes. Since the industrial revolution, the US has been the largest polluter in the world. You spent almost two hundred years burning fossil fuels to grow your economies and it really fucked over the rest of us.

B: Oh.

CONSCIENCE: My country endured floods that killed over 1,500 people last year and one third of our land is under water because of climate change. Who do you think is responsible?

A: Uh, I don't know. So, is this like, reparations?

CONSCIENCE: Call it what you will. It's for loss and damages.

A: I hear you. We totally hear you.

B: But, we are just college students. I mean, we weren't even here when all this polluting happened.

A: Yeah. We just voted for the first time this year.

B: I'm on work-study.

A: And I'm looking at years of student loans. When we found this cheap flight, we thought, wow. We have never been there. And we figured everything would be so cheap.

B: A!

A: Oh, I mean, no disrespect or anything. I meant within our budget.

B: No, no disrespect.

A: We're just broke-ass college students. Sorry. I mean, broke. Broke college students.

CONSCIENCE: Uh huh. Hmmm … let's see then.

They review in a book.

Form T.

B: T?

CONSCIENCE: T for tourist.

A, *to B*: Are we tourists? I mean, we came because of spring break. We didn't want to do the Cancun thing.

B: We came because we want to see the world. And what they aren't teaching in school.

CONSCIENCE: A laudable ambition. Right on.

B: To know our neighbors.

A: In the Global South.

B: Yes. The Global South.

CONSCIENCE: Ok. But here's the deal: We get a lot of you. Do you know that tourism is responsible for about eight percent of carbon emissions?

A: No way!

CONSCIENCE: Way.

B: Wow.

CONSCIENCE: Yeah, wow.

A: We're like, sorry …

B: Very sorry. We care about climate change. All the fires last year.

A: And the heat. It was so, so hot. And the temperature swings. Last fall, it was like eighty degrees one day and thirty, only two days later. And snowing! Crazy.

B: And we have been having flooding, too. We've been thinking about joining Sunrise on campus but there's just so much going on.

A: Reproductive choice and trans rights and Black Lives Matter. And we worked on campus outreach for the election.

CONSCIENCE: I am not sure what all that is but elections are good. Important.

B: They are.

A: More and more.

CONSCIENCE: Your elected representatives are not making it easy for us and you are one of the primary places responsible for the mess we are in. We are not churning out carbon at the rate you are. Like you have been doing for decades and decades.

B: I'm sorry. Maybe we shouldn't have come. If you don't want us here.

CONSCIENCE: You seem like nice people.

A: Thanks. We try.

B: You seem nice, too.

CONSCIENCE: You are very welcome here. We are one world.

B: Truly.

CONSCIENCE: And you are the future.

A: Yes.

CONSCIENCE: But what happens where you are affects us. It deeply affects everywhere.

B: Right.

CONSCIENCE: And you did promise to help pay.

A: We did??

CONSCIENCE: Your elected representatives. To help cover loss and damages and more preventative measures going forward. And we haven't seen much. So, …

They hand a paper to B.

B: Form T is for tourist. *(reading aloud)* "If you must travel, invest in certified carbon reduction programs. Make it part of your travel budget."

A: Carbon reduction programs.

B, *continues reading*: "These programs help offset carbon emissions by investing in wind farms, planting trees, and supporting green energy in other countries. *(to A)* Look, there's a QR code.

CONSCIENCE: And think about volunteering in the local community while you are there.

A: That's cool. We volunteer a lot. Food Outreach. Doorways.

B: We didn't know that was an option.

A: The local volunteering thing.

B: Yeah.

CONSCIENCE: Almost everything is an option if you dig deep enough.

A: Yeah, cool. Listen, we didn't catch your name. I'm A and this is B.

CONSCIENCE: I go by many names. But you can call me Conscience.

A and B: Oh.

CONSCIENCE: Namaste.

They bow and walk away.

◊ ◊ ◊

Joan Lipkin is an internationally recognized playwright, director, producer, educator, facilitator, and social activist based in St. Louis, Missouri, US. Joan is the founding artistic director of That Uppity Theatre Company, DisAbility Project, Dance the Vote, and Playback Now! She has worked on environmental justice for years, as a playwright, dramaturg, and educator, designing curriculum for teaching climate change and storytelling online. Some awards include Woman of Achievement, Visionary, Bravely, Arts Innovator, and the Ethical Humanist of the Year. Her work has been widely produced and anthologized, and featured in the rapid response theatre projects, *Every 28 Hours,* and *After Orlando*.
joan.lipkin@gmail.com

I HAD TO SEE

Eric Lockley

Mystical creatures – dragons, mermaids, trolls, and many others – reflect the human desire for an escape from reality, and simultaneously the desire to experience the rare and awe-inspiring. With climate change creating more endangered species, I considered the possibilities of a reversal: What mystical creatures could/would greet us once we reversed the effects of climate change, and what could they teach us about valuing our Earth?

Note

These are mystical "creatures" so they can be cast as any gender, race, creed, or age and can be as similar or as different from how the character is "assumed" to look or dress. PLAY!

◊ ◊ ◊

ARIEL, BIGFOOT, and ICEBERG walk into the space prepared to give a press conference.

They face the audience, though BIGFOOT easily gets distracted, so they may need to be redirected to face the audience from time to time. BIGFOOT holds a satchel from which they may pull props (signs, rodents, mirrors, etc.).

ARIEL, *with a princess wave*: Hello humans of the land!

BIGFOOT: Ohhhh. Heyroooaar.

ICEBERG: 'Sup.

ARIEL: We are thrilled to be here. You *might* recognize us, though generally we don't like to be seen. But this is a special occasion! *(waves like a princess again)* I'm Ariel – lovingly also known as The Little Mermaid.

BIGFOOT has wandered from center stage a bit.

ARIEL: Shucks. Come back, BF!

BIGFOOT gets back center.

ARIEL: This is Bigfoot.

Bigfoot gestures strangely.

He's a bit shy. And this is –

ICEBERG: Woah, I'll speak for myself, darlin'.

ARIEL: Totally get it. I had my voice stolen once.

ICEBERG: The world knows your backstory sweetheart, but me, I've never had the ears of the public. This press conference is my chance to set things straight.

ARIEL: Ok, but we're on intros so can we just stick to that for now?

ICEBERG: You've had the most interaction with their kind, so whatever you say, hun. *(begrudgingly)* Intro: I'm Marty the Iceberg … also known as the iceberg that sank the Titanic.

BIGFOOT gasps loudly.

ICEBERG: See, I can't help but rub people the wrong way.

ARIEL, *to audience*: We've called you here to thank you.

BIGFOOT was hiding some dead rodent or just something strange in a pocket or in his fur. He now offers it to the audience as a thank you.

BIGFOOT: Tank tank for chew.

ICEBERG: No Bigfoot, no one wants to see that! Look, the reality is all three of us have the same press agent and she begged us to join together to do a little kumbaya-celebrate-Earth type thing.

ARIEL, *with excitement brewing*: Because …

ICEBERG: Princess, you make everything sound like cotton candy and rainbows so please, you do the honor of sharing the good news.

ARIEL: Us, unique mystical beings, have shown up here/to celebrate that –

ICEBERG: Hold your seahorses, sweetie. I realize they need a little more context for why I, Marty the Iceberg, am mystical. *(proudly, to the audience)* Look, I know you never thought of the iceberg who sank the Titanic as fantastical or even sentient, but *I am*, ok? I'm a big effin deal. I am a loveable monster like ... like ... King Kong or the Kardashians. And let's be honest, you humans *love* the narrative of a fantastical creature defending its natural habitat against human invaders. But for some reason with the Titanic, y'all wanted to side with the unsinkable ship. That thing ran into *me*!

ARIEL: Oh, Marty! I think we're getting a bit off track. Sorry, humanity.

ICEBERG: You're apologizing to them? No, they need to hear this: Nature doesn't respond well to human arrogance!

ARIEL: But it *does* respond well to care! And we, fantastical beings, are actually here to thank and congratulate you, our human friends, for –

> *Suddenly, a single alien invader appears! The MARTIAN could come through the audience, from the audience, or from elsewhere offstage. Whatever the entrance is, it should be surprising and fun!*
>
> *Our mystical beings are on-guard – prepared to defend themselves.*

MARTIAN, *speaking to all*: Negligent humans and other species of Earth, I come from a far, far distant universe, XOEN. I am Martian, but you can call me Marty for short.

ICEBERG: Hey fella, that's my name.

MARTIAN: Martian?

ICEBERG: No, Marty.

MARTIAN: Well, I don't think people will get us confused.

ICEBERG: And hopefully, you won't be here for long.

ARIEL: Whatever do you want, Martian?! Please don't take my voice. Someone always wants my voice!

MARTIAN: I'm here to use your planet better than you have. I heard that humans are ruining Earth – completely depleting it of its natural resources, abhorrent carbon footprints all around, overconsumption up the wazoo –

ARIEL: No, no, that was our past.

BIGFOOT goes over to MARTIAN, takes a big sniff, then smiles and gives a big thumbs up – implying the air is good.

ICEBERG: Yeah, dude, whoever you're getting your intel from needs a system update. *(to audience)* This guy's still runnin' Windows 95!

ARIEL: Yeah, our announcement, which you rudely interrupted, Marty –

ICEBERG: I always get blamed for thi – Oh. Not me.

ARIEL: Our announcement is that Earth has finally reached: *(singing in the style of* Part of Your World*)* DRAAAAAAAW DOWWWWN.

Pause for coherence.

MARTIAN: Beautiful voice, but what's that?

ICEBERG: Drawdown is when greenhouse gases in the atmosphere have stopped increasing. As of now, those gases are on the decline.

ARIEL: This is the beginning of a brand new day, and a brighter future on Earth. Us three came out of hiding to announce it to the press.

BIGFOOT does the American Sign Language gesture for "thank you" towards the audience.

MARTIAN: But how?!

ICEBERG: Let the big bad iceberg tell ya while Ariel and BF get artsy! Humanity has committed to using renewable energy.

ARIEL proudly sings in the tune of Part of Your World *while BIGFOOT does an interpretive dance (ideally representing the lyrics – use props or don't).*

ARIEL: *Wind for power*
We use the sun too

ICEBERG: *Wind and solar power*

ARIEL: *Dams make electricity*
Better than fossil fuels do

ICEBERG: *Hydro power*

ARIEL: *Water from underground*
Biomass that lay around

ICEBERG: *Geothermal and biomass power*

ARIEL: Drawdown's achieved …
We cleaned the air and yes, we cleaned the seeeeeeeeeeeas …

Suddenly, MARTIAN interrupts as ARIEL almost makes it to her big finish!

MARTIAN: Hey! I came here to take Earth cause the people were treating it so badly, but since you're all doin' right by it, and now that I hear this young lady's lovely voice … *(starts to move towards ARIEL)* instead of your planet, I'll take Ariel's voi –

ICEBERG trips MARTIAN. MARTIAN falls and is knocked out.

ICEBERG: Oops. Call me accident prone.

For a brief moment ARIEL, ICEBERG, and BIGFOOT stare at MARTIAN on the ground. Suddenly MARTIAN pops up!

MARTIAN: I see that you're all pretty passionate about this place and each other. I'll leave without taking anything *this time*. But you *all* better take care of what you've got, or else I'll be back!

MARTIAN walks a few steps away and then …

MARTIAN: And I *mean it!*

MARTIAN exits.

BIGFOOT: Phew! Group hug!

They start to move into each other, but –

ICEBERG: Wait! Mermaids, Bigfoots, and Icebergs wouldn't still be here if it weren't for humanity committing to using renewable energy. They deserve to be in on this hug!

BIGFOOT: Group sing!

ARIEL: Great idea, Bigfoot! A singalong! And, look at you Iceberg, you're warming up to people.

ICEBERG: I came out here to make an announcement, not to save the world or save your voice, but now that I've done all that … it's kinda chill.

ARIEL: Each and every one of us must take serious responsibility for this wild world we live in, where both the natural and the mystical, the scientifically proven and the beyond explanation, co-exist. Let's keep finding ways to show up for this planet and make it the best it can be for everyone!

BIGFOOT, *sweetly*: Awwwwwww.

ICEBERG: Are we singin' or what? Ya know, I saved that voice of yours.

ARIEL: Ok, and I'm very grateful. Alright, everybody, repeat after me:

ARIEL, *singing*: *I had to see*

Audience repeats.

ARIEL: *It's up to meeeeee*

Audience repeats.

BIGFOOT pulls out a sign that reads: "TO PROTECT OUR WOOOOORLD"

ARIEL, *spoken*: You sing with me now! Everybody, let's all sing it together.

ARIEL and EVERYONE: *To protect our world*

ARIEL, BIGFOOT, and ICEBERG pose for a big, happy finish!

◊ ◊ ◊

Eric Lockley is a US-born, Harlem, New York-based, OBIE and AUDELCO award-winning writer, actor, and producer. Eric's plays and solo shows include dark comedies *Blacken the Bubble* and *Last Laugh*. His Afro-futuristic pieces *We The People (Not the Bots)* and *Sweet Chariot* have been showcased on the New York Off-Broadway scene. Lockley is a founder of and produces with The Movement Theatre Company and Harlem9, creating opportunities for artists of color to be expansive in their play. www.iamericlockley.com

THUNDERBIRD

Jo MacDonald

Legends tell us Thunderbirds were either protectors of the people and/or made thunder by the flapping of their wings. Every direction now experiences thunderstorms, including way, way up North, as in the Arctic. The increase of thunderstorms in that region is a direct result of climate change. We can act to help our planet. We can walk in a good way and set in motion for all good things to begin. Together.

Characters

WOMAN: Wears a colorful blanket/shawl – blue and green
THUNDERBIRD: An eaglelike spiritual creature wearing a blanket similar to the WOMAN's
Four BEINGS representing the four directions:
North wearing a white blanket
East wearing a yellow blanket
South wearing a red blanket
West wearing a black blanket

Notes

Music can be regional and completely up to the artists.

Small pouches can be made from any material and contain small items or traditional plants of the artists' region. (Traditional Anishinaabe medicine pouches were made from hide/leather and contained cedar, sage, and tobacco, sometimes sweetgrass.)

Darkness.

Light slowly illuminates the center stage; gentle, inspirational music begins. A WOMAN with long hair, wearing a vibrant blue and green blanket/shawl, is sitting in the center. She rises, spins slowly, happily beckoning THUNDERBIRD to join her.

THUNDERBIRD enters.

It dances with her. Stops. They embrace. It releases her and dances slowly around her. Moves away. Then exits.

The four BEINGS enter.
They gently move/dance to center stage from the four directions.
They sit. Close but far enough that the WOMAN can continue dancing and spinning.

She notices them. Stops, reaches down, and picks up four pouches.
She offers each of them a pouch *(starting in the East)*. They take them quickly, rise together, and begin dancing happily for a moment. They see more pouches and begin grabbing more. They start fighting over the pouches. The WOMAN offers them more and more, but the BEINGS continue grabbing from each other. The music is slowly changing to the harsh sounds of traffic, construction, bulldozers, trees being chopped down, explosions, etc.

Slowly, they all lose their original blankets, and they are replaced by a gray/brown heavy blanket that weighs them down. They try to hold on to the pouches but drop them. They try to get away and are forced to crawl to the sides of the stage.

Light slowly fades as the WOMAN tries to remain standing but she too, is weighed down.

Darkness.

Sounds – traffic, construction, trees being chopped down – become white noise.

A small light appears in the center.

THUNDERBIRD reappears, screeches, frantically circling, looking for the WOMAN in all directions. Angrily screeching at the BEINGS.
The BEINGS cower. Thunderbird continues screeching, stomping, flailing in all directions.

The WOMAN struggles and manages to raise an arm with a pouch. She waves it in the air. Hoping for THUNDERBIRD to see it. It does and stops screeching. It reaches for her. It takes the pouch, and they clasp hands. The woman lets go and motions for THUNDERBIRD to go.

THUNDERBIRD hesitates but leaves and sprinkles the contents in the four directions. It returns to the center and lays near the WOMAN to comfort her.

The four BEINGS slowly crawl to the center. THUNDERBIRD sits up. Watching the BEINGS. They come close to the WOMAN and help her up.

The traffic/construction sounds soften but don't completely disappear.

Each BEING helps remove the gray/brown blanket off the WOMAN. They place her beautiful shawl back on her. She gifts them with more pouches.

They accept with gratitude and humility this time.

They offer her and THUNDERBIRD a pouch. THUNDERBIRD doesn't accept. Instead, THUNDERBIRD stands and spreads its blanket and envelops the woman with it.

The BEINGS sit down, holding the pouches. They offer each other their pouches and exchange.
The construction noises fade. Gentle music is heard.

The BEINGS slowly raise the pouches to the sky.
Sounds slowly disappear till silence.

Light fades.

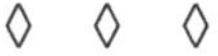

Jo MacDonald (she/her) is Anishinaabe and living on Treaty 1 Manitoba, Canada. She is a beader, short film creator, and playwright. She created *Winn Nipi*, an audio piece for PTE's Winnipeg Stories Safe at Home Manitoba Project. Her play *Neechie-itas* won the Native American New Play contest and was produced by Oklahoma Indigenous Theatre Company. The digital production of *Neechie-itas* has been shown across Canada, New Zealand, UK, and US.

LIFE AND DEATH AND LIFE AND DEATH AND LIFE AND DEATH AND LIFE

Thomas McKechnie

This play was inspired by the home worm-composting station I created during the early days of the pandemic. I derived a lot of wisdom from the way the worms were able to transform rotting garbage into new life. It made me reflect on cycles of nature, including death, and how constant growth, an essential component of capitalism, is both the source of climate change and also a fatal flaw within many of the proposed solutions to climate change.

Note

Can be performed by any number of actors – four is maybe a good minimum because of the vocal harmony, but you could do it with one voice or you could do it with a whole choir. Some or all of this could be sung or set to music. If that would make it too long, you could cut lines to allow more singing.

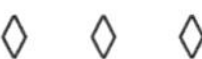

"Let's talk of graves, of worms, and epitaphs;
For God's sake, let us sit upon the ground
And tell glad stories of the death of kings"

All good things must begin
Sometimes they must begin with death
What feeds the plants?
Worms turning death into new life
What feeds the worms?
Animal carcasses, plants uprooted, poops excruted[1]
Death feeds the worms
The worms feed the plants
The plants feed the animals
Even the arrogant *Homo sapiens*

The start of new life is death
La petite mort à la française

---

[1] "Excruted" is a word I made up to rhyme with "uprooted." It means expelled.

But also, the death of so many before us who had to come and go so we could
Come and go
Life is not a line from birth through school, and working to retirement
and death
Life is a wheel with no beginning and no ending, just endless repetitions
Spring, summer, fall, winter
Rainy, dry, rainy, dry
Life and death and life and death and life and death and life

In capitalism, we don't like the death part
We like growth, growth, growth, growth
Endless summer where the sheaves of wheat just get fatter and fatter
And the potatoes keep coming out of the ground no matter how many
times you go back
As though we can dig and build and mold and take and never lack

But in nature, the only thing that grows and grows and never shrinks
Is cancer
And it does so by eating the host
And most take a dim view of it

But still, we're told we need more growth, green growth
Maybe some oil in the present tense to pay for all the future green,
green growth
But death is actually the answer to our problems
Death that brings new life

Not the death of bodies, overpopulation is a fascist myth when ten percent
of the world's population does seventy percent of the emitting
But we can't keep living how we're living
We can't keep compelling others, on pain of extinction, to adopt the
eternally growing mode of life
To recreate a world in our own image
We need life
For life needs death of ideas, death of structure, death of eternally
increasing growth
We need death

Let's take a moment to feel death coming
Because it's coming either way
The death we choose or the death that chooses us

It's one or the other
Let's take a minute and feel death

The actors all take different postures and listen or feel for death
One by one, the horror of it overtakes them and they begin to make various sounds of fear and panic
Eventually, everyone is just screaming
Eventually, the screaming finds its way into a beautiful musical harmony
This eventually ends with a collective out-breath

I actually feel much better now
I'm glad we did that *(responses of agreement)*

Beneath the pavement, the beach
Beneath the highways, the wetlands
After the death, new life

But we're still so afraid of death
We avoid death in every way we can
California says there will be no new gas-powered cars by 2035
But there will still be cars
So many cars
And freeways
Endless concrete rivers to endless vinyl suburbs
Greenly widened regularly to greenly keep up with green traffic

Which means it's just a matter of time
Till we invade Bolivia just like we invaded Iraq
Till we make new wars on the Navajo to cover the whole of northeast Arizona in solar farms
Till we cover our tanks and aircraft carriers in solar panels for net zero resource wars
So we never for a second need to slow down
To die

All these ideas, all the green new deals, promising new growth, green growth
All those fingers in all those ears screaming
DEATH WON'T COME FOR ME I'M CANADIAN[2]
All that denial

[2] Replace with whatever nation the play is being performed in.

What if our first step was death?
Not a march, not a petition, not a visit to your representative's office
Not a hopeless, desperate plea for someone, anyone, to do something, anything
What if the first step was death?

This is healthy, this is normal, too many wolves makes too few deer, which makes wolves starve, which makes deer safe, which makes too many deer, which makes good hunting for wolves, which makes the cycle start again
Not a little red line growing, growing upwards into infinity
Life death life death life death life

Before you tell me your plan to save the world
Tell me about the death that will clear way for new life
Tell me about the forest fire that will clear away the deadwood and add nitrogen to the soil
Tell me about death
Tell me about the death of the world we live in
And the life of the world to come

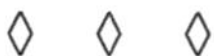

Thomas McKechnie is a Toronto-based playwright and organizer, and a settler. Writing credits include: *The Jungle* (co-written with Anthony MacMahon), *12 Letters from Your Lover, Lost at Sea* (co-written with Hannah Kaya), *Worm Moon*, *4 1/2 (ig)noble truths*, and *Remembering the Winnipeg General.* They helped organize a first-of-its-kind union for app-based food delivery workers and are a founding member of Artists for Climate and Migrant Justice and Indigenous Sovereignty.

WHERE THE GREENS GROW THICK

Anna Maria Nabirye

This play was inspired by a series of works I co-created with Metis Arts in the UK. The first piece was called *We Know Not What We May Be*, and was about imagining a future that was possible. We spent four years dream-building this world and imagining the folks who inhabited it, their stories, journeys, and roots – and Pea was part of that world. When I got this brief, I knew it was them who could take on the task of *beginning*. I also had just visited my stepdad's grave in Uganda for the first time after he passed two years prior, at the start of the pandemic. Being there and feeling so connected to my ancestral land, then having to leave and feel a deep separation from it and those it holds, made me think about connections to land and what we hold with us no matter where we are.

Notes

When OLDER PEA enters the scene, younger PEA can swap places with OLDER PEA, leave the space, or enhance the scene in whichever way feels right.

DAADA is the word for "grandparent" in Lusoga, a language of Uganda. It is not a gendered title.

/ indicates the next line starting.

A middle-aged woman sits on a stool watching the following scene.

DAADA, an elder, shuffles around the kitchen. They are cooking, making a flat bread dough. One hand is covered in flour and mixture, forcing them to use their elbows and create strange shapes in order to pick up jars, open cupboards, etc. PEA, their grandchild, sits on a stool, watching, helping, and trying to resist helping.

DAADA: I can do it!

PEA: I know you can. I was just helping. Making it easier.

DAADA: Easier isn't always better.

PEA: I know. How could I not know!

DAADA continues kneading the dough.

DAADA: Water? Bring me a little water – it's too dry, the day is too warm. We should have started earlier.
Cold from the cellar. If it was warm water I wanted, I could have got it myself.

PEA: Here.
You are going to need to start packing up. We've only got five days and there's / so much to do.

DAADA: I am not going anywhere. I haven't suggested anything of the sort!

PEA: *Daada*, I know this is hard for you. It's hard for me too

DAADA: But you already left. Didn't seem / hard at the time!

PEA: That's not fair / I didn't want to go.

DAADA: What is not fair is my own grandchild working to get me out of my home, taking my land, everything that has ever meant anything to me. Your mother was born right here in the corner, you next door. Our ancestors are buried in this very earth – when that was still possible. Now scattered in the land – they are in the bark of those trees, the grain in the earth. That is my journey. And no one, not the government or my very own seed is going to tell me otherwise.

Silence. DAADA continues to work. PEA continues to watch. DAADA covers the dough with a towel. DAADA washes their hands in a pail. PEA pours water for DAADA to rinse.

DAADA: I'm going to collect some herbs.

PEA is about to follow.

DAADA: Start on the sauce. You know how or do I need to supervise?

PEA: Of course, I know how!

DAADA: Good because I am getting old. Now don't over-dry the fish. Remember, straight on the coals, / fragrant leaves make a fragrant fish.

PEA: "Fragrant leaves make a fragrant fish."

DAADA leaves.
PEA cooks.
She looks out to see if she can see DAADA returning. Nothing.
She calls for her out the kitchen door in the back. Nothing.
It's dark. PEA is alone in the kitchen.

The woman on the stool watching has been affected by PEA and DAADA. She gathers herself, stands, puts on a mic, and pulls out a clicker from her pocket. She adjusts a slim phone-looking device and addresses the screen, clicking every now and then, activating images for an audience.

OLDER PEA: Hi, my name is Pea Kabalyia and this is my story. My home – rewilded eighteen years ago. No human has been back until today. Under the Rewild 2080 Nature Reclamation Act, a group of scientists, ornithologists, field botanists, and a lottery-drawn group of civilians, both with and without connection to the land, returned for an evaluating window of three weeks. My ticket was not drawn.
But I don't feel sad. I get to visit my homeland whenever I want through the Memory Bank Auto-Creation VR Simulator 8.50, and everyone I knew and hold dear is still there. Knowing my community's efforts and sacrifices have enabled us to reach 3.8 degrees, species not seen for decades are thriving, and water quality is only at forty percent microplastic, is something to be proud of. I am not here to tell you it is easy, but I am here to say it is possible and it is one hundred percent worthwhile!

OLDER PEA smiles. Clicks her clicker – the lights change. She stops smiling. She takes off her headset and sits.

OLDER PEA: Memory Bank, replay moment 2178: 28th March 2082, 3:18 p.m., full immersion mode.

OLDER PEA sits on the stool inside the kitchen scene.

The opening scene plays out again. DAADA says the same words but their delivery is different in response to OLDER PEA.

DAADA, an elder, shuffles around the kitchen. They are cooking, making a flat bread dough. One hand is covered in flour and mixture, forcing them to use their elbows and create strange shapes in order to pick up jars, open cupboards, etc. OLDER PEA sits on a stool, watching, and trying to resist helping.

DAADA: I can do it!

OLDER PEA: I know you can.

DAADA: Easier isn't always better.

OLDER PEA: Yeah. I agree.

DAADA continues kneading the dough.

DAADA: Water? Bring me a little water – it's too dry, the day is too warm. We should have started earlier.
Cold from the cellar. If it was warm water I wanted, I could have got it myself.

OLDER PEA: That cellar! What a great design, no power, just earth and forethought about the journey of the sun. Do you remember it being built? Or has it always been here? I've wanted to replicate it for years now – but I couldn't remember it in enough detail.

DAADA: I am not going anywhere. I haven't suggested anything of the sort!

OLDER PEA: You don't have to go anywhere. This is our home / our root

DAADA: But you already left. Didn't seem hard at the time!

OLDER PEA: But it was, it is. I miss it every day. But it's not mine. I am proud of leaving. Of leaving … something. That's fair, no?

DAADA: What is not fair is my own grandchild working to get me out of my home, taking my land, everything that has ever meant anything to me. Your mother was born right here in the corner, you next door. Our ancestors are buried in this very earth – when that was still possible. Now scattered in the land – they are in the barks of those trees, the grain in the earth. That is my journey. And no one, not the government or my very own seed, is going to tell me otherwise.

Silence. DAADA continues to work. OLDER PEA walks over and leans her head on DAADA's shoulder. She places her hands over DAADA's. They cover the dough with a towel. DAADA washes their hands in a pail. OLDER PEA pours water for DAADA to rinse.

DAADA: I'm going to collect some herbs.

OLDER PEA is about to follow.

DAADA: Start on the sauce. You know how or do I need to supervise?

OLDER PEA: I know how. You taught me well.

DAADA: Good because I am getting old. Now don't over-dry the fish. Remember, straight on the coals, / fragrant leaves make a fragrant fish.

OLDER PEA: "Fragrant leaves make a fragrant fish."
Daada? Will you pick some greens too – the thick ones that grow behind the big mango tree by the fast river?

DAADA leaves.

It's our favorite spot.

OLDER PEA sits. She looks out and tries to remember how sweet those greens tasted and the sound of the rushing water of the fast river.

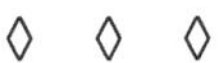

Anna Maria Nabirye is a British-Ugandan writer, multidisciplinary artist, and director. Nabirye co-founded Afri-Co-Lab, a creative community dreaming space in her now hometown of St. Leonards-on-Sea, and slow fashion brand AfroRetro. As an actor, her credits include The National Theatre, Shakespeare's Globe, The Almeida, and BBC & Film4. Nabirye is a passionate educator and has directed, taught, and created programs for theatre, music, and visual arts institutions. Her current work, *Up In Arms*,

makes space for transformative conversation in interracial friendships. Co-created with Annie Saunders, it was commissioned by The De La Warr Pavilion, UK, and includes a social practice experience, solo exhibition, film, and performance. Anna Maria and Annie are currently working on a book of the project.
Without joy there can be no revolution.
annamarianabirye.com

FROM WITHIN THE DARKNESS

Lana I. Nasser

Technology is developing faster than our ability to grasp its repercussions. "Renewable" is the buzzword, but we're still functioning from within the same consumerist paradigm that wants to extract, mine, and excavate. An insatiable hunger. Having domesticated the wild cow and sucked her dry, we turn to suck at the sun. But what if the sun itself could be depleted? As a star, the sun is predicted to die in about eight billion years.[1] But what if our interventions have sped up the process to only a century … a decade? An absurd premise, indeed.

This play is inspired by a *Saidi* porter in Cairo, whose face I will never forget, and by the tears of the sun god Ra', which fell on desert sand and transformed into honey bees. It is dedicated to those who wake up to greet the morning sun and those who seek to restore our balance with nature.

Characters

W: Female. Young and cheerful. Innocent. Childlike. Dressed in casual/modern garb. (Bee.)

E: Male. Old/ancient. Destitute porter in a tattered *jellabiya* garment. Hands trembling with Parkinson's and hardship. (Grand)Father sun.

DV: Disembodied voice(s). News reports, sometimes advertisements. Quasi-neutral, high tempo, and always delivered with a "smile." At least three distinct styles/voices. I imagine DV as voiceovers, but feel free to choose otherwise, as long as they remain disembodied.

The DV lines are one long stretch, punctured by static, that underpins the actions (or non-actions) of W and E. The reports come in mid-sentence and can overlap at times, as long as the main point is made clear. Play with it.

Setting

A futuristic world divided into two parts: Smart cities enclosed by green walls that generate energy, gather water, and regulate temperature and air; unwalled districts that provide raw materials for gadgets and a dumping place for old batteries.

[1] "Death and New Life." *Life and Death of a Planetary System*. NASA. https://science.nasa.gov/exoplanets/resources/life-and-death/chapter-7

On stage:
West: An apartment within a walled city. Quiet, except for the hum of electricity. A hot day.
East: A busy platform between two train tracks, in a muggy city outside the walls. A cold day.

The two realities function autonomously on either side of the stage until the characters meet in the center in darkness.

Before the darkness: A crescendo of news reports and buzzing of electricity; a sensory overload juxtaposed with the calmness on stage.

After the darkness: Stillness and long pauses; empty space waiting to be filled.

The setting does not have to be portrayed per se, but can simply be imagined and interacted with.

Notes

Optional sounds may include:

- Zoom of high-frequency electromagnetic waves/electricity that begins very low and rises to unbearable, leading up to darkness.
- Hum of a beehive. At the end, ideally generated by actors(s) and audience.
- Static. Like an old radio, a walkie-talkie – a sound that intersects the reports.

If it's not possible to achieve total darkness, devise a creative way to temporarily deprive actors and audience of sight.

Reuse, recycle. Buy nothing new for this play. Substitutions allowed.

◊ ◊ ◊

DV1 slowly fades in.
E steps onto the stage pushing an empty luggage cart and waits.

DV1: … the last days are upon us, according to a data leak in central AI. Batteries are running out. Power is in shortage. The price of portable oxygen tanks has doubled overnight. Dead bodies are on the streets with no QR codes to identify them. Cast forth into mass graves in silence –

An avalanche of boxes crashes onto the other side of the stage, spilling the contents, sweeping W along (perhaps she falls on top).

DV2: … Don't let this happen to you. Get chipped today for free. Vote Yes on TTI: Trackable, Tracible, and Identifiable – *(static)*

W gathers herself and begins inspecting the mess.
The reporting continues as she empties boxes in a pile, untangles cables, and sorts out things. She begins energetically, but as the reports continue, her movements gradually slow down, becoming robotic.
Meanwhile, E inches his way towards center stage at a constant snail speed.

DV3 … with more than ninety-six percent of roofs decked. Companies' shares have skyrocketed. High-capacity, long-life batteries are being developed. Environmental groups are engaged to find appropriate dumps for worn out – *(static)*

DV1: … fire that broke out in the central seed bank has been contained with no human casualties. The seeds have been destroyed. Leading bioengineering companies are working on new patents. The fire was attributed to a power outage – *(static)*

DV3: … released their newest invention. A lightweight implant in the back of the neck that filters air into breathable oxygen, with a battery smaller than a grain of rice that's powered by walking. Available soon for all chipped cit – *(static)*

DV2: … "Panels, Not Walls" is unanimously adopted. The initiative will fully utilize new city walls to collect sun energy. This will not only close the grid at one hundred percent renewable, but will increase our surplus to two hundred percent, thus securing our – *(static)*

DV1: … malfunctioning of twelve nuclear plants. Total capacity of the shelters has been reached, with only twenty percent of the population left stranded. An electrical – *(static)*

DV3: … as conspiracy theories. Air quality and power generation are stable within the walls. Residents are advised to keep their chips uploaded and avoid – *(static)*

DV2: … Floods are continuing to sweep away villages around the main rivers as a result of heavy rains and dam failures. The underlying causes might be terrorism or computer errors that – *(static)*

DV3: … collision of three trains in the city center, with sixty-two casualties. The temporary power outage might have been – *(static)*

E is center stage. The tremor in his hands is worse as oxygen levels drop. It's freezing.
W begins lethargically piling the boxes on the porter's cart. Temperature is rising.
W and E do not interact (each is in a different reality).
The buzzing of high-frequency electricity is louder.

DV1: … are baffled at what seems like a depletion of the sun's power to produce energy – *(static)*

DV3: … is pushing to mandate for booster panels to avoid blackouts and a global catastrophe – *(static)*

DV2: … The air and water regulation system has been breached. Technicians are working to – *(static)*

DV1: … suggest that our beliefs about the sun itself might be faulty. *(static)* Not infinite. The light can also be depleted. *(static)* The sun is shrinking. Renegade scientists *(static)* suggested a correlation between the depletion of the sun and inflation of solar panels *(static)*.

DV3: … dropping levels of oxygen, the government is urging citizens to breathe less by taking shallow breaths. Avoid exerting any effort while – *(static)*

DV2: … transportation systems, banks, and the internet are laid flat – *(static)*

DV1: … You're running out of battery. *(long static)*

Unbearable buzzing. W covers her ears. E is subtly suffocating.

Sudden and complete darkness.
Silence. Not even breath.
W breathes deeply as if emerging from under water.

W: Grandfather?

E: Yes, child.

W: Where are you?

E: I'm standing where you left me.

W: How can you still be standing?

Silence.

W: Where is everyone?

Silence.

W: I can't see anything.

E: The light has retreated.

W: Will it come back?

Silence.

W: Grandfather … Will you –

E: Child …

W: What's happened?

E: Everything. Nothing.

W: But I'm still here. You're here –

E: Only briefly. You're the last –

W: What –

E: – one.

Silence.

W: What now?

E: Imagine.

W: What?

E: The future.

W: But there's only darkness.

E: That's where the dreaming happens.

Silence.

W: Where do I begin?

E: Where does a day begin?

Silence.

W: With the bird. The one with big eyes nestled above the tree canopy … excited to start anew. Whistling and whistling, waking all the other birds up, to greet the sun into being. But … all the birds are gone. *(beat)* A drop of water. *(beat)* Grandfather, why are you crying?

E: You are so pure, child. *(beat)* Begin your song.

W: But I can't sing. *(beat)*
Grandfather? Grandfather … *(no response)*
Alone I cannot beckon the sun.
Grandfather … who will join my song? Grandfather … grandfather sun …

Silence.

W begins to whistle like a bird, and then to hum, hesitantly at first, but then believing that it's possible. She makes up melodies as she goes along.
Inviting the audience with her intention in song.
Perhaps they join her, perhaps they don't.
She/they hum and hum until the light comes on.

◊ ◊ ◊

Lana I. Nasser is a writer and performing artist dancing barefoot between three languages. A dreamworker, facilitator, and beekeeper, she is an ecofeminist with a passion for mythologies and a belief that peace is possible. Born in Jordan with Palestinian blood, she studied and lived across the US for many years, before planting herself in the south of the Netherlands – for now.
www.lananasser.com

WILD PARSNIPS

Tira Palmquist

This play was inspired by an *Ologies* podcast episode in which Alie Ward interviewed Alexis Nikole Nelson (@BlackForager). They talked about how the practice of foraging goes beyond just taking (with impunity) from the natural environment, and, at its best, inspires a greater sense of stewardship of the natural world.[1]

Characters

A: A forager
B: An "environmentalist"

Time

Now?

Setting

Along a public trail

Note

Since this was inspired by the larger foraging community, it would be great if A was played by a BIPOC woman.

◊ ◊ ◊

Somewhere in a wilder place (not wilderness, but close to it).

A has a basket, a large gardening knife, shears – other good tools for foraging – and is in the process of loosening the root of a wild parsnip when B comes down the path.

B: Whoa! Hey! You can't do that!

A: … Excuse me?

B: Can you do that? I don't think you can do that.

[1] Ward, Alie. "Foraging Ecology (EATING WILD PLANTS)." *Ologies*, May 18, 2021. https://www.alieward.com/ologies/foragingecology

A: You don't think I can do … what, exactly.

B: The *digging*. Of the *plants*.

A, *holding up the root*: You mean this?

B: Yeah. That.

A: Do you know what this is?

B: Well – no. I don't know exactly what it is. But a wildflower.

A: Well, it's not – though it will flower, eventually. It's how it propagates.

B: *Ok*. But I don't think you can do any of *(gesture)* that – out here.

A: And this assertion is based on what?

B: What?

A: Your assertion. That I can't do this. Is based. On what.

B: These are wild lands –

A: Point of fact: Not that wild.

B: And you can't mess it up by taking that away from the rest of us.

A, *holding up the root*: And yet you don't even know what this is.

B: It's … a *plant* – that was growing there, and you just –

A: *Pastinaca sativa*. Wild parsnip. A non-native plant. Or, as you might say, a weed.

B: Ok – alright – but still – should you just be … doing that?

A: I am doing the world a solid by eating this.

B: You're going to … eat that?

A: Well, yes. That's the point.

B: The point of what?

A: Of what I'm doing. Here along this pathway, on these *public lands*, digging up all the wild parsnips.

B: To eat them. Do you have permission to do that?

A: Wow. You're awfully fixated on that.

B: It's just – you know. If everyone came through here, digging everything up –

A: Well, that would be wrong.

B: Right. Yes. That would be wrong.

A: But I'm not "digging everything up." I'm removing a couple of invasive plants – a limited number, I might add, because even though I love a good wild parsnip, even I can't eat that many – which will, in turn, be better for the native species.

B: Better how.

A: I'm removing some of the competition. Invasive plants are good at … invading.

B: Like … kudzu?

A: Like that! Which is also delicious. Also, garlic mustard, dandelion, burdock –

B: And you eat all that.

A: This disturbs you.

B: It could be … dangerous. You don't know.

A: I do know, actually – but maybe danger is a matter of perspective. Is eating this more dangerous than eating food from a grocery store, that came from who knows where, trucked in from who knows how far, grown and harvested by who knows what methods?

B: Ok – hold on –

A: Whereas me – I walked here to these public lands – which are not even wild or protected lands – to harvest a few delicious little pests, which would crowd out the delicious native plants that could otherwise thrive.

B: Native plants such as –

A: Wild onions, ramps, wild asparagus, miner's lettuce, milkweed –

B: You … know a lot about plants. *(A nods)* And you eat all that?

A: Sure. But I don't eat all that. I mean – I forage … intentionally. I only take some, while leaving the plant to continue to propagate, or to cast some seed, to ensure a future crop.

B: Well, good. I mean, I was, you know, just concerned about the environment.

A: The environment that you don't seem to know that much about.

B: Hey! That's unfair!

A: But you didn't know about this. *(holding up the parsnip root again)*

B: No, I didn't know –

A: Or that it was, in fact, a weed.

B: No –

A: Or that you could eat it.

B: Ok! No! No, I didn't. *(beat)* You got me. Fine.

A: Would you … like to?

B: What?

A: Eat this.

B: I'm not going to take your parsnip.

A: I could show you how to find your own parsnip. I could show you how to find a lot of things.

B: Whoa whoa whoa. That seems like – a lot.

A: It doesn't need to be. I could teach you to find one delicious thing.

B: And then what.

A: Then you'll want to find other delicious things. And then you'll see the world in a different way. Wanting to make sure that public lands continue, and thrive.

B: By eating them.

A: It's a good place to begin.

A hands B the wild parsnip. Lights fade.

◊ ◊ ◊

Tira Palmquist, based in Southern California, is known for plays that merge the personal, the political, and the poetic – such as *Two Degrees*, which premiered at the Denver Center and is available through TRW Plays. Her newest play, *The Body's Midnight*, premiered at Boston Court Pasadena in April 2024 (a coproduction with IAMA Theater Company). Tira's current projects include *Memory of Winter*, a play continuing her series of plays about Minnesota, also about climate change; and *King Margaret*, an adaptation of the Henry VI cycle, which was featured in the 5 Directors, 5 Plays reading series with Oregon Shakespeare Festival in July 2021. Other plays include *The Worth of Water, Safe Harbor, The Way North, Ten Mile Lake, Age of Bees, And Then They Fell,* and *This Floating World.* www.tirapalmquist.com

BARBERMAN

Sigmund Roy Pecho aka 『siglo』

As we were both mourning a loss and celebrating an upcoming milestone, oil tanker *MT Princess* sank off Naujan, Oriental Mindoro, causing a widespread oil spill in some islands of southern Luzon, Philippines. Barbershops across Batangas, Laguna, Mindoro, and other nearby provinces, pledged a donation drive of hair as a strong absorbent of oil.

Characters

BARBER LINO (late 50s): A skilled barber
JOSE (15): Junior high school student
PEDRO (15): Junior high school student
JUAN (15): Junior high school student
A chorus of high school boys, teens, and junior high school students

Note

The script may be interpreted in different creative ways, but it is meant to convey that the lines are being spoken simultaneously.

Lights snap up.
An overture of percussive and rhythmic sounds. We hear the sound of scissors swiftly cutting.

The scene takes place in a barbershop just across the premises of Barangay Our Lady of Lourdes High School. Outside, a queue of junior high school students is seen. They all tap their feet impatiently, unknowingly, monotonously.

At one end of the stage, we see a classic barbershop setup – vintage barber chair, the barber's desk with a mirror, and adorning the desk, are the barber's tools. The barbershop has been cutting hair since 1986, as seen in one of the posters.

At the other end, we see the waiting chair.
Next in line, inside the barbershop, are one of the freshies in high school and three classmates, JOSE, PEDRO, and JUAN.

BARBER LINO: Next!

With a ruler, BARBER LINO ensures that the right length for the boy's haircut is met. The previous customer finally takes off the overweight barber cape. The youngest in the line is pushed by JUAN to go next.

JOSE, *to PEDRO who is busy scrolling on his smartphone*: Damn, Barber Lino with the ruler again.

Come sit. *(to the next customer)* Stop texting, will you? I will confiscate that. Report you to the disciplinary officer.

(to BARBER LINO) Hey, you can't do that!

You grow too much hair – I can extract vinegar! Can you even afford proper shampoo? Too thick, eh!? This is good for lice nesting! *(chuckles)*

PEDRO: He can. He gets a commission each time.

JUAN: *Sana* all! But nope, I'm not your corrupt officer.

PEDRO: HA! And look at you, falling in line with us.

What's your haircut? What?

Ah, don't mention it, I don't have to know. Because everybody knows. Everybody comes here for Barber Lino. For sure, you will get a good score with the girls. You boys should take it from Barber Lino.

JOSE: It's really three by four inches! How the fuck can we score with the girls if we always look the same? We all look like brothers. LOL.

School ain't cool!

Fuck this school!

Do you wanna know why I'm a sweeter lover than those Jeepney drivers? Because I make people look good, look decent. *(chuckles)*

JUAN: And the barber, too!

But you know, in two thousand-I forget-exactly-when, there were many people lining up here. No, not students. They were volunteers. Like for blood donation. But I'm a barber, y'know, and a good one, so you won't lose any blood or ear from my razor-sharp scissors, oh no no no. *(coughs)* I felt like Barberman. Y'know, a Marvel DC-like hero.

BARBER LINO takes the barber cape off the current customer, and spreads it in the air, shaking off the hair and dandruff.

It was like yesterday.

Shadowplay begins. The mirror becomes a surface where images of coastal areas affected by sunken oil tankers and oil spills are projected. The images show an almost Revelation-like scene from the Bible, but in the depths of the ocean. Marine life is killed by the oil.

Outside, the long queue of school boys develops a percussive accompaniment to the scenes narrated inside.

BARBER LINO takes his time. He is in his element. He takes his cutting tools, and wields them like a surgeon, then like a caricature superhero.

JOSE: Hey, Pedro, Juan, Barber stories are gold. Listen.

PEDRO: Good Lord!

JUAN: I know, right?

PEDRO: No. Look! *(points at his phone)*

JOSE, *reads fast, and mumbles through some words:* February 28 – that's yesterday – Oil spill. So?

PEDRO: Dude, what's wrong with you – "So?"

JUAN: Yeah, show some empathy, man. You're not the renegade Student Council Officer for nothing.

PEDRO: I was rooting for you, *pre*!

JOSE: No, I mean, "so" as "what should we do next?" Organize a hair donation drive?

With the school?

JUAN: Sounds good, and bad.

JOSE thinks about it for a time, while PEDRO shows

his phone to JUAN. They are both glued to the news.

It was in this very barbershop that I felt like *The* Barberman. People lined up, until the stars were all out. A line like there was no tomorrow.

JOSE: I mean, I can work on it now!

Look, there's a huge line outside! Lots of hair to start with.

It was a moment when you felt like the sun was about to shine. All things must start, especially the good ones. But of course, they have to end too, for a new start. Every day is a new day. But that day felt like forever.

JUAN: Not gonna lie: I love the idea, but the school will think they are way too cool to be the heroes here!

I was cutting for all sorts of people. Girl, boy, *bakla*,[1] tomboy, *butiki*,[2] *baboy*.[3] *(chuckles)*

JOSE: Fuck the school, Juan! It's not about being cool.

There was an affected area in one of the ports where oil companies housed their source of income! Heh! All for money, those people sure are greedy!

JUAN: Jose, there's nothing much we can do.

JOSE: C'mon! Juan, you always try to be a defeatist.

JUAN: And you are always the superhero? Thinking every rise of arms is an additional energy source for Son Goku's energy ball.

Blood is thicker than water? Well, there is one more thing thicker than water: It's oil! And they are not friends. In the depths of the ocean, it's like the Revelation in the Bible for the fish.

JOSE: Well, that's exactly the point! At least it's not nega energy! You're too *maasim*,[4] Juan! Make it sweet and sour, dude!

Armageddon. Like, how many times do schools of fish experience

[1] Filipino word for "gay."
[2] Filipino word for "lizard."
[3] Filipino word for "pig."
[4] Filipino word for "sour."

the end of the world? And how many times do they start again? And I've been an angel to many of them. *(chuckles)*

But you know what, the hair is the healing.

See? I'm a hero in my own right. What could have been done to stop it, had we not responded quickly?

The hair movement had to start quickly. It can't go down from here.

And I won't stop helping.

Some say it's nothing, but to me, it's a barberman thing. Every little cut is important.

JUAN: Yeah, sweet and sour *pork*, ok? Not fish, not now.

JOSE: So what? No fish until the oil spill is totally cleared up?

PEDRO: Why, look at Twitter. Lots to see about the spill. Damn, Mindoro. It's all going south and to some of the neighboring provinces. Oh, how about Coron!

JUAN: Oh no, Coron. How about Boracay?

JOSE: Well, guys! Stop it. All good things must get a full start!

JUAN: Like what, Jose? How? When? Where?

PEDRO: Ah, look. It's such a huge tanker! Oil floats on water. Damn oil is thicker than H_2O. Locals from Mindoro are now having an oily day. Pun intended.

JOSE: Dude, stop it.

PEDRO: What?!

JUAN: Jose, if you wanna do something now, I'm sorry but you can't. We are here in this god forsaken barbershop, waiting for our turn to have our three-by-four and comply with school rules. But it's always cool to help out, I know.

PEDRO: Yeah, I just think we are too stuck on Twitter.

Someone is calling?

JOSE: Barberman?!

Jose grabs the scissors.

The seas are calling. Oil is thicker than water.

Oil is thicker than water.

Shall we?

(nods) We shall.

JOSE goes outside and shouts:

NEXT!

The scene ends with a "timelapse" movement of BARBER LINO and JOSE cutting hair.

A movement piece shows villagers in coastal towns with buckets trying to scoop out oil from the sea, and progresses into villagers becoming the students ritualistically offering buckets of hair to the sea.

◊ ◊ ◊

Sigmund Roy Pecho aka 『siglo』 (b. 1992, Philippines) works with shadowplay – a contemporary form of shadow puppetry – as a medium for creative expression and an act of solidarity with social movements and advocacies. He has joined various puppetry and mixed-media performances with shadowplay as a tool for collaborative creation. He is curious to

investigate dynamic relationships of social actors and the systems they participate in.
https://sigpecho.wixsite.com/siglo

YOU ARE NOT ALONE

Nicole Pschetz

My inspiration comes from the ideas shared by Ailton Krenak, an Indigenous movement leader, writer, poet, and philosopher of Krenak ethnicity (state of Minas Gerais, Brazil). In his work, he often speaks about our relationship with what we call "nature," saying that, for instance, what is called "humanity" has purposely dissociated itself from it, from planet Earth itself. Destruction, domination, and endless desire for power come from that estranged relationship. This touches me profoundly because I believe we only start acting upon something if we feel connected with it, if we really care. And changing the course of things will depend on this feeling of connection: If a part of a whole dies, we are also losing a part of ourselves. Krenak's thoughts and ideas have shed a ray of light in dark times. This play is an attempt to do the same.

Characters

RIVER: A person of any gender.

OLDER RIVER: Same as above, but with an important age gap between them. This character can be an actor on stage, a recorded voice, or even be performed by the same actor who plays RIVER.

WIND: A portrayal of a natural element. It could be a recorded voice, a recorded voice combined with a video projection, or an actor on stage.

Setting

This play takes place in the near future. The main character goes through and/or visualizes different locations.

Notes

I wrote this play thinking it would be a physical theatre piece, with movement and/or dance conveying the main character's shifts in their inner state, as well as shifts in locations. Sound design and/or music could help "make visible" the different locations. This could also be done visually with lighting design and/or video projections. But it could just as well be a radio play. Or a straightforward reading – a character's testimonial given in any setting or space. The possibilities are endless.

◊ ◊ ◊

An empty, quiet space. As RIVER speaks, the space around them changes progressively.

RIVER: I don't know when it all started. Perhaps it was with those strange dreams. They weren't the usual thing. I had the sensation they were real. I know. You'll say that's what happens when we dream. But those were different. The images were so vivid. And the fear was too. The first dream was perhaps the scariest. Because it was the first of many … I opened my eyes and my bedroom was in an abandoned state. There was orange light coming through the broken window. Ragged curtains were flowing in the wind. The room was empty; there was silence. I didn't see anything else, but I had the feeling that if I opened the door, and if I went outside the house, I would see the whole neighborhood abandoned, destroyed.

Complete change of location. RIVER is outside.

Next, I started seeing things. As I rode my bike to go to work, I would see the trees move in a strange manner. It was the wind, of course. But it wasn't just that. In a way, I understood the trembling leaves were sort of whistling a message to me. It couldn't be translated into words because no human words could express that. Those trees are older than me and you together. They have seen a lot, you know? And now, they seemed to be warning me of what was coming. I tried to decipher it. I didn't manage. Do you think it's madness? Me too. I thought it was madness.

Complete change of location. RIVER is in a café.

Then, the unexpected happened. I was in a café, looking out the window, enjoying the sensation of warm sunshine in December. I got distracted by the birds singing, and started thinking about how our winters haven't been the same in the past few years. Lingering fears came back to my mind. I had finished my coffee but I still had a glass full of water in front of me. I saw it trembling. At first, I thought it was an earthquake. I looked around me but nothing else was moving. I looked again at the glass and I saw tiny waves moving back and forth. It was like a miniature ocean. Then somehow … I dove in. Into the glass.

Complete change of location. RIVER is outside, in the middle of a river. Water is flowing around them. The character is/could be completely drenched.

When I emerged, I was no longer in the café. I was swimming in the middle of a river. Someone called my name. I turned around and … I saw myself. Standing on the riverbank. It was me, but older. Much older. We stared at each other.

OLDER RIVER: Not only do you need to start paying real attention to what you see, but you also must start believing in it. What you see are indeed messages. But they are not messages from the future. They are messages from the present. You need to understand that there are other ways to read what's around you. And other living things are capable of doing that. If you allow yourself to connect with them, with the world around you, you will understand the meaning of what you are seeing.

Suddenly, RIVER is back in the café. They could be completely drenched, which would accentuate the strangeness of the situation.

RIVER: And then, I was back in the café. I looked around me and life was going on as usual. I guess no one noticed my absence. I looked again at the glass and the waves had stopped. At that moment, I realized the sky had gone from blue and bright to dark and thundery. The rain started falling. Raindrops were hitting the window. Water started to accumulate on the pavement. It was rising and rising … Strong winds were blowing the rain around. Everyone was staring out. Not me. I walked out.

Change of location. RIVER is standing in the stormy rain.

I stood in the middle of the storm. I felt the cold water soaking my clothes. The wind was blowing my hair around and I could hear it whispering to me.

WIND, *whispering*: It will be alright. You are not alone. We are many. And many more are joining us. At this exact moment, they too are outside, eyes wide open, not afraid.

RIVER: There's no one here! Only me. Look at them! Scared inside that building, and that one, and that one! I can't do anything alone. Please, stop.

WIND, *whispering*: You are not alone.

RIVER: Suddenly, something else happened. The rain became a sort of a wall, a water curtain.

Pause. Change in the way the rain falls (or in how it's being represented).

I looked through it and I saw them – all of them – spread over our planet: People, but also wild animals running free in vast fields, birds flying over the top of dry mountains, huge whales jumping in the middle of the ocean, trees growing, plants twisting and shaking in order to reach the sunlight, clouds of insects flying and buzzing, rivers running through rocks and sand, the desert at night. I saw eyes gazing at me. I heard other living beings breathing. I felt the Earth moving. I felt its heartbeat. It was synchronized with mine. I understood that I was part of something much bigger. I understood that despite all the horrors, all the destruction, there is still hope. This huge thing we call nature is also me, it's also you.

Blackout.

RIVER and OTHER CHARACTERS/VOICES, *whispering*:
You are not alone.

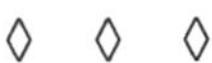

Nicole Pschetz is a French-Brazilian theatre maker and performer based in Paris. She has created shows in Brazil, the UK, Italy, Portugal, and France. Since 2015, she has been the artistic director of *Poulpe Électrique*, a physical theatre and multimedia company that focuses on contemporary themes through a critical and poetic dialogue between physical expression and the digital arts.
https://nicolepschetz.com
https://poulpeelectrique.net/en/home

KIDS FOR SAVING EARTH CLUB #121

Gab Reisman

I've been thinking of my earliest memories around the climate movement – how was I taught to be conscious of our impacts on the Earth and then, later, how I've been directly impacted by both climate change and our choices around it. My partner and I are beginning the process of having a baby this year, which takes some forethought as queer women; so, I've also been thinking about what it means to deliberately choose something so simultaneously joyful and difficult.

◊ ◊ ◊

GAB 1, GAB 2, and GAB 3.
Are they on a playground? Are they on a stage?
Their speech moves at a gallop.

GAB 1: Hi, it's me, it's Gab, it's 1993, I'm at a meeting of the Kids for Saving Earth club, I'm ten.
My neighbor's mom organized this club and it's great. We talk about ways to recycle and reuse? We talk about why you shouldn't use aerosol hairspray, about the ozone layer, and the dolphins? We go on camping trips and eat wintergreen Life Savers and see how they spark in our mouths –
We all have a little card we can put in our wallets; it has the club's mantra on it and at the beginning of every meeting, we sing the mantra as a song, it goes:
The Earth is my hooooome.
I prooooomise to keep it –
healthy and beauuuuutiful.
I will love the land, the air, the water –
It's a terrible song.
It doesn't rhyme. It has no beat. The entire club is *far* too sincere. It feels like church.
But. I make sure our peanut butter jars and cans are washed out and put in separate bins.
And I really like seeing my friends every week. It's the only time we go in their house.
And I like having the card in my wallet. It's laminated.

GAB 2: Hey, it's Gab, it's 2005, I'm on my porch in New Orleans, I'm like twenty-three?
There are *huge* piles of trash on the street, these two-story-high piles of drywall and wet carpet and flooring and just stuff Hurricane Katrina destroyed?
Every morning, my boyfriend and I sit on the porch and watch workers in hazmat suits walk down the street, watch guys in hazmat suits drive bobcats around and push the trash into larger piles till a truck comes and shovels it up.
We think, "Should we be in hazmat suits?"
We're living in this dust that coated everything when the water went down.
It's streaked with old motor oil and gas and whatever was in people's garages, and everyone is sick with a nasty cough but it feels like no big deal?
Because everything else was so much worse – people were trapped, people died, and so many animals – you see their bodies still stacked in the rubble.
So much is gone, there's no mail or gas or hot water or streetlights – there are no *children* allowed in the city.
So, a cough that everyone has at once … That's really no big deal.

GAB 3: I'm Gab, it's Earth Day in 1990, I'm in first grade, and we made this play about not throwing trash on the ground. And also, probably, about dolphins.

GAB 1: I'm in India, I'm twenty-nine, and the woman next to me on the bus takes my empty bag of chips and throws it out the window into the ditch. The family across from us at the restaurant throws their napkins onto the sand floor and the man we're staying with burns his garbage every night in a little spot just off of the kitchen.
"This never used to be a problem," the man says. "Everything used to go back into the earth. We need new systems in place."

GAB 3: It's Earth Day, it's 1990. We made this play with Barbara Peacock. Barbara Peacock is the playground monitor and she's in her forties. She used to be a soap opera actress – she still gets residual checks to prove it. She's got dyed red hair and bright green eyes and her lips always curled into a secret smile. I think she's completely *gorgeous*.
Everyone in our elementary school sees the play.

GAB 2: Hey, it's Gab, it's now, I'm forty. My partner wants to have a baby.

GAB 1: I'm Gab, it's 2015 I think, I just started dating this coastal ecologist – who will later become my partner – and we're driving through the marsh in Louisiana and she's telling me about points of no return – like

the line where a forest can't recover from a fire and becomes a prairie, or a marsh loses too much land and becomes a lake.
Those moments where one thing crosses over to become another –

GAB 1 and GAB 3: I think I'm in love.

GAB 2: "We can't wait any longer," my partner says. "I'm not getting any younger. I know it's not the ideal time, but when is?"

GAB 3: It's Gab, it's 2021, there's just been another hurricane here.
The same date Katrina hit, the same day of the week, and I know it's not the same but – it feels – it feels – we're driving through trees on the Northshore, thirty miles outside of New Orleans.
The roof of our bedroom blew off. The bed is covered in mildew.
But we're lucky, we evacuated, it's not so bad, no one was hurt.
We stop at the Lowe's to get bleach and I can't breathe. I can't breathe, I feel like I'm back there again – in the dust with the garbage and hazmat suits, the slick of dried mud and dead rabbits – the dead rabbits in a cage on top of a pile of trash and I can't, I can't!

GAB 2: It's Gab, I'm nineteen, in Berlin. It's like 2001 and the sky is full of cranes. I love it here.
The city is in a construction boom. We have a *kohlenheizung* in the room I'm staying in – an old coal-burning oven to heat the space. My friend and I put little coal briquettes in and we lounge around all day. We can't move. We're tired and dizzy and don't know why.
We go outside later and everything's really loud and we realize it's carbon monoxide poisoning. "We're lucky we didn't die," my friend says.
Though I know someone who died like that, at sleepover in Pakistan, it was his birthday –

GAB 3: It's me, it's 2011, I'm in grad school, I'm driving a friend home and we're talking about global warming and he says, "Yeah, where's the proof though, really."
I stop the car – I'm furious. I say, "You can walk." And we are both surprised his casual dismissal cut so close to the bone.

GAB 2: I'm really freaked out, to have a baby. Not even because of the world they'd grow up in. Because we're all gonna have to take part in that. I'm just …

GAB 1: You'd be a good parent.

GAB 2: I know.

GAB 1: I always thought you'd be such a good parent /

GAB 2: It's not that! It's not that I think I can't do it.
It's just like, is this the right choice? Are me and my partner making the right choice?
Should we have a kid together?
How do you know you should do a thing when it doesn't happen accidentally?

GAB 3: My whole life has been falling into danger and then cleverly muscling a way out of / it

GAB 2: Narrowly avoiding a way out of it.

GAB 3: How do you have the faith to choose to do something that lasts on after you?

GAB 1: Hey – here.

GAB 1 hands wintergreen Life Savers to the others. She drapes a blanket over all of their heads – raising it up and letting it fall over them like a parachute.
Or maybe they turn the lights off.

GAB 1, *under the blanket*: See if you can see a spark.

The noise of them biting on wintergreen Life Savers.

GAB 2: I saw it!

GAB 1 takes her head out from under the blanket.

GAB 1: It's 1990, it's Earth Day, I'm seven.
The play ends just as the dismissal bell rings and everyone streams out of the cafetorium. There's trees – two hundred tiny trees on a table in the hall and every child grabs one, small, sprouted trees in brown paper bags – and we pour out the school doors onto the playground –

GAB 3, *under the blanket*: Oh! I saw it!

GAB 1: It's raining but the sun is out – a sun-shower, a rainbow and it feels, as I remember it – like everyone amasses in a giant crowd. Like somehow everyone's circling with their little paper bag trees around Barbara Peacock and me.

GAB 2: Here –

GAB 2 and GAB 3 have taken their heads out of the blanket.

GAB 1: It feels like a film and I look up into the rain and I'm *so* happy to be alive. I'm so overwhelmingly happy. I feel like I'm turning into light –

GAB 2: Triboluminescence – is the thing that makes Life Savers spark in the dark.
It happens because of sugar and friction. It's pretty much the same shit as lightning, but that's all I know. I never fully get physics.

GAB 3: All I can do is go day by day. Be loving, be open –

GAB 1: Look up into the rain sometimes

GAB 2: Try and summon lightning in my mouth.

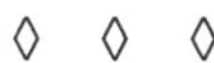

Gab Reisman is a New York-based playwright whose work explores the connections between geography, history, and identity, and what it means to live on the continual precipice of chaos. Besides her own plays, Gab builds immersive and devised performances in non-traditional spaces, most recently with utopia-based trio Bender/Mars/Reisman. She has developed work with Clubbed Thumb, Page 73, Actors Theatre of Louisville, Fusebox, Sundance, MacDowell, The Orchard Project, The NOLA Project, and The Playwrights' Center among others.
www.gabreisman.com

SELLING BABY PRAIRIE

Mark Rigney

Ten years ago, I dug up a large chunk of my backyard and turned it into a native plant "garden." It now hosts something like twenty different species of Midwest-native flowers, plus a few grasses. But what happens if I move elsewhere? What will happen to Baby Prairie?

Characters

BLAKE: Addicted to gardening, homeowner, PARKER's spouse. This actor also plays QUINN, the prospective buyer.

PARKER: Supportive of gardening, homeowner, BLAKE's spouse. This actor also plays RILEY, the realtor.

CUP PLANT: A very tall, square-stemmed plant with yellow, daisy-like flowers. Best done as human puppet? With flowers on both hands?

CONEFLOWER: A stiff, slightly sharp plant with droopy, lavender-purple flowers. Best done as human puppet? With flowers on both hands?

Setting

A "yard" behind a house. Straggly flowers reaching for sunlight.

Time

First, now, then a now just a little farther in the future.

Note

A five-minute play for four actors, or six actors (if QUINN and RILEY are not played by the same actors who portray BLAKE and PARKER), or more if the company would like to showcase a "garden of live flowers." Gender in casting is open; adjust pronouns as needed.

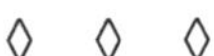

Lights up on a backyard and a tangle of mostly native plants. BLAKE is trying to make it maximally beautiful. PARKER is losing patience. CUP PLANT and CONEFLOWER eavesdrop.

PARKER: Blake, come on. You've always said that half the point is to just let Baby Prairie do its thing.

BLAKE: Not an option right now.

PARKER: You know how this works, right? When we find a new house, one we really like, there will be aspects that we want to change. And that cuts both ways. Something like eighty percent of homebuyers – they rip out the kitchen, start over.

BLAKE: But if the kitchen is beautiful. Updated.

PARKER: Pulling weeds and dead-heading will not turn Baby Prairie into anybody's idea of a fully updated kitchen.

BLAKE: Parker, if I do this right, maybe I can convince some stranger that this is worth keeping.

PARKER: Some things in life are out of your control.

BLAKE: Not this. Not today.

PARKER exits. BLAKE digs in.

CONEFLOWER: I keep wanting to like her.

CUP PLANT: Ok, listen, you know I've got my roots to the ground, right?

CONEFLOWER: I wish for once you'd be plant enough to know your limitations.

CUP PLANT: There is nothing wrong with a little detective work.

CONEFLOWER: You are a cup plant. I am a coneflower. Our only legitimate "work" is to stay upright long enough to make a few thousand beautiful baby seeds.

BLAKE gives up. Time for lunch. BLAKE exits.

CUP PLANT: Ok, look. These are the facts: Blake, there – our gardener – lives in that house.

CONEFLOWER: The what?

CUP PLANT: You know, that wood dark rectangular blank huge thing over there that he spends so much time in. But the thing is, he's moving to a different house, far away – and when he does, someone new will move into the dark blank rectangular big house thing. And that someone might prefer a perfectly mown nice evenly green all-looks-the-same lawn.

CONEFLOWER: You mean, some other gardener might prefer a lawn to us.

CUP PLANT: Exactly.

CONEFLOWER: But why? Lawns are like – they're deserts with extra chlorophyll.

CUP PLANT: Lawns make humans think life is safe. Orderly.

CONEFLOWER: But we're the ones that belong!

CUP PLANT: Do you really think that the people who love lawns give two flying foxgloves about you being native?

CONEFLOWER: I host pollinators! I feed birds! I don't need to be watered, and my petals delight all who gaze upon me!

CUP PLANT: True. Pity about your crippling vanity, but otherwise, true.

CONEFLOWER: I aerate the soil! No, we aerate the soil! We hold it in place! We ameliorate flooding!

CUP PLANT: How can you toss around a word like "ameliorate" and not know what a house is?

CONEFLOWER: I will not be ripped out in favor of a lawn.

CUP PLANT: Then if I were you? I'd start blooming like you have never bloomed before.

CONEFLOWER: Yes. I shall grow. Flourish. I shall attract ten thousand gorgeous swallowtail butterflies!

CUP PLANT: Probably best if we let me handle the swallowtail yellow gorgeous ten thousand butterflies angle. Your job is: Don't droop. Hang on to your petals a little extra long and do your best to look generally fabulous.

CONEFLOWER: I shall be the most drop-dead stunning coneflower in history.

CUP PLANT: And pass the word, yeah? Every flower here, even the ones who already bloomed –

CONEFLOWER: Oh, like that silly little columbine –

CUP PLANT: – we all need to be on the same page.

CONEFLOWER: The same what?

CUP PLANT: Doesn't matter. We need to look spectacular! All of us. Leaves, stems, the works.

CONEFLOWER: Done. We are now the best-looking native plant garden *ever*.

Enter QUINN, a realtor, and RILEY, a potential homebuyer.

QUINN: And here we have the backyard. Mature trees, attractive border beds, azaleas every spring.

RILEY: Why is there a scraggly mess right in the middle of the lawn?

QUINN: Yeah. About that.

RILEY: It's like they just plunked it down.

QUINN: So, the seller, I don't want to speak ill, but the guy is like nine cans short of a six-pack.

RILEY: I don't even know what half these flowers are.

QUINN: Doesn't matter. It's not an architectural feature, and it won't take long to dig up.

RILEY: It's definitely not, I don't know. Landscaped.

QUINN, *removing a letter*: I told the man, roll out some sod, make it look decent. Instead, he hands me this letter. I'm supposed to read it. Aloud.

RILEY: O-k.

QUINN, *reading aloud*: "Hello. My name's Blake. Ten years ago, I joined a small but growing revolution. I dug up the only sunny patch in the backyard and began planting flowers and grasses native to this part of the country. The result is Baby Prairie, with over twenty species present, and they come up every year all by themselves. The only maintenance required is digging up the cup plant in summer (it spreads too fast) –"

CUP PLANT: I do not!

QUINN, *still reading*: "– and cutting the stems back to ground level in December. I spend less on gas for the mower, and I get more bees, birds, and butterflies than every other yard in this neighborhood combined."

RILEY: Really?

CONEFLOWER: Come on, everyone! Bloom! Bloom harder!

QUINN, *still reading*: "I realize that if you buy this property, it'll be yours to do with as you please, but for the sake of what lived here before houses took over, I'm hoping you'll keep Baby Prairie intact. All best, Blake Ward."

RILEY, *to Quinn*: Any chance you've seen this yard in winter?

CUP PLANT: Oh, no, no, no. Don't ask that.

QUINN, *to Riley*: Honestly? In winter, Blake's precious prairie looks like a muddy sty.

CONEFLOWER: We're doomed.

RILEY, *to Quinn*: Well, it might look like a muddy sty to us. But I wonder …

A brilliant swallowtail appears on CUP PLANT. A goldfinch appears on CONEFLOWER. RILEY takes note.

QUINN: We should do another walkthrough. Inside.

RILEY: No, I want to meet this guy. The seller. Blake whatever.

QUINN: That's not typical. Can I ask why?

RILEY: I want a first-hand introduction to every plant in Baby Prairie.

QUINN: So … you're buying.

RILEY, *a bit of an epiphany*: No. I'm caretaking.

More butterflies. More birds. Rabbits. Squirrels. Mice. Raccoons. Baby Prairie blooms.

◊ ◊ ◊

Mark Rigney's plays have been produced in twenty-three states plus Australia, Austria, Canada, Hong Kong, and Nepal. In New York, his work has played off-Broadway at 59E59. US-born, he is a member of the Dramatists Guild and has won multiple contests, including the John Gassner Award, the TNT Pops! Playwriting Competition, the Panowski Playwriting Award, and the Maxim Mazumdar New Play Competition. His published work is available from Playscripts, Inc., Next Stage Press, and Smith & Kraus's *The Best Ten-Minute Plays*.
www.markrigney.net

THE GLOWING RED PLANET

Carmen Rivera

Famines are not new. There have been famines throughout human history. But as a result of 20th and 21st century human-made climate change, there are nearly 41 million people suffering through famine.[2 3]

Contributing factors to human-made climate change are war, contamination, exploitation of our resources, and a blind disregard for the health of our planet. Ironically, as the rate of human starvation increases, our world produces more food than has ever been produced in human history. Much of it is tainted with chemicals and poisonous substances, rendering our food supply harmful for consumption.

The Glowing Red Planet is inspired by my love of the television show, *The Twilight Zone,* and my anxiety over the refusal of the "powers that be" to accept climate change as a global crisis, and their lack of will to take action.

Characters

MAMÁ: Mother, mid-thirties.
PAPÁ: Father, mid-thirties.
MARISOL: Daughter, ten years old. She will become the seventy-year-old ABUELA MARISOL.
ABUELA MARISOL: Grandmother, seventy years old.
GRANDDAUGHTER: Ten years old. The actor who plays MARISOL can also play the GRANDDAUGHTER.

Setting

A desolate land – a dry, hard, lifeless Puerto Rico. It used to be a fertile island many years prior.

Time

Sometime in the future.

[2] "Famine knocking at the door of 41 million worldwide, WFP warns." *United Nations*, June 22, 2021. https://news.un.org/en/story/2021/06/1094472
[3] Davies, Lizzy. "Famine: what is it, where will it strike and how should the world respond?" *The Guardian*, July 6, 2022. https://www.theguardian.com/global-development/2022/jul/06/famine-what-is-it-where-will-it-strike-and-how-should-the-world-respond

Note

The tree frog *coquí*, native to Puerto Rico, is referenced in the play. Its name is derived from the sound it makes.[4]

◊ ◊ ◊

MAMÁ is digging on dry and hardened ground. PAPÁ enters.

PAPÁ: Stop it. We have to leave.

MAMÁ: No. I'm not leaving without burying the baby.

She continues digging.

PAPÁ: Stop it! Stop it!

MAMÁ: NO! The baby needs to be buried. He needs to be buried properly!!

PAPÁ bends down and hugs her in an effort to stop her.

PAPÁ: *Ya, amor*. STOP! Look at your hands. They're cracked and bloodied.

MAMÁ loses her strength and collapses in his arms. She's angry and continues crying.

MARISOL enters and watches the scene.

PAPÁ: We can't bury him. You can't dig into the earth. The dirt is so dry and hard … it's like digging into cement.

MAMÁ: I killed him. He was only six months.

PAPÁ: You didn't kill him.

MAMÁ: I fed him my milk. If I had known my milk was poisoned, I would have bought the milk in the black market.

PAPÁ: *Mi amor*, that milk is also poisoned. He would have died anyway. He's in the best place he can be – in our home here in Puerto Rico, in his crib, wrapped in the blanket you made for him.

[4] "Coqui Sound Puerto Rico Relax." YouTube, uploaded by Puerto Rico Real Estate, December 24, 2020. https://www.youtube.com/watch?v=P44T5xrqWH0

MAMÁ continues crying. MARISOL approaches her parents.

MARISOL: Mamá, don't cry. The baby looks like he's sleeping.

MAMÁ: *Ay*, my dear beautiful girl Marisol … And today is your birthday. *Ay m'ija* … I love you … *Happy Birthday to you … Happy Birthday to …*

MAMÁ tries to sing Happy Birthday *to MARISOL, but her fragile emotional state will not let her. PAPÁ softy finishes singing the song.*

PAPÁ: *Happy Birthday, dear Marisol … Happy Birthday to you …*

They all hug.

PAPÁ: We will have a party for you at the space station. But right now, we have to be ready for the transport.

MARISOL: Papá, I don't want to leave.

PAPÁ: Marisol, I don't want to leave either. If we stay, we'll starve to death. The water is radiated, the air is poisoned, and the land is dead. The animals are all gone … You can't even hear the *coquíes*. Nothing grows on Earth anymore.

MARISOL: I love the *coquíes*.

PAPÁ: There's no time. Come … the transport has arrived.

PAPÁ helps MAMÁ gather herself, and they, along with MARISOL, exit.

Lights shift.

A space station, sixty years later.

ABUELA MARISOL and her GRANDDAUGHTER are looking through a telescope for a beat. ABUELA MARISOL sits down. It is clear she's upset.

GRANDDAUGHTER: Abuela Marisol, why are you sad? You should be happy. Today is your birthday.

ABUELA MARISOL: I am happy and sad. I was ten years old, exactly your age now, when my family left Earth and came to live here. We were some of the lucky ones who survived through the nuclear war … My mother's grief was so deep, she died weeks after we arrived here.

GRANDDAUGHTER: We learned about the nuclear war in school. The teacher said the fires could never be extinguished. They will burn forever.

ABUELA MARISOL: Papá was an engineer working on the space station when the nuclear war happened. People were already living in space, but no one thought that Earth would be destroyed. Look here through the telescope; do you see that red dot with the bright reddish orange *glow* around it?

The GRANDDAUGHTER looks through the telescope.

GRANDDAUGHTER: I see it.

ABUELA MARISOL: That's Earth. That was my home.

GRANDDAUGHTER: It looks like a shiny, beautiful red light in space. In school, we learned that Earth used to be called the Blue Planet. They showed us pictures of when the planet was blue, with water. Is that really true?

ABUELA MARISOL: Don't you get tired of my stories?

GRANDDAUGHTER: No, Abuela. I love to hear your stories. You're the only person left in the space station who remembers life on planet Earth.

ABUELA MARISOL: Sometimes at night, I look through the telescope, and I hope to see a blue planet again.

GRANDDAUGHTER: Tell me about the ocean.

ABUELA MARISOL: The beach was near my house in Puerto Rico. The sand was soft and white. The water was clear. I used to collect shells and rocks and bring them home.

GRANDDAUGHTER: And the sky was blue.

ABUELA MARISOL: Yes, it was. The most amazing and brightest sky-blue color … Earth was perfect – beautiful oceans, beaches, forests full of animals, rainforests full of rivers and waterfalls. There was a tree frog, the *coquí*, which made the most adorable sound …

GRANDDAUGHTER: Abuela, make the sound, sing like the *coquí*.

ABUELA MARISOL: *Coquí … coquí …*

GRANDDAUGHTER/ABUELA MARISOL: *Coquí … coquí …*

ABUELA MARISOL: There were farms that grew fruits and vegetables. We had everything we ever needed. We had a mango tree in our backyard. Can you imagine the largest and sweetest mangoes that you ever tasted? It was a perfect world until the greed of the corporations polluted the Earth. And then they declared nuclear war on each other for the resources.

GRANDDAUGHTER: You're lucky to be here, Abuela.

ABUELA MARISOL: Yes, I am. I love you, *querida*.

GRANDDAUGHTER: I love you too. HAPPY BIRTHDAY, Abuela Marisol!!

They hug.

ABUELA MARISOL: Thank you, my beautiful girl.

GRANDDAUGTHER: You're going to be seventy years old today.

ABUELA MARISOL: Seventy years. I've lived sixty years on this space station.

GRANDDAUGHTER: Make a wish for your birthday.

ABUELA MARISOL: I wish I could go back to a Blue Earth.

GRANDDAUGHTER: Me too. I wish I could go with you. *Mami* says we can go anywhere we want when we meditate.

ABUELA MARISOL: Your *mami* is right.

GRANDDAUGHTER: So, let's meditate … Close your eyes.

ABUELA MARISOL: Ok.

They both close their eyes.

GRANDDAUGHTER: Think about the place you want to go to.

ABUELA MARISOL: Ok.

GRANDDAUGHTER: What do you see?

ABUELA MARISOL: I see a white beach, blue ocean, I hear the waves … and I hear the *coquíes* …

GRANDDAUGHTER: *Coquí, coquí* …

Lights fade as the sounds of the waves and the sounds of the coquíes get louder.

◊ ◊ ◊

Carmen Rivera is a New York-born, Puerto Rican playwright and screenwriter. Her play, *La Gringa,* which was part of the OBIE Award Winning Series "New Voices," premiered in 1996 and is now the second longest-running play in Off-Broadway history after *The Fantasticks.* Both English and Spanish versions are available at Concord Theatrical Productions. She is also co-director of Educational Play Productions (EPP), which brings plays about social issues into public schools.
www.carmenrivera-writer.com
www.educationalplayproductions.com

HURRICANE

Juan C. Sanchez

This piece was inspired by Hurricane Andrew, which struck Florida, Louisiana, and the Bahamas in 1992. The greatest impact was felt in South Florida's Homestead, passing through the city, and stripping many homes of all but their concrete foundations. After four months of the city's residents living in tents, a school was quickly rebuilt to get students back in class. My piece, Hurricane, imagines one teacher's experience on that first day of school.

◊ ◊ ◊

TEACHER: As I drove to the school this morning, I felt overwhelmed. First of all, the drive was chaotic, with no traffic lights or stop signs and the military guiding and controlling everything. Debris and fallen trees were still lining the streets. When I passed by Carlo's Pizza – our go-to spot for date nights – I had to pull over. To catch my breath, you know? Because it was gone. The whole thing is gone. And so, I'm in the car, breathing, trying to stay calm. But I can't get over the pizza place gone. And not just the pizza place, the whole block is gone. And then I'm crying for Carlo, for the city, for the neighborhood, for you, for me, for the lives lost, for those who are still missing … and then it really hits me: What the hell am I going to say to the kids? These sixth graders who've been living in tents or shelters for the last four months now because they lost their homes, their possessions … their sense of security. And today, they're getting bussed to this brand-new school, and not just the regular students, but kids from other districts, strangers to each other, and to me, their teacher … for who knows how long? And I had the lesson plan, of course. Ideas about turning this disaster into a learning opportunity to help them understand and process, but when I get to the school, it's *chaos*. Cameras everywhere. Reporters, microphones, photographers. And bodyguards. And at the center of it all – in the middle of this circus – is the governor, yeah, the governor … *and* the senator … yeah, *that* one, posing for pictures, shaking hands and talking about budgets, about how they worked a miracle to get the school ready for this opening. I wanted to tell them that this catastrophic hurricane was a product of a changing climate, a result of the greenhouse gases we've been pumping into the atmosphere for decades, but I didn't. I couldn't. Not today. Not on deaf ears. Look, you know me. As a teacher I believe in the power of education. But these two, and those like them … their stubborn resistance to the truth, their dismissal, their inability to grasp that human activity does, in fact … I mean, their refusal to even mitigate the effects that climate … and it's there, the studies, the facts, the proposals … And now they're at the school, looking sharp and shiny, in our vulnerable community, which was all but decimated because … But forget them for now … it's what happened in the classroom that's important. So, forget them.

Now, the classroom was overcrowded with familiar faces, and new ones, like I expected. I gotta tell you, it took self-control to not lose it, you know? Most of them looked happy, if a little rattled … even the new kids. So that was a relief, that they were – I never told anyone this, but, uh … during the storm, when the eye was hitting, with the thunder and lightning and stuff flying outside … and that sound like a horn, like a wail, like a scream from some deep, dark place … I ran into the closet with my spouse and our three-year-old … and in that closet, with a little radio between us, as we held each other, the three of us … our eyes shut tight … holding each other for dear life … right at that moment when I was the most scared I've ever been … I saw the face of every single student I ever had in class. The face of every student who's ever walked by me in the halls. As we held each other, as we protected each other from danger … I prayed for the students. That each one of them was safe right now … feeling protected, being shielded … being *held. (beat)* Part of me wanted to tell them that, so they knew what they meant to me. How important their life, their safety, is to all of us, and, uh … but, of course, I didn't. I mean, the minute I said the word "hurricane," their faces froze. The room went silent. That's when I really felt what they were experiencing inside: They were nervous, still scared, even a little guilty that they were in a building with running water and electricity, while some of their families didn't have it. And we stood inside that silence for a few moments. Until this one student – one of the new students – raised their hand and shared, with a breaking, cracking voice, that their older brother was still missing. The student went on to describe the brother in case we saw him, or ran into him, and I … I mean, the brother was probably … and I didn't know what to say. What *could* I say? But I didn't have to say anything. Because without any prompting, or any words from anyone … every child in that classroom stood up, walked to the student, huddled around them, and hugged them. It was like the instinct to take care of each other was in them … and they knew what had to be done. The instinct to comfort, it was … it lived inside them naturally. And as they loved and cared for their fellow student … I'm … well, I'm thinking about the governor and the senator, and I wonder: When did *they* lose that instinct? Where did their sense of community go? When – and *who* – stopped them from growing? Who made them forget, I mean – And the door flies open. Camera crew rushes in, followed by the governor and the senator, who want pictures with the children. And they're oblivious … and I … still in my thoughts, I feel this emptiness take over me and I just … cry. A little. But I look at the kids again, still embracing their hurting, worried, frightened classmate … someone they have never met before … and I don't feel so lost anymore.

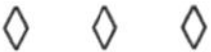

Juan C. Sanchez is a Cuban-born, Miami-based playwright dedicated to writing stories that explore the cultural diversity and social issues of Miami. He has written plays for a variety of platforms – from traditional theatre stages to immersive, site-specific performances set in historical motels, virtual stages, climate-change themed productions, and radio plays. Plays include the *Miami Motel Stories* series, *Long Distance Affair*, *Versace Era*, *A Grey Divide*, *Paradise Motel*, and others.

A LITTLE GREEN
Charly Evon Simpson

When I think about good things and beginning again, I think about my grandparents. Looking back to them helps me look forward. They could see possibility in despair, change amidst stagnancy, growth alongside death.

Characters
GP: A grandparent
GC: A grandchild

Setting
A climbable tree on the top of a hill.

◊ ◊ ◊

GP and GC stand at the bottom of a tree.

GP: Can you climb?

GC nods and begins climbing the tree.
GC gets nice and high and then looks down to GP.

GC: Can you get up here?

GP: Does the tree feel sturdy?

GC bounces a bit. The tree sways.

GC: For now, I think.

GP: Alrighty then.

GP carefully takes hold of a branch and carefully steps on the trunk.
And then they breathe in and out.

GC: I think you can do it.

GP: I used to be able to do it.

GC: I think you can do it now.

GP: I might fall.

GC: I might fall!

GP: My fall may cause permanent damage.

GP lets go of the branch and takes a few steps back from the tree.

Tell me what you see.

GC: Where?

GP: Out there. Over this hill. In the distance.

GC looks into the distance.

GC: Well, I see the forest.

GP: What do you see about the forest?

GC: Trees. Lots of trees.

GP: And what do those trees look like?

GC: Depends on where you look in the forest.

GP: Mmhmm. Tell me more.

During this, GP attempts again to climb the tree several times.

GC: Well, it is so big. It looks like it goes on forever. For miles and miles, just trees. And some of the trees are thick and short and others are tall and lanky. And some are green, but a lot are … black. Gray. They look like sticks.

GP: Like sticks?

GC: Yes, like sticks. Those are from the fire?

GP: Yeah, they are.

GC looks out.
GP successfully manages to pull themself up to a lower branch.

GC: You can make it higher.

GP: That's ok. Look again in the trees, in the ones that look like sticks.

GC: Ok …

GP: Look amidst the sticks.

GC: Like in-between them?

GP: Yeah.

GC: They're so far away.

GP: Use your superhuman eyes.

GC: I don't have superhuman eyes.

GP: We all do. There's so much we can see if we actually look.

GC tries to look with their superhuman eyes.

GC: I don't see anything.

GP: Fine. Close 'em.

GC: My eyes?

GP: Yes.

GC closes their eyes.
GP keeps their eyes open, staring into the distance.

Nothing has made as much sense as the air
As the wind moving the clouds above
As the sun hitting the leaves just so
As the steadiness of the waves hitting the shore
As stopping and breathing and taking it all in

Do you know what I mean?

GC: No.

GP: Hopefully one day you will.

Many times, along the way, life has not made much sense
And a pause and a look up
or a look down or a look forward or a look back
has provided all that I needed.

GC: You probably need more than that. What about food?

GP: Sure, sure. I'm speaking broad strokes. Are your eyes still closed?

GC: Yes.

GP: Ok, keep them closed but begin to look down and up and forward and back.

GC: What?

GP: Eyes closed. And look.

GC: But –

GP: No buts. Just look.

GC grumbles.
They do their best to look back and forward, up and down.
They do this by exaggerating their head movement as they try to look in different directions.

What about looking while staying still?

GC: C'mon.

GP: Try.

GC deeply sighs and tries to look again. This time GC is still. So still. And then:

GC: When I look forward, I see the trees. The ones that look like sticks.

GP: Ok.

GC: When I look more forward, in-between the trees, I can begin to make out the ground.

GP: Good. And?

GC: And, on the ground, there's a lot of dirt and dust and ash and …

GC stops.

GP: And?

GC: A little green.

GP: Ah. Now open your eyes.

GC listens.

Do you see the green in between the trees?

GC looks hard. They squint.

GC: I'm not sure.

GP: That's ok. You know it's there. You know it's possible. Sometimes you have to look in other ways. It's like how I can't get as high as you in this tree, so I have to use my mind's eye.

GC: But how do you know if it's real?

GP shrugs.

GP: Sometimes it won't be real until you make it real, but if you don't see it, if you can't picture it, then how are you going to go about making it real?

GC: I'm not sure I get it.

GP: You will.

GP exhales.

Alright now. My bones need a rest. You want to come down?

GC thinks and then shakes their head.

GC: I'm going to keep looking.

And with that, GP carefully climbs out of the tree.
But GC stays, eyes closed, looking back and forward, up and down.

◊ ◊ ◊

Charly Evon Simpson is a New York-based, Black American playwright, TV writer, and teacher. Her work has been seen and/or developed with Vineyard Theatre, WP Theater, Ensemble Studio Theatre, The Eugene O'Neill Theater Center, South Coast Repertory, and others. She's a recipient of the Paula Vogel Playwriting Award and Lanford Wilson Award. In TV, she has worked on shows for Showtime, HBO, and Netflix. She holds a BA from Brown University, an MSt from University of Oxford, New College, and an MFA from Hunter College.
www.charlyevonsimpson.com

THE COMMITTEE TO EXPROPRIATE, A REVENGE FANTASY

Darrah Teitel

I've lived in a rental building on the edge of one of the wealthiest neighborhoods in Toronto since 2019. Throughout the pandemic, my young family and I spent hours walking up and down tree-lined streets filled with massive mansions, trying to spy into their windows through massive hedges, wondering about the wealth hoarded inside and the people who possess it. This practice has led to a game I play with my partner: We design our plans for which mansions we would expropriate and how many families and workers these homes would be given over to. We design intentional communities with daycares, food co-ops, and massive communal backyards that include all the public swimming pools, tennis courts, food and flower gardens, a neighborhood could wish for. We imagine a political reality, not too long from now, where climate catastrophe and excellent organizing have led to a genuine eco-socialist government being democratically elected to make urgent changes in society. We call this fantasy game: The Committee to Expropriate. It's the inspiration for this play.

◊ ◊ ◊

In the entranceway of a residential mansion in a wealthy neighborhood in any big North American city. A man in his fifties answers the doorbell while speaking at the same time to someone through a Bluetooth headset. A woman in her mid-thirties, wearing a casual but stylish green uniform, is standing on his stoop.

DAVE: No.

FLORA: Yes.

DAVE: Get out.

FLORA: Today is the day. *(checks notes)* Mr. Sherman? David?

DAVE, *to phone*: Fuck. Listen, Christine? I've got to call you back.

FLORA: Can I come in?

DAVE, *to phone*: Because the fucking expropriation Nazi's on my porch. *(to FLORA)* No! You can't come in. What do you think? This is my house.

FLORA: I'm coming in.

DAVE, *to phone*: She's coming in ...

FLORA: It's extremely hot out here. *(the cooled air hits her face)* Wow ... It's like a walk-in freezer in here. What's your AC at?

DAVE: I have a private generator.

FLORA: Bullshit, this is above code limits for AC, for sure. Oof, it's really nice ... Did you hang up your call? *(he doesn't respond)* Good. Do you need to see a warrant? Are you ready to go?

DAVE, *starts to videotape himself*: My name is David Sherman on April 2nd 2036 and I am invoking my Charter right under Section 6 and under the civil statute –

FLORA: That's not going to work. Did you watch that stupid thing that told you that this will work?

DAVE: I have a Charter right to private –

FLORA: It's not going to work. I'm sorry. The Charter was torn up years ago. You must have heard ... Those statutes don't exist anymore. Climate Emergency Measures Act has been in place since then, and I'm a government agent, so ... You don't need me to explain all this. Aren't you a lawyer?

DAVE: Yes.

FLORA: Good. We can save a lot of time and distress if you accept what is happening, Mr. Sherman.

DAVE: Please don't talk to me like I'm a –

FLORA: Well, it sounded for a moment like you are confused.

DAVE: I'm not confused. I'm …

FLORA: What?

DAVE: Defiant!

FLORA: Ha! Sorry, that's funny. You're not packed, Dave.

DAVE: I'm not funny.

FLORA: There are two ways for this to go, as I'm sure you and your neighbors have observed: Either you vacate this house with your belongings today and allow us to seal the door in advance of state-issued cleaning, subdivision renovation, and reassignment, or we forcibly remove you from your home and seal the door. The difference between these two scenarios is that if we forcibly remove you, you forfeit the contents of this house for us to reassign to the new occupants and/or liquidate in an estate sale, the proceeds of which will be given to the new occupants. It's entirely up to you.

DAVE: You think I'm just going to give you everything?

FLORA: Not me, Dave. This will all go to the three families who will be living here from now on. *(checks notes)* The Maceda-Maciels, the Panoses, and the Brogans.

DAVE: I'd rather die.

FLORA: That's your choice, but have you considered what you will do with all this stuff?

DAVE: Excuse me?

FLORA: You are going to a one-bedroom suite in Saint James Town, correct?

DAVE: No. Incorrect.

FLORA: It's big for one person, Dave! Twelve hundred square feet! How'd you swing that?

DAVE: I have two kids.

FLORA: One weekend a month … Anyway, the floor plan will accommodate a tiny fraction of the belongings you've accumulated here over what must be generations of wealth hoarding.

DAVE: Fuck you.

FLORA: I suggest you choose the contents of one or two rooms. *(looks around)* No. One. Max. And before you make a stupid choice to rent three trucks and schlep stuff out like a madman, remember there are no air-conditioned storage facilities anymore. Those have been outlawed. The average temperature is above fifty degrees Celsius for more than eighty days in a row most years and you can add twenty degrees inside any storage can. Your belongings will be destroyed, Dave. All the wood will be eaten by maggots, all the stuffing by moths and mites, all the appliances and electronics will just melt. Let it go, Dave. Let it go, like Elsa said. It will be used. It will be loved. It's needed. Can you see it in your heart to do that?

DAVE: Over my dead –

FLORA: For the Maceda-Maciels, the Panoses, and the Brogans. They're good people.

DAVE: You're fucking monsters.

FLORA: They're not. Maybe I am. I'm not them. I have much more power in this world than they do. At any rate, it's your choice. I'll wait here.

DAVE: Say that again?

FLORA: I'll wait here.

DAVE: No, say: It's your choice.

FLORA: Why?

DAVE: Just say it. Smiling like that …

FLORA, *smiling brilliantly*: It's your choice.

DAVE: You … I …

FLORA: Yes.

DAVE: I know you?

FLORA: Yes. I was hoping you'd recognize.

DAVE: Holy shit. What's your name? Francis?

FLORA: Flora.

DAVE: Every six weeks for ten years. "… it's your choice, Mister."

FLORA: "Almond, nougat, or truffle?"

DAVE: "It's your choice …" Well, fuck me …

FLORA: Yes.

DAVE: Andrea, my bitch ex-wife, would tell me not to open the door, but I always did. Ha! I liked you.

FLORA: You liked the almond bars.

DAVE: Flora … Did you pocket the money or did you actually give it to … what was it? A church? You people are all Catholic, right?

FLORA: Right. All of us.

DAVE: I didn't care, you know. I knew you might be pocketing the cash. Let her have it, I thought. If you had the gall to come to my door and lie about a church charity for three-dollar chocolate bars … Far as I'm concerned, you worked for it.

FLORA: Thanks.

DAVE: Unlike now. This is just theft.

FLORA: I worked for this too, Dave.

DAVE: No – I did. I worked for this house. This sofa.

FLORA: You're a lawyer in your father's firm, right?

DAVE: You think lawyers don't work?

FLORA: How hard did they work for their client … Suncor? Suncor stands out on their list of clients, doesn't it? It's fucking hot outside, Dave. You gotta agree. Your client must agree it's way too hot, right? But then, when were you last outside for more than five minutes?

DAVE: Know what? You're right. We worked hard and well. *(points his finger out the window)* Proof fucking positive that I'm a hard worker.

FLORA: Ooh. Dark. I'm getting to you, huh? I'm getting to the real you. I like this part.

DAVE: Don't say we didn't work. We fucking won.

FLORA: My mother worked too.

DAVE: Which house?

FLORA: That one.

DAVE: The Blair's?

FLORA: Yes.

DAVE, *collapses, resigned*: They were the first. You came for them first.

FLORA: Yes. *(smiles brilliantly)* So? Did you decide? It's your choice.

◊ ◊ ◊

Darrah Teitel is a playwright, socialist, and labor organizer living in Toronto. She is a graduate of The National Theatre School of Canada's Playwriting program. Her most recent credits include *Forever Young* (Great Canadian Theatre Company, 2022), *The Omnibus Bill* (Counterpoint Players, 2019), *Behaviour* (Great Canadian Theatre Company, 2019), *Corpus* (Teesri Duniya, 2014), and *The Apology* (Alberta Theatre Projects, 2013). Darrah is the winner of several awards for her plays and has been nominated for Dora, META, Betty Mitchell and Prix Rideau awards for best new play. She was a member of the 2007, 2011, and 2012 Banff Playwright's Colony, The MacDowell Colony, The Gros Morne Playwrights Residency, and the Asylum Arts Peleh Family Artists Residency.

WE ALMOST DIED, WAITING

Chris Thorpe

I think a lot about what story a better future would tell about us, if it looked back at the stories we told, and how we told them. I love Octavia Butler's *Parable of the Sower*, and it's definitely influenced the form here.

◊ ◊ ◊

To be performed by as many people as there are, in whatever way you want to do it.

In the movies we used to make
There was usually a human –
Uniquely blessed, uniquely able
To stand against the savagery
Unleashed by the end-times –
To say, no, this is wrong
Stop eating your neighbors
Stop crowding into your compounds
With whatever makeshift weapons you've collected.

I am here to lead you to a better place, they'd say –
I will clean the dirty politics
Pilot the plane out of the fatal dive –
I will pull your family from the burning woods
Or twist molecules into an antidote –
I have this innate spark, you see
That emerges, equips me
To illuminate the path through chaos
So, take my hand, I'll show you.

And this taught us to expect them –
That moment, those inspiring words
Falling out of the clouds
Emerging from the rubble
To dance through the web of bullets –
They were coming to save us

Sometimes by averting disaster
Sometimes by rebuilding after it –
Always the center of gravity.

So, the thought no one was coming
Crawled in, almost too late –
Our minds, still open to the savior
Couldn't register the hand-holds
We'd been falling past so long –
Eyes scanning the horizon, we were
Waiting for the grand entrance
Focused on the distant point
We thought salvation came from.

It wasn't till the ground came rushing
And we saw it coming, those last few seconds
The trick became apparent –
Projecting this concentrated hope –
The best of ourselves, outside of ourselves
Had led us powerless to disaster –
Our own arms caught us, and we hung
Half-joyful with the thought –
Nobody is coming after all.

So come outside now, kids –
Now today's heat has faded
And the air so free of dust for once
We can see each other's faces
In the light we've stored so carefully –
Kick your shoes off in new soil we made
Under the new trees we constructed to live in it –
Come and hear the story that explains
Why we don't tell those stories anymore.

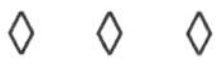

Chris Thorpe is a writer and performer from Manchester, UK. His work has touched on nationality and borders, political and social systems and their relationship to confirmation bias, our collective psychology around the climate crisis, and most recently, the construction of cultural hierarchies and Iranian pop music (*Things Hidden Since The Foundation of the World* with Javaad

Alipoor), and nuclear disarmament and global diplomacy (*A Family Business* and *Talking About The Fire* with Staatstheater Mainz and China Plate).

AND WHEN I LOOK INTO THE FUTURE, I SEE NOTHING

Harley Vale

When our shields of Hope and Wishful Thinking are finally set down, and the cherished but scientifically and politically impossible mirages of bright green futures are wrestled from our minds, all that is left is the suffering and potential of this present moment. The world screams for us to move beyond sheer activism and into real struggle. We fight, then, because we must. We fight because to do anything else means certain death. We fight to win, because no *deus ex machina* is coming to save us. Just beyond the utter terror that this new knowledge brings, rests the possibility for unimaginable joy, love, and life – if only we reach out and grab them.

This play is for Tortuguita (Little Turtle), a warrior murdered by the Georgia State Patrol for defending the Weelaunee Forest, and for all of the heroes, human and nonhuman, doing everything they can to fight for life on this planet.

If this play is paired with a political action, I challenge you to think beyond the world of petitions and donations and into the realm of tangible actions that adequately address the scale of the problems we are facing. Push beyond your capacity for daring.

Characters

ACTIVIST
CLOTHO/CHILD
LACHESIS
ATROPOS

Notes

All characters can be played by anyone of any age, gender, or ethnicity (adjust the pronouns as needed). The Child can be played by Clotho or, if a separate actor is used, Clotho will accompany her. The Fates are predatory, impish, and brutal. Their dialogue comes fast, almost overlapping with one another at all times as if only one being were speaking. This play exists on the verge of a nightmare; keep it scary, strange, magical, and vicious. Comfort must be earned here.

On pronunciation: The first spell is a combination of several divination spells from the Greek Magical Papyri; a summoning of the Fates in standard Greek; and the naming of the Fates in Greek, Norwegian, and Latin. The spells from the Greek Magical Papyri "are written in Old Coptic, which used Greek letters, so you will do best if you think Greek" for pronunciation.[1]

The prayer of protection is an ancient Greek spell that wards against evil.[2]

◊ ◊ ◊

A freshly clear-cut forest under a full moon.

An ACTIVIST sits on the ground, surrounded by the elements of an ancient ritual. He is quite bloody, beaten, bruised, and dirty, his Greenpeace shirt torn. He mutters the following spell ad nauseum.

ACTIVIST: *Eeim to eim alale'p barbariath menebreio arbathiao'th ioue'l iae'l oue'ne'iie mesommias, na mou érthei to moiraí kai as min fýgei méchri na tin apeleftheróso. O Klóstis, o Parachoritís, kai to Akampto. Skald, Verthandi, og Urth. Nona, Decima, et Morta. Evlogiménos Moiraí. Harmiouth lailam cho'ouch arsenophre' phre'u phtha harchentechtha.*

A clock tower somewhere strikes three. The final toll sounds eerie and strange. Clouds roll over the moon. The ACTIVIST stops, his breath suddenly cold.

He stands. The sound of rustling, of a branch snapping.

ACTIVIST: Who's there?

The wind blows. The ACTIVIST mutters a prayer of protection:

ACTIVIST: *Aski kataski haix tetrax damnameneus aision.*

A breathy, raspy laugh from the darkness, soon followed by a second elsewhere, then a third.

[1] For more information on pronunciation and the Greek Magical Papyri, visit https://hermetic.com/pgm/ecloga-I.

[2] For more information on this spell, read *The Witches' Book of the Dead* (2011, p. 138) by Christian Day, and Craig Conley's *Magic Words: A Dictionary* (2008, p. 111).

ACTIVIST: Who's there?

CLOTHO: *You*

LACHESIS: Summoned

ATROPOS: *Us* …

LACHESIS: Did you not?

ACTIVIST: I …

CLOTHO: Poor boy.

ATROPOS: Poor, sad boy.

CLOTHO: Has Fate been unkind.

LACHESIS: So unkind.

ACTIVIST: Show yourself.

They do.

ACTIVIST: My god.

CLOTHO: You look tired.

ATROPOS: At the end of your rope.

LACHESIS: So lost.

CLOTHO: So needy.

ATROPOS: So desperate.

LACHESIS: What is it you desire?

ACTIVIST: I want to know the future.

The Fates fade back into the darkness, their laughter airy and echoing through this dreamscape. The wind picks up with a brewing storm, and their voices seem to fly in from all around the space.

LACHESIS: This fool.

ATROPOS: We don't give that gift to anyone.

CLOTHO: Not to anyone.

ACTIVIST: Please! I need to see …

ATROPOS: Oh, he *needs* it!

ACTIVIST: When I look now, I see nothing. It's empty, it's a black hole, I / don't –

LACHESIS: Oh no, the mortal's divination powers are failing?

CLOTHO: It sounds like they're working just fine.

ACTIVIST: I need to know if we can win.

LACHESIS: Win?

CLOTHO: The humans always win.

ATROPOS: But everyone else …

LACHESIS: What a waste of our time.

ACTIVIST: Please! If there's no future for us, then I'm not going to stick around. So, I need to know.

LACHESIS: Is that so?

ATROPOS: He bluffs.

He pulls out a gun.

ACTIVIST: I'm not. I can't do this anymore.

LACHESIS: Oh, look at him!

CLOTHO: I think he's serious.

LACHESIS: Well, don't waste the bullet.

They take his gun.

ATROPOS: I can cut your string right now.

LACHESIS: If you'd like.

CLOTHO: One less thread for Gaia to choke on.

A glowing thread is produced.

LACHESIS: Won't she be pleased.

ATROPOS: Look at his life.

LACHESIS: So pretty.

ATROPOS: So marred.

LACHESIS: So taut.

ATROPOS: Just one snip …

CLOTHO appears just behind him.

CLOTHO: Boo.

The ACTIVIST jumps. The Fates cackle.

LACHESIS: So brave, this one.

ATROPOS: So stalwart.

CLOTHO: A natural hero.

LACHESIS: Ha!

ATROPOS: We used to have *real* heroes.

CLOTHO: Remember them?

LACHESIS: Where did the swords go?

CLOTHO: The ferocity?

ATROPOS: We need them back.

LACHESIS: True heroes.

ATROPOS: To give my hands a rest.

LACHESIS: Not this pathetic excuse for courage.

ATROPOS: Look at his signs.

CLOTHO: Look at his petitions.

LACHESIS: The little songs he sings.

The Fates laugh and laugh.

ACTIVIST: Show me the future.

ATROPOS: No.

ACTIVIST: Just a part of it.

LACHESIS: No.

ACTIVIST: Humans can't live without hope. Without dreams. / Without –

ATROPOS: They live plenty.

ACTIVIST: I can't go on like this! Nothing's working.

CLOTHO: Your signs and marches aren't working?

ATROPOS: How shocking.

LACHESIS: Spread the news.

CLOTHO: Warn Hercules!

LACHESIS/CLOTHO: Don't petition the Titans!

ACTIVIST: I've tried everything.

ATROPOS: No, you haven't.

LACHESIS: Not even close.

They put the gun back in his hands and point it outwards.

CLOTHO: Pick up your sword, child.

LACHESIS: There's so much you haven't tried.

ATROPOS: So much you're afraid to try.

LACHESIS: Try.

LACHESIS/CLOTHO: Try.

ALL THREE: Try again.

ACTIVIST: I'm a pacifist.

ATROPOS: You're a coward.

LACHESIS: For it's not your home on the line.

CLOTHO: Not your family.

ATROPOS: Not your life.

ALL FOUR: But violence solves nothing.

The Fates mock him.

ACTIVIST: It doesn't.

CLOTHO: Tell that to the violent.

LACHESIS: Tell that to the dead.

ATROPOS: To the Right Whale Nation.

LACHESIS: The dying.

CLOTHO: The Golden Frog Nation.

ATROPOS: The Weelaunee Nation.

LACHESIS: The Javan Rhino Nation.

CLOTHO: The Ogoni Nation.

LACHESIS: The Socorro Dove Nation.

CLOTHO: Oh, the Socorro Dove.

ATROPOS: There is a true hero.

LACHESIS: Worthy of the stars.

CLOTHO: Worthy of honor.

ATROPOS: She fought like hell too.

LACHESIS: All of the Dove People did.

ATROPOS: They, whose future's truly been stolen.

LACHESIS: They, who have nothing left.

CLOTHO: Still, she fights.

ATROPOS: With all she has.

CLOTHO: With a ferocity you'll never understand.

ATROPOS: She thinks not of *peace*

LACHESIS: But of *life*.

Another bell toll, far off in the distance.

CLOTHO: We leave now to cut her string.

LACHESIS: The final string.

ATROPOS: The last one.

CLOTHO: We mourn her.

LACHESIS: How we mourn her.

ATROPOS: *Gods,* we mourn her.

LACHESIS: But not you.

CLOTHO: Never you.

ATROPOS: My hands hurt. My shears grow dull.

ALL THREE: I'm so tired.

ATROPOS: Leave us be, coward.

ALL THREE: We have grave work to do.

They turn to leave.

ACTIVIST: You're the coward.

ATROPOS wheels around and smacks him across the face. Hard. With righteous anger. The wind picks up.

ATROPOS: You disgusting *fool.*

ALL THREE: YOU WANT TO SEE YOUR FUTURE?

ATROPOS: Fine.

ALL THREE: Here it is.

The Fates throw a small book at his feet.

CLOTHO: Open it!

LACHESIS: Take a look!

ATROPOS: But first a warning:

ALL THREE: This Is How It Ends.

The world changes. Red and blue flashing lights. The Fates are riot cops. ATROPOS is holding the gun now to the ACTIVIST's head. Loud chaos of police over a loudspeaker and people screaming.

DISEMBODIED MALE COP VOICE: Get fucking down.

Chaos.

DISEMBODIED MALE COP VOICE: I SWEAR TO GOD, I WILL FUCKING KILL YOU.

Shouting. ATROPOS pulls the trigger. Gunshot. Dark.
The world changes. A fiery hellscape.

CLOTHO: This Is How It Ends. Fires stealing all you know.

People screaming all around them, burning alive.

CLOTHO: Still do you fight?

The world changes. A massive storm, floods washing away a town.

LACHESIS: This Is How It Ends. Waters, rising, overflow. Still do you fight?

The world changes. A prison cell door closes over the ACTIVIST. Sounds of sorrow, of pain.

ATROPOS: This Is How It Ends. Damned down a dark, dank hole below. Still do you fight?

The world changes. A beautiful sunny day. Birds singing. Wildlife flourishing. All is good.

LACHESIS: This Is How It Ends.

ATROPOS: Everything destined to work out.

LACHESIS: Still do you fight?

ATROPOS: You want to see the future?

LACHESIS: Then here.

LACHESIS/ATROPOS: Talk to it.

The world changes. A desolate wasteland. A CHILD (CLOTHO) huddles around a garbage fire. When she speaks, a child's voice echoes through the dream, horrific and out of place in her mouth. The wind is cutting and merciless.

ATROPOS: This is how it ends.

ACTIVIST: Who are you?

The CHILD pulls out a makeshift knife crafted from the shards of a solar panel.

CHILD: Stay back.

ACTIVIST: Ok. Ok, I –

CHILD: STAY BACK.

He steps away.

ACTIVIST: I'm not going to hurt you.

ATROPOS: Ask her what she's burning.

ACTIVIST: What are you burning?

CHILD: You.

ACTIVIST: What?

CHILD: It's a curse. On you and everyone like you. For not doing enough. For letting this happen. I pray this wind carries it back to you.

A bell tolls.

ACTIVIST: I tried to –

CHILD: STAY BACK.

LACHESIS: Ask her what she's burning.

ACTIVIST: What are you burning.

CHILD: An offering. To you and everyone like you. You who toppled the gods before they could consume the world. You saved us. I pray that you find your peace, and that we may once again reclaim your strength.

A bell tolls.

ACTIVIST: I don't –

CHILD: STAY BACK.

ATROPOS: Ask her what she's burning.

ACTIVIST: What are you burning.

CHILD: It's a curse. On you and everyone like you. For not doing enough. For letting this happen. I pray this wind carries it back to you.

The CHILD's voice echoes on the wind as she and the fire fade into darkness.

THE FATES, *whispering*: Still do you fight.

A bell tolls.

ATROPOS: This is not a question of future, but one of *character*.

LACHESIS: The future is not yours to know.

CLOTHO: This is all you get.

LACHES: And here –

ATROPOS: in the present –

LACHESIS: there's suffering enough for a *billion* heroes.

CLOTHO: So much to be done.

ACTIVIST: I … *(pause)* And if I'm afraid?

Pause.

LACHESIS, *softer*: Then be afraid. But be afraid –

THE FATES: and *fight*.

LACHESIS: Because it is right.

CLOTHO: Not because you can win.

LACHESIS: But because you *must*.

ATROPOS: Fight for the suffering of now.

CLOTHO: The death of now.

LACHESIS: The murder of entire worlds before your eyes.

ATROPOS: That must be enough.

ACTIVIST: What do you want me to do.

ALL THREE: You're the hero.

They press the gun back into the ACTIVIST's hands.

CLOTHO: Get creative.

LACHESIS: Find others.

ATROPOS: Make it big.

LACHESIS: Make it count.

CLOTHO: Think not of peace

ATROPOS: But of *life*.

CLOTHO: Look at him.

He stands shell-shocked and frightened.

LACHESIS: So strong.

CLOTHO: So sure.

ATROPOS: So whole.

CLOTHO: Born anew.

ATROPOS: Alive again.

LACHESIS: You want your future so badly, hero?

THE FATES: THEN TAKE IT.

They vanish, leaving the ACTIVIST alone with the book and his gun.

◊ ◊ ◊

Harley Vale is a horror writer, blues musician, and biodiversity conservationist living in New York City.

50 WAYS TO END MOTHER EARTH – IN UNDER FIVE MINUTES!

Kirby Vicente

I'm actually inspired by the idea that if we put things on a very tight deadline, maybe that's where significant changes begin. I believe great stories should not be confined to structured narratives, especially if we aim to sharpshoot some facts straight to our audiences (and to our players in this context). This was also inspired by a conversation with a friend on what will motivate her to start taking action for the planet, to which she answered "fear."

For context, most of the numbered parts are *based on facts* and come from real-life events that happened (I don't even know why, but HEY) in the Philippines. *Players who are unlucky enough to choose this play are highly encouraged to inject their own local context into this script.* Feel free to replace, shuffle, and play with all fifty parts. *There are no wrong moves in performing this piece.*

The challenge is to perform all fifty parts in just five minutes. If you succeed, then pat yourself on the back, hug your co-actors and director (with CONSENT), grab a beer or something, and prepare to do it all over again.

Whether you finish or not is the point of the script.

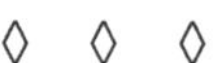

1. Proclaim that the climate crisis you're currently experiencing is fake news.
2. Even better, just keep undermining it. Believe in what politicians say about the climate crisis. They PROBABLY KNOW WAY BETTER than any of us. EVER!
3. Build, Build, BUILD! For mobility, for economic growth, for the golden age of infrastructure, for more buildings, for, for, for MORE BUILDINGS, basically buildings because they look cooler than trees.
4. If there's an oil spill, just ignore it. Because as Marcos Jr. said, "So there's no need. You see, there's no need to organize something for everything."

5. And if there's climate change, let the farmers ADJUST their crop schedules. Because they DEFINITELY NEED to adjust to the times, RIGHT?
6. Join Global Summits, write a script for your speech, or hire a writer instead because you're not that articulate about the global climate crisis, and finally look good for like a week or so.
7. When NGOs call you out on your empty promises, just ignore them.
8. Displace farmers.
9. Displace Indigenous peoples.
10. Displace squatters.
11. Invest more in foreign estate rather than actually address the climate situation.
12. Build a fake beach in Manila.
13. Build a casino near the fake beach in Manila.
14. Let foreign investors own more land on the fake beach near the casino in Manila.
15. Allot millions for the fake beach's maintenance.
16. Clean up our beaches AKA attract more foreign estates and displace local establishment owners FOR THE ECONOMY.
17. Invest more in environmentally unfriendly reclamation projects FOR THE ECONOMY.
18. And just say that you have mitigating systems for these reclamation projects and be VERY VAGUE ABOUT IT.
19. Smoke a pack of cigarettes every day. And make sure to throw the cigarette butts everywhere.
20. Or vape.
21. Or use every e-cigarette as long as there is smoke (except for the nebulizers of our hard-breathing friends).
22. When you buy more "eco-friendly" products. (Most of them are scams and just weak attempts at corporate social responsibility – GET OUT OF OUR FACE!)
23. When you stomp on plants.
24. When you don't hug trees.
25. When you drink a lot of alcohol and don't recycle your bottles for a sustainable art school project that is due on Monday.
26. When you say that you hate trees! Or everything about nature.
27. When you're not paying attention. Take notes, my friend.
28. Make a political campaign ad where you throw trash in the river and attempt to make fake footage of you cleaning it – you BASTARD.
29. Laugh at kids when they speak up about the climate crisis. You've been warned Greta Thunberg haters.

30. When you enjoy too much almond milk and oat milk. Stop killing the bees, my friends. Yes, they are harmful to the bees – look it up!
31. When you kill eco-defenders. The Philippines remains one of the most dangerous places for eco-defenders and activists.
32. When you kill farmers.
33. When you kill people just for your mining operations to continue.
34. When we constantly believe that bettering the economy will always be at the expense of the environment.
35. When we participate in shady foreign deals to "address" the water crisis by building a dam while simultaneously displacing communities near that dam site.
36. When we make more spaces for the rich and none for the poor.
37. When we bank on empty promises to address climate change.
38. When we get angry about all of these things and we don't do something about this anger.
39. When we hesitate to take action.
40. When we keep on waiting for higher powers to lead us to this change, for divine intervention, for politicians to finally get off their asses.
41. When we stop singing songs like *We Are the World*.
42. For real. It's because we're not taking it seriously.
43. When we let politicians get away with these transgressions towards us, our fellowmen, and the environment.
44. When we laugh at young people when they do some crazy shit just to make ignorant adults listen. Like that tomato sauce thrown at the Van Gogh painting.
45. When we believe that kids like those are just clout-chasers.
46. Or misled.
47. Crazy even.
48. When we don't see the point of all these things we've just told you.
49. When we are comfortable enough to finish this show, go back to our own homes, and live life the same way as ever before.
50. That's where we fail. When we stop talking about the elephant in the room and just willingly put ourselves in this slow-burn mass genocide.

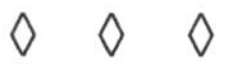

Kirby Vicente (they/them) is a performance maker and storyteller with a stark fascination for participatory work and multi/anti-disciplinary research. Channeling the erratic, explosive, and inquisitive energy of play, their creative practice revolves around various disciplines, embracing their desire to become a multi-hyphenated artist and storyteller. They are one of the pioneers of Jungle Gym Play Laboratory, a Manila-based playground for developing multi-arts performances and collective creations that explore the intersections of art, games, and social justice.

(UP)ROOTED

Caity-Shea Violette

This piece was inspired by the solarpunk movement and their goal to imagine an optimistic future in which humanity sees itself as part of nature. I wanted to get a glimpse into a hopeful and healing moment of connection, community, and ritual in the face of simultaneous societal and personal distress. I also wanted to explore the internal pressure that comes from wanting to do the most good – when your time or money is limited, should you focus your activism locally or support initiatives for distant communities with fewer resources? Finally, I wanted to reimagine how we could see the end of our human life as a return to the deeply alive Earth from which we came.

Characters

ONE: Devoted, stable, deeply rooted at home, any ethnicity, any gender identity, age eighteen or older

TWO: Adventurous, mission-driven wanderer who always returns home, any ethnicity, any gender identity, age eighteen or older.

MOURNER: A person remembering their loved one, any ethnicity, any gender, age thirty or older

TREE SPIRIT(S): Optional one or more dancers of any ethnicity, gender identity, and age. Timeless memories of people who awaken into a dance ritual when remembered by loved ones.

Notes

All props and set pieces should suggest the environment, but do not need to be realistic. Depending on casting availability, you can have multiple tree spirit dancers awaken at the end, just one, or just have the glow of the candle be the final beat.

Dusk. A large grassy hill overlooking a vast lush forest with a winding hiking path leading up to the top. ONE and TWO approach the top. ONE is winded and carries an oversized backpack. TWO effortlessly bounds to the top without breaking a sweat.

TWO: See? That wasn't so bad.

ONE: I'm literally going to die. At least, I came to the right place.

TWO, *stifling a laugh*: Shh – there are like families around.

ONE: You're the one who likes coming here.

> *They sit atop the hill and ONE pulls out reusable water bottles from the oversized pack. The two sip water and drink in the sun setting over the expansive verdant vista.*

TWO: I told you we really didn't have to come here. If I knew everything that was going on, I wouldn't have suggested it.

ONE: No, it's fine. I'm starting to get it. Returning to the earth when you're gone. Seeing people come to be with their people again. Plus, bonus points for not making people go broke to fill the ground with non-biodegradable chemicals.

TWO: And a great hiking trail.

ONE: See? Lots of perks. Plus: Your going away party, your choice.

TWO: I feel guilty going now.

ONE: You absolutely shouldn't.

TWO: If I knew what was going on for you, I would have pushed my volunteer deployment.

ONE: Which is why I didn't tell you. She's *my* mom. It's on me, not you.

TWO: But I love Mama O. I was at your house enough growing up for her to practically raise me too.

ONE: She's just one person. You're going to save the world.

TWO: It feels like a bit of an overstatement to say building community gardens will save the world.

ONE: Not for the people who live there. Community gardens were the turning point in the food shortage.

TWO: I guess that's true.

ONE: You're volunteering to help these people you've never even met around the world. Deflect all you want, but I'm still going to be proud of you so you might as well let me.

They sip and look out in a tender, comfortable silence. On the hill, we see a MOURNER laying out a picnic blanket in front of a large tree. They reach into a tote bag and take out a piece of cake, a music box, and a candle.

ONE: I heard they're going mausoleum-style for the bigger trees. Digging by the base to add new ashes to the roots. Really leaning all the way into that family tree metaphor.

TWO: I like that. Give more space to more people.

ONE: Keeps it affordable for everyone now that the old cemeteries are full.

MOURNER searches for something in their bag, but can't find it.

TWO: You know, for someone who allegedly found this place spooky, you know a lot about it.

ONE: Guess I'm seeing this place in a different light with everything going on. Figure if we bury her here, we'd have another reason to get in some hikes up here.

TWO: Ok, now I feel twice as guilty for bringing you here.

ONE: Your guilt doesn't make me feel better.

TWO: Family shows up for each other when things fall apart. I want to be there for you.

ONE: You are.

TWO: If anything happens while I'm gone –

ONE: I'll call you. I promise.

TWO: I just don't want you to be alone.

MOURNER approaches ONE and TWO on the hill.

MOURNER: Do you two have any –

ONE and TWO jump.

MOURNER: Sorry – Didn't mean to startle you. I just wanted to see if you might have some matches.

ONE: Let me check …

MOURNER: Of course, I remember the candle, the cake, the music box – everything but the matches.

TWO: Is it your birthday?

MOURNER: It was my husband's. Still come out here to light a candle for him every year. It's a silly little ritual, but it makes me feel closer to him.

TWO: I think it's lovely.

ONE pulls out a small matchbook.

ONE: Here you go.

MOURNER: I'll bring them right back.

ONE: Keep them, please. Thrilled for any excuse to carry fewer things.

MOURNER: Thank you.

MOURNER walks back to their tree.

TWO: Ok, I retract my mocking of your backpack.

ONE: Never leave home unprepared.

TWO: I'm too impatient for that.

ONE: Guess that's why you're able to go globetrotting to do good.

TWO: Doesn't do much good for stranger candle-related emergencies.

ONE: That's what I'm here for.

ONE and TWO sit in a comfortable silence as the sun continues setting. Below them, we see MOURNER strike a match to light a candle by their tree. They wind the music box and let it play – closing their eyes, remembering. As they do, the TREE SPIRIT of their husband awakens from within the tree and moves freely, elegantly, once again dancing with life as the day turns to night.

TWO: I'm proud of you too, you know.

ONE: I do carry matchbooks with the best of them.

TWO: I'm serious. The gardens that raised us need as much tending as anywhere else.

ONE: Sure, but –

TWO: You're just here to do it.

ONE: I suppose they do.

ONE lifts their water bottle to make a toast.

ONE: To staying. And also, to leaving.

TWO raises their bottle too.

TWO: To returning.

ONE: To remembering without needing to forget.

ONE and TWO clink water bottles and sip in the setting sun. Maybe the final beat is just the glow of the candle, the clink of the bottles, the music box, and old friends. Maybe TREE SPIRITS from all around them come out from their trunks and join the MOURNER's TREE SPIRIT in joyful, effortless movement. Either way, it is beauty and it is tenderness and it is hope.

◊ ◊ ◊

Caity-Shea Violette is a US-based playwright whose work explores the intersections of disability, sexuality, capitalism, and intergenerational healing. She has won the Jean Kennedy Smith Playwriting Award, Kennedy Center's ACTF Harold & Mimi Steinberg Award, Samuel French OOB Festival, National Partners of the American Theatre Playwriting Award, and more. Her work has been presented at Portland Stage Company, Roundabout Theatre Company, the Kennedy Center, Boston Playwrights Theatre, and more. She holds an MFA in Playwriting from Boston University.
www.caitysheaviolette.com

TRANSMISSION

Kevin Matthew Wong

This is a monologue of hope. I welcome any and all voices to perform this text (you definitely don't have to be a Hakka Chinese-Canadian … that would be a very small pool of actors). Feel free to translate and transform this speech into your local language/lexicon/way of communication. The goal is to create direct and immediate acknowledgment and connection between performer and audience. You are me. I am you. You are beyond my wildest imaginings. Oh, and please feel free to send me any recordings of your performances!

◊ ◊ ◊

KEVIN: Hi everyone! My name is *(insert performer's name).*
I'm a *(insert descriptors as desired, i.e., height, gender/pronouns, hairstyle, cultural background, career, etc.).*
I'm your friendly, neighborhood performer, *(insert other descriptors if helpful to the audience such as cycling enthusiast, bubble tea aficionado, chronically anxious, etc.).*

But for today, I am Kevin Matthew Wong.

A 5'7"
Hakka Chinese-Canadian man,
Usually seen in long sleeve, button-down shirts
And the writer of this play.

The performer looks around.

Well … ok. I'm not actually Kevin Matthew Wong.

But for today, for the next few minutes, I really am … Kevin Matthew Wong.

Magic! *(perhaps a flourish, like performing a quick magic trick if the performer knows one)*

Anyway, it's great to be here in *(insert name of specific town/city/neighborhood/building).*

I bring you this transmission.
It's about you, and me.
I've always yearned to share this with you.
But I'd never found the words.

So let me begin by saying …

Here we are. Together.
Flesh. Skin. Blood. Bone.
I'm right here!
But, obviously … I am also not here.

I am many people. Many beings who came before.

I am my parent's child – for better or worse.
I am a toddler stumbling around, learning to walk, to speak.
I'm a sage in meditation.

I am a woman – *who is not yet my grandmother* –
who drives a speeding car,
drives it through the streets of Hong Kong,
in search of sanctuary.

I AM CANADIAN! *(optional line, this is a popular beer slogan in Canada. Feel free to omit and/or replace for your local context)*

I am a brainstorm.
I am an existential crisis.

I'm the heat in fire, and the purest cold.
I am sea breeze *and* Sea Biscuit.
(That's the name of a horse, by the way.)

I'm a nervous beam of light
who comes to this planet from a distant star;
who finds a quiet spot, in a little garden,
and rests upon a crisp green leaf – the front door to a flower's home.
I knock gently on the door, and hope to be let in.

I am inaction. I am self-doubt.
I am a revolutionary. I am revolutions.
I am violence, lust, and greed.
I am terrified.

I am terror itself.

I am love's patience and pettiness.
Love's rage and convictions.
I am pure hatred.
I am hopeless affection.

And, yes, you may say,
"Ok, ok, Kevin, I get it … I get it … *we all contain multitudes* … Yes! Fine! Whatever …"

And I say:

> *Beat – perhaps suddenly more severe, perhaps more relaxed, perhaps flippant, as long as it feels real to you, the performer. Play with time here, if it helps.*

I am a turning point.
I am a leap of faith.
I am the admission of failure.
I am a heroic act.
I am sun becoming soil, becoming wind, becoming volcanoes and rainforests, becoming flesh and sound.
I am the tussle between courage and cowardice.

I'm Kevin and I'm not. I'm *(performer's first name)*, and not *(performer's name)* too.

And we – you and I – are connected.
Connected beyond the waves of my voice echoing around these *(insert type of room, i.e., theatre, living room, classroom)* walls.
Connected beyond our breaths meeting and dancing in the air between us.
You are me; and I am you, too.

And *we* are everything that *has been*,
Everything that *can* be,

And everything that ever *will be.*

Beat.

Who can say that the worst is yet to come
when every choice, every action,
every stumble and misstep,
every dream and hope …
every *possible future is within us.*

In front of us.

Perhaps a moment of recognition – really seeing and acknowledging the audience.

Magic.

◊ ◊ ◊

Kevin Matthew Wong (he/him) is a Hakka Chinese-Canadian theatre creator, producer, dramaturg, and video artist who creates, produces, and tours work internationally and across Canada. Kevin has collaborated with organizations like Barbican Centre (UK), National Arts Centre (Canada), Music Picnic (Macau/China), Blooming Ludus (UK/Korea/Canada), Gardarev Center (USA), and Festival Theaterformen (Germany). Kevin is the Director of Producing and Creative Associate at Why Not Theatre, and the co-founder and Artistic Director of Broadleaf Creative. Kevin's multidisciplinary works entitled, "Benevolence," celebrates Hakka-Canadian history and includes a documentary created with ReelAsian International Film Festival, a solo show with the Tarragon Theatre, and a museum installation at Toronto's Market Gallery.
www.kevinmatthewwong.com

SCAR TISSUE

XANA

Inspiration: Lack of maternal care for Black mothers, poor housing, and highest rate of air pollutants in Global Majority neighborhoods currently affecting and killing children.

In decades to come, will rain be able to land on our skin or will it burn at the touch? Will we look up at the sky and try to imagine stories or hide from its storms and color? Will we be looking at children and explaining how we watched the world burn?

What if the child in each of us woke up and took over, gave us our connection again so we don't harm the world but care for it? So we are more curious to connect than to destroy, and can be the guardians of our planet?

Albums that I listened to while I wrote this piece:
Love Deluxe by Sade
Operation Doomsday by MF Doom

> Wan ti wan ti cyah get ti, get ti get ti an nuh wan ti.
>
> —Jamaican Saying

> We'll have to be very careful how we allow our needs to shape us.
>
> —Octavia E. Butler, Parable of the Sower

> Until you dig a hole, you plant a tree, you water it and make it survive, you haven't done a thing. You are just talking.
>
> —Wangari Maathai

Characters

RIFT: Non-Global Majority Person, any gender
IDOLATRY: Global Majority Person, any gender
CALAMITY: Non-Global Majority Person, any gender
HUNGER: Global Majority Person, any gender
SURFACE: Non-Global Majority Person, any gender
DEPTH: Global Majority Person, any gender
TIME: Global Majority Person, any gender
CROSSING: Global Majority Person, any gender

CHILD: Global Majority person, any gender
MUMMY: Global Majority person, any gender
HEALING: A recorded voice or spoken by an audience member

◊ ◊ ◊

Infinity enters. Six characters stand in a circle facing the audience: RIFT, IDOLATRY, CALAMITY, HUNGER, SURFACE, and DEPTH. The other two, TIME and CROSSING, are in the center. They speak in music – their mouths are open and moving but we cannot comprehend until later. We can only feel the sound as they sing an opening chorus.

It is the trial of TIME and CROSSING. They have fallen in love. CROSSING is carrying a possibility. TIME looks over at their lover, exhausted for the first time in their awareness.

TIME and CROSSING's connection provided Earth with a reprieve and a large number of the keepers have stopped slumbering in the walking state for the first time. The keepers are now starting revolutions and anarchist cells, distracting from the infinity to be able to feed off of the keepers' own self-destruction.

Scene 1 - The Earth's Atmosphere

IDOLATRY: To punish for attempting to bring life. When life is what we do … Playing with it. Eating off of it. A strange sensation.

HUNGER: But we exist in a flux.

SURFACE: A flux that gives us all many layers of agency …

RIFT: And our only rule.

SURFACE: Our only rule is …

CALAMITY: Never stop feeding.
SURFACE: Yes.

HUNGER: It upsets the balance and now look at the canvas we built.
DEPTH: Dismantling –

CALAMITY: … the careful palette we have perfected.

HUNGER: Not a morsel of amoral decadence with which to admire.

DEPTH: The hosts are stupefied in their own liberation. Impossible feats are tipping into balancing their world. We have all seen these tiny overgrown land masses … felling giants of industry. It is only the beginning.

CROSSING: Not a giant. A falsehood. The keepers –

RIFT: Hosts. They know what they want and we respond when their desires are strongest. The hosts will applaud at the progress they build with our guiding appetite.

CROSSING: The keepers of the world want this to stop. They want their waters back, their grasslands. We have to stop feeding our base desires and allow them to reset. The keepers who fight know the value of their world and now more keepers –

IDOLATRY: No.

TIME: No?! We are a wound! This *(points to CROSSING's stomach)* is the healing. We have to let this be and finally allow all the keepers to truly see what is being done around them. Let them sever their egos and be a community!

HUNGER: Impossible.

SURFACE: Incensed.

RIFT: A wound? You act as if scar tissue doesn't also have possibility. Scars tell stories, do they not? A memory of –

CROSSING: Pain. When this child is born, with them an old consciousness will unite the keepers. They will blend; they will see their distinctions and define equities. The keepers will finally live globally so all of the Earth is all of their weight to hold.

TIME: If we continue to whisper progress in their ears at their sun's closing, without consequence, they will poison their waters beyond repair. Their young will not survive in the air surrounding them. They will consume all and build works that do not decompose. Fires will spread, more and more land will not sprout food. Our child –

DEPTH: Child?! Never. Do you remember what you are? We are the unseen, the felt and resented, what the hosts blame rather than look at, what they never seem to learn. It is them. Them alone.

IDOLATRY: Crossing. You help them move from this plane to the next. What would make you think walking by their side would mean they want to hold you in their arms?

RIFT: Enough! Time for this distortion of our rules. You will become a mass of slowing death. The hosts will do everything in their might to stop your growth. Crossing, your child will never be born. It will live inside you forever. You will feel it quake and claw, but it will never see the cosmos.

HUNGER: You will not rest and neither will the hosts.

TIME turns to CROSSING.

CROSSING: No matter how much doing nothing chokes me, I will not speak a word after this day. You are all going to feel the change my silence will bring.

Crossing keeps their promise. They don't speak again after that day.

Scene 2 - Pillars of Creation

Three hundred years pass. A feast is about to happen.
RIFT and CALAMITY are swirling their tendrils of curiosity across the Earth's atmosphere, causing storms. The infinity has gotten stronger as the keepers' connection with the Earth has weakened.

CALAMITY: Rift? How do you think they did it?

RIFT: Did what?

CALAMITY: You know. Brought about the will of life … here of all places
RIFT: …

CALAMITY: We can't touch. We are but refractions of light and choosing to be solid is one of the most grotesque acts we could do. So, how did they do it?

RIFT: What does it matter, Calamity? They chose ends and beginnings when we are the infinite. I suppose Time and Crossing believe the hosts are worth it, but they never gonna change. Just look at the metallic veneer surrounding their home – all because to reach the stars, they must shed themselves.

They all gather inside the nebula, exchanging laughs over the chaos their indulgences have supported across Earth. CROSSING, the cousin to sleep and shadows, isn't seen by the group until the last moment. They open their mouth and a glorious birth is made. Every silence, every prayer, every chant, every lament, every protest from the Earth – everything and all is opened. The birth is glorious.

This can be a dance, or sound and light. Designers and directors: Show us what the release of anger, protests, desire to save our world looks like. A voice emerges and the chorus cries.

HEALING: I am the crack of light breaking into the void.

CROSSING falls to the ground.
TIME emerges from their cage.
Chaos is still.

HUNGER, *screams*: I'm full!

DEPTH can only look up.
SURFACE tries to bury themselves.

CALAMITY, *cries for the first time in their existence*: Calm.

RIFT tries to repair, but nothing holds together.

HEALING: We will begin anew. Food will grow everywhere and replenish as it's picked, air will be cleaned so lungs can be in tomorrow, oceans will be clear and so full of abundance it will be impossible for resources to exist in silos. Keepers, you will stop your slumber and become the guardians you were always meant to be. Centuries of ill governance will come to a close.

You will all speak and hear one another, break into prisms of light and song, fill the space up and up.

HEALING turns to everyone, speaking in the minds of the keepers.

If a keeper attempts to destroy your home, you will bellow through the earth. Any keeper who attempts to harm the land will sink into it – in an instant, your body will take root and red will be your crown. You all see it now. We will walk among you. Your understanding and knowledge of each other will be rooted in love. You will love your world and ache to feed it with your souls. We are not gods. We are from you. From Agbogbloshie to the Antarctic, you will hear each other's song.

The infinity become bonded, sings its last chorus, and disperses.

Scene 3 - Kingston, Jamaica

Nature has gotten wild outside. People are whooping and hollering. The island has lifted further from the ocean and more landmass has appeared. A mother is stirring a pot of stew, oblivious to the symphony of life other than the one she is concocting in her pot.

CHILD: Mummy, Mummy, cum si!

MUMMY: Wa?

CHILD: A mango tree jus grow insida di living room!

◊ ◊ ◊

XANA is a freestyle live loop musician, spatial sound artist, poet, and vibrational sound designer. XANA composes music and designs accessible sound systems for theatres and installations. XANA's music-making process blends sound with sensory experiences such as scents, touch, and raw materials. XANA is a music science and technology lead at music research label, Inventing Waves, where XANA researches acoustic ecologies within climate change, and supports Black creatives with sustainable inventions. XANA is also a sound arts and music tech facilitator working with local communities, youth groups, and organizations.
xa-na.com

THIS PLAY IS WRITTEN IN MUSHROOM

Haeweon Yi

Fungi have lived on Earth long before humans, composing and decomposing life and death. Mushrooms are just a small visible fruiting part of fungi, and there is an incredibly large and complex network of mycelium beneath the ground that connects the world. This play was inspired by shaggy inkcap (*Coprinus comatus*) in a campus nook, which brought me great pleasure during my first few months in a new city. The mature inkcap mushroom's black liquid can be used as ink to write and draw. Sadly, this play is delivered to you in non-mushroom ink for the convenience of the editors and the publisher, but please use your imagination. The opening scene is an homage to Wolf Erlbruch's beautiful book, *Duck, Death and the Tulip*,[1] which shed new light on the tenderness of death and grief for young and old readers.

Characters

SOIL-HUMAN
THE DEAD
THE UNBORN

Setting

A bare ground with rubbles and ruins. This performance could be staged either indoor or outdoor. Let the creative team find connection with the land and ground itself using all their senses before the performance. I recommend that soil be sourced locally and disposed of responsibly.

Notes

The Dead (they/them) and The Unborn (they/them) can each be performed by one performer or by multiple performers as an ensemble.

Soil-Human can be performed by a puppet or other nonhuman materials.

◊ ◊ ◊

From inside the ruins of an old city, SOIL-HUMAN slowly moves its heavy body towards the front of the stage. Like a young toddler just

[1] Erlbruch, Wolf. *Duck, Death and the Tulip*. Gecko Press, 2011.

learning to walk, it wobbles and dribbles. Then after a few steps, it collapses. Limbs softly crash. There's only a pile of soil left on the stage.

Silence.

THE DEAD appears on the stage, walking consciously, holding a dead wild goose – the wild goose who happened to drink the contaminated water near an abandoned mine. THE DEAD softly strokes the goose.

THE DEAD: Oh, goose, my friend. Now is your time to return. Your friends must have departed already. I can smell the season changing, but the ground here is still bare. You must have been very thirsty from your long journey, right? But that one last sip you took … if only it had seeped deep inside your body and quenched all your thirst. They have stolen everything from the ground, and now they have taken your life, even your little life … I wasn't able to save you when I was alive and once again, like a coward, I greet you as a mere witness. Let's allow death to embrace us. Let us rot together and wait for new life to begin. *(beat)* Would you like one last laugh together? Well, *(a brief pause while thinking of a joke)* I don't have any jokes left for you. But, if I can think of any, I will come back, I will come back …

THE DEAD slowly folds their body and buries the goose using the pile of soil. Without any sounds, THE UNBORN comes closer to them. They help the burial of the winged companion. Soil warmly covers the bird's cold body. The flesh, beak, and flat feet that still hold light fatigue from a long journey finally disappear into the soil. THE DEAD takes out a wild goose feather from a pocket. They put the feather on the little grave and embrace it with two arms. THE UNBORN also folds their body and embraces the grave and THE DEAD together. Startled at the warmth of THE UNBORN's body, THE DEAD rises.

THE DEAD: You? How? How did you get here already? The time …

THE UNBORN: The time is not here yet. I came before its arrival.

THE DEAD: But, but you are …

THE UNBORN: … unborn. I am unborn.

Suddenly, an idea pops into the head of THE DEAD. THE DEAD points at the grave and then THE UNBORN, confused. Absurd silence.

THE DEAD: You … wait. Are you, already …?

THE UNBORN: No, no, no. I'm not the goose. I don't even know the bird. I just joined because the funeral was too quiet.

It starts to rain.

THE DEAD: Finally, my friend, you won't feel parched any longer. *(patting the grave while whispering an old story)* A Tree Frog made his mother's grave by the river and he cried every rainy day because he worried that his mother's grave would be washed away by the water. Ribbit, ribbit, ribbit. *(glancing at THE UNBORN)* Don't worry. It's just a story. Our friend will not be washed away … Not in the near future, I believe.

THE UNBORN: What happened to her?

THE DEAD: She drank contaminated water near an abandoned mine.

THE UNBORN: Oh … Where's your grave?

THE DEAD: Underneath your feet.

From the grave of the wild goose, a slender strand of fungal hypha begins to stretch out. Soon, others join in, merging and intertwining to form multiple layers of hyphae. These intricate lines busily weave through the ground, creating an expansive network of mycelium.

THE UNBORN: Who are they?

THE DEAD: Fungi. They are here to celebrate.

THE UNBORN: Celebrate what?

THE DEAD: The death, the return, and the journey of our feathered friend. They will whisper the news of mourning and grief across the forest, from here to there, from this tree to that tree, from me to you, and you to me.

Together THE UNBORN and THE DEAD trace hyphae with their hands and feet. Their steps turn into a dance. Their bodies get entangled. Every hypha contains memories and unheard stories. This scene can be longer and contain all the names to celebrate on the land where the performance is happening.

THE DEAD: I was a boar.

THE UNBORN: I will be an otter.

THE DEAD: I was a lizard.

THE UNBORN: I will be a dragonfly.

THE DEAD: I was a robin.

THE UNBORN: I will be a trout.

THE DEAD: I was a pine tree.

THE UNBORN: I will be a sorrel.

THE DEAD: I was you.

THE UNBORN: I will be you.

THE DEAD: But you will forget me. You will forget it all.

THE UNBORN: As you did.

The rain stops while they are dancing. A flock of wild geese fly across the sky.

THE UNBORN: It's them! Our feathered fellows!

THE DEAD: Did they come to say goodbye to their friend?

THE UNBORN: No. Goodbye has already been said. This is my time.

THE UNBORN tries to follow the flock in a hurry. THE DEAD quickly grabs THE UNBORN.

THE DEAD: Wait! Are you sure? The ground is bare and your wings haven't started growing yet.

THE UNBORN: I may not need them at all. I might grow fins, or antlers … or both? I just know that it's my time to go out into the world. *(beat)* Do you think I will be able to live?

THE DEAD, *after taking a moment*: You will, you will. Do you know where you are going?

THE UNBORN lies low putting their ear on the ground. THE DEAD does the same. Earth starts to roar. Birds start to sing. Fish start to make splashing waves. Small insects chirp and bigger animals stomp their feet. Trees swoosh their twigs and leaves while grass trembles. Fungi slowly stretch themselves under the ground. All living things make sounds.

THE UNBORN: Now I know. I am the first one to be born after the calamity.

THE DEAD, *nodding their head*: Because all good things must begin.

They both rise. THE DEAD picks up the feather from the grave and hands it to THE UNBORN.

THE DEAD: You will forget, but try to remember.

THE UNBORN: I will. Remember me too.

THE DEAD: I will. We will celebrate you from birth to death.

THE DEAD stares at their hands.

THE DEAD: My body is crumbling.

Mushrooms start to grow out of THE DEAD's mouth. They start covering THE DEAD's body. After one last hug, THE UNBORN leaves THE DEAD with the feather in their hand.

THE DEAD arduously moves their body to the goose's grave, almost dragging. Sitting on the grave, after a big exhale, THE DEAD slowly turns into mushrooms: a bundle of curious shaggy inkcap mushrooms (Coprinus comatus). *As an autumn breeze gently brushes their white and round caps, they can feel spores from faraway mushrooms freely surfing the wind. The audience can almost see the faint smile of THE DEAD. Very slowly, the mushrooms open their caps, revealing the edge of their soft black gills. They gradually begin to deliquesce to spread the spores. The shaggy inkcap will melt down to the ground even before the full moon. A drop of black ink, like a tear, drips from the gills. The wind starts singing and slowly, the stage goes to darkness.*

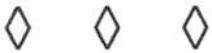

Haeweon Yi is an award-winning theatre maker, writer, and researcher from Korea, currently based in Manchester, UK. Her research explores human-fungi relationships and our interconnectedness with the planet through performance. As a co-founder and co-artistic director of Blooming Ludus, she has been creating participatory theatre projects that bring together communities, art, and the environment, with the goal of amplifying the voice of climate justice and advocating for a sustainable future since 2015.
www.bloomingludus.com

www.ingramcontent.com/pod-product-compliance
Lightning Source LLC
LaVergne TN
LVHW010637110826
845149LV00014B/2868

* 9 7 9 8 9 9 0 5 4 3 9 0 4 *